T0224297

Design Patterns in .NET 6

Reusable Approaches in C# and F#
for Object-Oriented Software Design

Third Edition

Dmitri Nesteruk

Apress®

Design Patterns in .NET 6: Reusable Approaches in C# and F# for Object-Oriented Software Design

Dmitri Nesteruk
St. Petersburg, c.St-Petersburg, Russia

ISBN-13 (pbk): 978-1-4842-8244-1   ISBN-13 (electronic): 978-1-4842-8245-8
https://doi.org/10.1007/978-1-4842-8245-8

Managing Director, Apress Media LLC: Welmoed Spahr
Acquisitions Editor: Joan Murray
Development Editor: Laura Berendson
Coordinating Editor: Jill Balzano

Cover designed by eStudioCalamar

Cover image designed by Freepik (www.freepik.com)

Distributed to the book trade worldwide by Springer Science+Business Media New York, 1 New York Plaza, Suite 4600, New York, NY 10004-1562, USA. Phone 1-800-SPRINGER, fax (201) 348-4505, e-mail orders-ny@springer-sbm.com, or visit www.springeronline.com. Apress Media, LLC is a California LLC and the sole member (owner) is Springer Science + Business Media Finance Inc (SSBM Finance Inc). SSBM Finance Inc is a **Delaware** corporation.

For information on translations, please e-mail booktranslations@springernature.com; for reprint, paperback, or audio rights, please e-mail bookpermissions@springernature.com.

Apress titles may be purchased in bulk for academic, corporate, or promotional use. eBook versions and licenses are also available for most titles. For more information, reference our Print and eBook Bulk Sales web page at http://www.apress.com/bulk-sales.

Any source code or other supplementary material referenced by the author in this book is available to readers on GitHub (https://github.com/Apress). For more detailed information, please visit http://www.apress.com/source-code.

Printed on acid-free paper

The forces of light shall overcome the forces of darkness.

Table of Contents

About the Author

Dmitri Nesteruk is a quantitative analyst, developer, course instructor, book author, and an occasional conference speaker. His interests lie in software development and integration practices in the areas of computation, quantitative finance, and algorithmic trading. His technological interests include C# and C++ programming as well as high-performance computing using technologies such as CUDA and FPGAs.

About the Technical Reviewer

As Microsoft Technical Trainer in Microsoft, **Massimo Bonnani**'s main goal is to help customers empower their Azure skills to achieve more and leverage the power of Azure in their solutions. He is also a technical speaker at national and international conferences, and public speaking is one of his passions. He likes dogs (he has one beautiful female Labrador that he loves), reading, and biking. He is Microsoft Certified Trainer, former MVP (for 6 years in Visual Studio and development technologies and Windows development), Intel Software Innovator, and Intel Black Belt.

Introduction

The topic of design patterns sounds dry, academically dull, and, in all honesty, done to death in almost every programming language imaginable – including programming languages such as JavaScript that aren't even properly object-oriented programming (OOP)! So why another book on it? I know that if you're reading this, you probably have a limited amount of time to decide whether this book is worth the investment.

I decided to write this book to fill a gap left by the lack of in-depth patterns books in the .NET space. Plenty of books have been written over the years, but few have attempted to research all the ways in which modern C# and F# language features can be used to implement design patterns and to present corresponding examples. Having just completed a similar body of work for C++,[1] I thought it fitting to replicate the process with .NET.

Now, on to design patterns – the original *Design Patterns* book[2] was published with examples in C++ and Smalltalk, and since then, plenty of programming languages have incorporated certain design patterns directly into the language. For example, C# directly incorporated the Observer pattern with its built-in support for events (and the corresponding event keyword).

Design patterns are also a fun investigation of how a problem can be solved in many different ways, with varying degrees of technical sophistication and different sorts of trade-offs. Some patterns are more or less essential and unavoidable, whereas other patterns are more of a scientific curiosity (but nevertheless will be discussed in this book, since I'm a completionist).

You should be aware that comprehensive solutions to certain problems often result in overengineering, or the creation of structures and mechanisms that are far more complicated than is necessary for most typical scenarios. Although overengineering is a lot of fun (hey, you get to *fully* solve the problem and impress your co-workers), it's often not feasible due to time/cost/complexity constraints.

---

[1] Dmitri Nesteruk, *Design Patterns in Modern C++* (New York, NY: Apress, 2017).
[2] Erich Gamma, Richard Helm, Ralph Johnson, and John Vlissides, *Design Patterns: Elements of Reusable Object-Oriented Software* (Reading, MA: Addison-Wesley, 1994).

Who This Book Is For

This book is designed to be a modern-day update to the classic GoF book, targeting specifically the C# and F# programming languages. My focus is primarily on C# and the object-oriented paradigm, but I thought it fair to extend the book in order to cover some aspects of functional programming and the F# programming language.

The goal of this book is to investigate how we can apply the latest versions of C# and F# to the implementation of classic design patterns. At the same time, it's also an attempt to flesh out any new patterns and approaches that could be useful to .NET developers.

Finally, in some places, this book is quite simply a technology demo for C# and F#, showcasing how some of the latest features (e.g., default interface methods) make difficult problems a lot easier to solve.

On Code Examples

The examples in this book are all suitable for putting into production, but a few simplifications have been made in order to aid readability:

- I use public fields. This is not a coding recommendation, but rather an attempt to save you time. In the real world, more thought should be given to proper encapsulation, and in most cases, you probably want to use properties instead.

- I often allow too much mutability either by not using `readonly` or by exposing structures in such a way that their modification can cause threading concerns. We cover concurrency issues for a few select patterns, but I haven't focused on each one individually.

- I don't do any sort of parameter validation or exception handling, again to save some space. Some very clever validation can be done using C# 8 pattern matching, but this doesn't have much to do with design patterns.

You should be aware that most of the examples leverage the latest version of C# and generally use the latest C# language features that are available to developers. For example, I use `dynamic` pattern matching and expression-bodied members liberally.

At certain points in time, I will be referencing other programming languages such as C++ or Kotlin. It's sometimes interesting to note how designers of other languages have implemented a particular feature. C# is no stranger to borrowing generally available ideas from other languages, so I will mention those when we come to them.

Preface to the Second Edition

As I write this book, the streets outside are almost empty. Shops are closed, cars are parked, public transport is rare and empty too. Life is almost at a standstill as the country endures its first "nonworking month," a curious occurrence that one (hopefully) only encounters once in a lifetime. The reason for this is, of course, the COVID-19 pandemic that will go down in the history books. We use the phrase "stop the world" a lot when talking about the Garbage Collector, but this pandemic is a *real* "stop the world" event.

Of course, it's not the first. In fact, there's a pattern there too: a virus emerges, we pay little heed until it's spreading around the globe. Its exact nature is different in time, but the mechanisms for dealing with it remain the same: we try to stop it from spreading and look for a cure. Only this time around it seems to have really caught us off guard, and now the whole world is suffering.

What's the moral of the story? Pattern recognition is critical for our survival. Just as the hunters and gatherers needed to recognize predators from prey and distinguish between edible and poisonous plants, so we learn to recognize common engineering problems – good and bad – and try to be ready for when the need arises.

Preface to the Third Edition

Design patterns are, for me, a subject of continuous research. Even though the core set of patterns remains more or less unchanged (though I *did* include a new one, Value Object, in this edition), the exact implementations keep varying as new framework and language features are introduced. With C#, the language has recently made an effort to focus on conciseness: getting more done with less. On the other hand, features such as Source Generators also simplify some of the approaches where code repetition is inevitable. Sadly, we've not yet reached the stage where we have a fully functioning metaprogramming system, so we have to make do with what's essentially plain-text code generation.

This edition also includes a lot of new material related to pattern interactions. Normally, when using patterns, you're likely to use more than one anyway, and sometimes these patterns interact in weird and wonderful ways. Sometimes it's difficult to determine *exactly* what pattern is represented by a particular code because it seems to be covering so many at once. I've made explicit in the names of sections which patterns are involved in an interaction.

Patterns are a fun topic to experiment with and delve into those "what if?" questions regarding how an implementation can be improved – whether in terms of maintainability, testability, thread safety, or some other criterion. On the other hand, comprehensive solutions often result in overengineering, which can weigh down implementations and make them more difficult to understand and maintain. I encourage you to consider carefully how much engineering embedded into patterns you actually need for your purposes. Do not be afraid to cherry-pick, experiment, and adjust things to your needs.

Oh, and if you find some interesting approach that this book does not cover, be sure to let me know!

PART I

Introduction

CHAPTER 1

The SOLID Design Principles

SOLID is an acronym that stands for the following design principles (and their abbreviations):

- Single Responsibility Principle (SRP)

- Open-Closed Principle (OCP)

- Liskov Substitution Principle (LSP)

- Interface Segregation Principle (ISP)

- Dependency Inversion Principle (DIP)

These principles were introduced by Robert C. Martin in the early 2000s – in fact, they are just a selection of five principles out of dozens that are expressed in Robert's books and his blog.[1] These five particular topics permeate the discussion of patterns and software design in general, so before we dive into design patterns (I know you're all eager), we're going to do a brief recap of what the SOLID principles are all about.

Single Responsibility Principle

Suppose you decide to keep a journal of your most intimate thoughts. The journal is used to keep a number of entries. You could model it as follows:

```
public class Journal
{
  private readonly List<string> entries = new();
```

---

[1] https://blog.cleancoder.com/

© Dmitri Nesteruk 2022
D. Nesteruk, *Design Patterns in .NET 6*, https://doi.org/10.1007/978-1-4842-8245-8_1

```
// just a counter for total # of entries
private static int count = 0;
}
```

Now, you could add functionality for adding an entry to the journal, prefixed by the entry's ordinal number in the journal. You could also have functionality for removing entries (implemented in a very crude way in the following). This is easy:

```
public void AddEntry(string text)
{
  entries.Add($"{++count}: {text}");
}

public void RemoveEntry(int index)
{
  entries.RemoveAt(index);
}
```

And the journal is now usable as

```
var j = new Journal();
j.AddEntry("I cried today.");
j.AddEntry("I ate a bug.");
```

It makes sense to have this method as part of the Journal class because adding a journal entry is something the journal actually needs to do. It is the journal's responsibility to keep entries, so anything related to that is fair game.

Now, suppose you decide to make the journal persist by saving it to a file. You add this code to the Journal class:

```
public void Save(string filename, bool overwrite = false)
{
  File.WriteAllText(filename, ToString());
}
```

This approach is problematic. The journal's responsibility is to *keep* journal entries, not to write them to disk. If you add the persistence functionality to Journal and similar classes, any change in the approach to persistence (say, you decide to write to the cloud instead of disk) would require lots of tiny changes in each of the affected classes.

I want to pause here and make a point: an architecture that leads you to having to do lots of tiny changes in lots of classes is generally best avoided if possible. Now, it really depends on the situation: if you're renaming a symbol that's being used in a hundred places, I'd argue that's generally OK because ReSharper, Rider, or whatever IDE you use will actually let you perform a refactoring and have the change propagate everywhere. But when you need to completely rework an interface…well, that can become a very painful process!

We therefore state that persistence is a separate *concern*, one that is better expressed in a separate class. We use the term *Separation of Concerns* (sadly, the abbreviation SoC is already taken[2]) when talking about the general approach of splitting code into separate classes by functionality. In the cases of persistence in our example, we would externalize it like so:

```
public class PersistenceManager
{
  public void SaveToFile(Journal journal, string filename,
    bool overwrite = false)
  {
    if (overwrite || !File.Exists(filename))
      File.WriteAllText(filename, journal.ToString());
  }
}
```

And this is precisely what we mean by *Single Responsibility*: each class has only one responsibility and therefore has only one reason to change. Journal would need to change only if there's something more that needs to be done with respect to in-memory storage of entries – for example, you might want each entry prefixed by a timestamp, so you would change the Add() method to do exactly that. On the other hand, if you wanted to change the persistence mechanic, this would be changed in PersistenceManager.

An extreme example of an anti-pattern[3] that violates the SRP is called a *God Object*. A God Object is a huge class that tries to handle as many concerns as possible, becoming a

---

[2] SoC is short for System on a Chip, a kind of microprocessor that incorporates all (or most) aspects of a computer.

[3] An *anti-pattern* is a design pattern that also, unfortunately, shows up in code often enough to be recognized globally. The difference between a pattern and an anti-pattern is that anti-patterns are common examples of *bad* design, resulting in code that's difficult to understand, maintain, and refactor.

monolithic monstrosity that is very difficult to work with. Strictly speaking, you can take any system of any size and try to fit it into a single class, but more often than not, you'd end up with an incomprehensible mess. Luckily for us, God Objects are easy to recognize either visually or automatically (just count the number of member functions), and thanks to continuous integration and source control systems, the responsible developer can be quickly identified and adequately punished.

Open-Closed Principle

Suppose we have an (entirely hypothetical) range of products in a database. Each product has a color and size and is defined as

```
public enum Color { Red, Green, Blue }

public enum Size { Small, Medium, Large, Huge }

public record Product(string Name, Color Color, Size Size);
```

Now, we want to provide certain filtering capabilities for a given set of products. We make a `ProductFilter` service class. To support filtering products by color, we implement it as follows:

```
public class ProductFilter
{
  public IEnumerable<Product> FilterByColor
    (IEnumerable<Product> products, Color color)
  {
    foreach (var p in products)
      if (p.Color == color)
        yield return p;
  }
}
```

Our current approach of filtering items by color is all well and good, though of course it could be greatly simplified with the use of LINQ. So our code goes into production, but unfortunately, sometime later, the boss comes in and asks us to implement filtering by size too. So we jump back into `ProductFilter.cs`, add the following code, and recompile:

```
public IEnumerable<Product> FilterBySize
  (IEnumerable<Product> products, Size size)
{
  foreach (var p in products)
    if (p.Size == size)
      yield return p;
}
```

This feels like outright duplication, doesn't it? Why don't we just write a general method that takes a predicate (i.e., a `Predicate<T>`)? Well, one reason could be that different forms of filtering can be done in different ways: for example, some record types might be indexed and need to be searched in a specific way; some data types are amenable to search on a Graphics Processing Unit (GPU), while others are not.

Furthermore, you might want to restrict the criteria one can filter on. For example, if you look at Amazon or a similar online store, you are only allowed to perform filtering on a finite set of criteria. Those criteria can be added or removed by Amazon if they find that, say, sorting by number of reviews interferes with the bottom line.

Okay, so our code goes into production, but once again, the boss comes back and tells us that now there's a need to search by both size *and* color. So what are we to do but add another function?

```
public IEnumerable<Product> FilterBySizeAndColor(
  IEnumerable<Product> products,
  Size size, Color color)
{
  foreach (var p in products)
    if (p.Size == size && p.Color == color)
      yield return p;
}
```

What we want, from the preceding scenario, is to enforce the *Open-Closed Principle* that states that a type is open for extension but closed for modification. In other words, we want filtering that is extensible (perhaps in a different assembly) without having to modify it (and recompiling something that already works and may have been shipped to clients).

How can we achieve it? Well, first of all, we conceptually separate (SRP!) our filtering process into two parts: a filter (a construct that takes all items and only returns some) and a specification (a predicate to apply to a data element).

We can make a very simple definition of a specification interface[4]:

```
public interface ISpecification<T>
{
  bool IsSatisfied(T item);
}
```

In this interface, type T is whatever we choose it to be: it can certainly be a Product, but it can also be something else. This makes the entire approach reusable.

Next up, we need a way of filtering based on an ISpecification<T> – this is done by defining, you guessed it, an IFilter<T>:

```
public interface IFilter<T>
{
  IEnumerable<T> Filter(IEnumerable<T> items,
                        ISpecification<T> spec);
}
```

Again, all we are doing is specifying the signature for a method called Filter() that takes all the items and a specification and returns only those items that conform to the specification.

Based on this interface, the implementation of an improved filter is really simple:

```
public class BetterFilter : IFilter<Product>
{
  public IEnumerable<Product> Filter(IEnumerable<Product> items,
                                     ISpecification<Product> spec)
  {
    foreach (var i in items)
```

---

[4] At this point, an interesting question is whether you want to use interfaces or abstract classes. If you do go for interfaces, you lose out on some options (such as custom operators), but you get being able to use record structs, which absolutely make sense for specification inheritors. Your choice.

```
    if (spec.IsSatisfied(i))
      yield return i;
  }
}
```

Again, you can think of an ISpecification<T> that's being passed in as a strongly typed equivalent of a Predicate<T> that has a finite set of concrete implementations suitable for the problem domain.

Now, here's the easy part. To make a color filter, you make a ColorSpecification:

```
public class ColorSpecification : ISpecification<Product>
{
  private Color color;

  public ColorSpecification(Color color)
  {
    this.color = color;
  }

  public bool IsSatisfied(Product p)
  {
    return p.Color == color;
  }
}
```

Armed with this specification, and given a list of products, we can now filter them as follows:

```
var apple = new Product("Apple", Color.Green, Size.Small);
var tree = new Product("Tree", Color.Green, Size.Large);
var house = new Product("House", Color.Blue, Size.Large);

Product[] products = {apple, tree, house};

var pf = new ProductFilter();
WriteLine("Green products:");
foreach (var p in pf.FilterByColor(products, Color.Green))
  WriteLine($" - {p.Name} is green");
```

Running this gets us "Apple" and "Tree" because they are both green. Now, the only thing we haven't implemented so far is searching for size *and* color (or, indeed, explained how you would search for size *or* color or mix different criteria). The answer is that you simply make a *combinator*. For example, for the logical AND, you can make it as follows:

```
public class AndSpecification<T> : ISpecification<T>
{
  private readonly ISpecification<T> first, second;

  public AndSpecification(ISpecification<T> first, ISpecification<T> second)
  {
    this.first = first;
    this.second = second;
  }

  public override bool IsSatisfied(T t)
  {
    return first.IsSatisfied(t) && second.IsSatisfied(t);
  }
}
```

And now, you are free to create composite conditions on the basis of simpler ISpecifications. Reusing the green specification we made earlier, finding something green and big is now as simple as

```
foreach (var p in bf.Filter(products,
  new AndSpecification<Product>(
    new  ColorSpecification(Color.Green),
    new  SizeSpecification(Size.Large))))
{
  WriteLine($"{p.Name} is large");
}

// Tree is large and green
```

This was a lot of code to do something seemingly simple, but the benefits are well worth it. The only really annoying part is having to specify the generic argument to AndSpecification – remember, unlike the color/size specifications, the combinator isn't constrained to the Product type.

Keep in mind that, thanks to the power of C#, you can simply introduce an `operator` & (important: single ampersand here – && is a byproduct) for two `ISpecification<T>` objects, thereby making the process of filtering by two (or more!) criteria somewhat simpler. The only problem is that we need to change from an interface to an abstract class (feel free to remove the leading I from the name):

```
public abstract class ISpecification<T>
{
  public abstract bool IsSatisfied(T p);

  public static ISpecification<T> operator &(
    ISpecification<T> first, ISpecification<T> second)
  {
    return new AndSpecification<T>(first, second);
  }
}
```

If you now avoid making extra variables for size/color specifications, the composite specification can be reduced to a single line[5]:

```
var largeGreenSpec = new ColorSpecification(Color.Green)
                   & new SizeSpecification(Size.Large);
```

Naturally, you can take this approach to extreme by defining extension methods on all pairs of possible specifications...

```
public static class CriteriaExtensions
{
  public static AndSpecification<Product> And(this Color color, Size size)
  {
    return new AndSpecification<Product>(
      new ColorSpecification(color),
      new SizeSpecification(size));
  }
}
```

---

[5] Notice we're using a single & in the evaluation. If you want to use &&, you'll also need to override the `true` and `false` operators in `ISpecification`.

...with the subsequent use:

```
var largeGreenSpec = Color.Green.And(Size.Large);
```

However, this would require a set of pairs of all possible criteria, something that's not particularly realistic, unless you use code generation, of course. Sadly, there is no way in C# of establishing an implicit relationship between an enum Xxx and an XxxSpecification.

Figure 1-1 shows a diagram of the entire system we've just built.

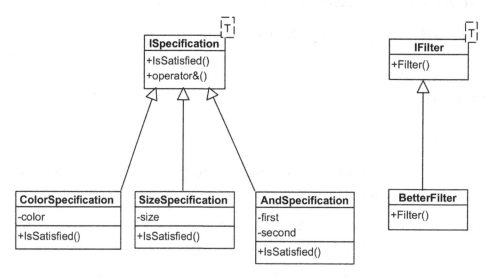

Figure 1-1. *Specification pattern class diagram*

So let's recap what the OCP is and how this example enforces it. Basically, the OCP states that you shouldn't need to go back to code you've already written and tested and change it. And that's exactly what's happening here! We made ISpecification<T> and IFilter<T>, and from then on, all we have to do is implement either of the interfaces (without modifying the interfaces themselves) to implement new filtering mechanics. This is what is meant by "open for extension, closed for modification."

One thing worth noting is that OCP conformance is only possible inside an object-oriented paradigm. For example, F#'s discriminated unions are by definition not compliant with the OCP since it is impossible to extend them without modifying their original definition.

Liskov Substitution Principle

The Liskov Substitution Principle (LSP), named after Barbara Liskov,[6] states that if an interface takes an object of type Parent, it should equally take an object of type Child without anything breaking. A more formal definition of the LSP is as follows:

> Let $\phi(x)$ be a property provable about objects x of type T.
> Then $\phi(y)$ should be true for objects y of type S where S is a subtype of T.

This requirement for so-called *behavioral subtyping* cannot be enforced in an automatic fashion, though some automated code checks can theoretically be performed to avoid it being broken. The LSP is therefore best treated as an informal rule rather than a strict OOP dogma.

Let's take a look at a situation where the LSP is broken.

Here's a rectangle; it has width and height and a bunch of getters and setters calculating the area:

```
public class Rectangle
{
  public int Width { get; set; }
  public int Height { get; set; }

  public Rectangle() {}
  public Rectangle(int width, int height)
  {
    Width = width;
    Height = height;
  }

  public int Area => Width * Height;
}
```

---

[6] See https://en.wikipedia.org/wiki/Barbara_Liskov

Suppose we make a special kind of Rectangle called a Square. This object overrides the setters to set both width *and* height:

```
public class Square : Rectangle
{
  public Square(int side)
  {
    Width = Height = side;
  }

  public new int Width
  {
    set { base.Width = base.Height = value; }
  }

  public new int Height
  {
    set { base.Width = base.Height = value; }
  }
}
```

Your intuition is probably telling you that this code is not great and potentially erroneous, but you cannot see any problems just yet because it looks very innocent indeed: the setters simply set both dimensions (so that a square always remains a square), and what can possibly go wrong? Well, suppose we introduce a method that makes use of a Rectangle:

```
public static void UseIt(Rectangle r)
{
  r.Height = 10;
  WriteLine($"Expected area of {10*r.Width}, got {r.Area}");
}
```

This method works just fine when used with a Rectangle:

```
var rc = new Rectangle(2,3);
UseIt(rc);
// Expected area of 20, got 20
```

However, an innocuous method can seriously backfire if used with a Square instead:

```
var sq = new Square(5);
UseIt(sq);
// Expected area of 50, got 100
```

This code takes the formula Area = Width × Height as an invariant. It gets the width, sets the height to 10, and rightly expects the product to be equal to the calculated area. But calling the preceding function with a Square yields a value of 100 instead of 50. I'm sure you can guess why this is.

So the problem here is that although UseIt() is happy to take any Rectangle class, it fails to take a Square because the behaviors inside Square break its operation. So how would you fix this issue? Well, one approach would be to simply deprecate the Square class and start treating some Rectangles as special case. For example, you could introduce an IsSquare property:

```
public bool IsSquare => Width == Height;
```

Similarly, instead of having constructors, you could introduce factory methods (see Chapter 4) that would construct rectangles and squares and would have corresponding names (e.g., NewRectangle() and NewSquare()), so there would be no ambiguity.

As far as setting the properties is concerned, in this case, the solution would be to introduce a uniform SetSize(width,height) method and remove Width/Height setters entirely. This way, you avoid the situation where setting the height via a setter also stealthily changes the width.

This rectangle/square challenge is, in my opinion, an excellent interview question: it doesn't have a correct answer, but allows many interpretations and variations.

Interface Segregation Principle

The discussion around the Interface Segregation Principle calls for an admittedly contrived example that is nonetheless suitable for illustrating the problem. Suppose you decide to define a multifunction printer: a device that can print, scan, and also fax documents. So you define it like so:

```
class MyFavouritePrinter /* : IMachine */
{
  void Print(Document d) {}
```

```
  void Fax(Document d) {}
  void Scan(Document d) {}
};
```

This is fine. Now, suppose you decide to define an interface that needs to be implemented by everyone who also plans to make a multifunction printer. So you could use the Extract Interface refactoring in your favorite IDE, and you'll get something like the following:

```
public interface IMachine
{
  void Print(Document d);
  void Fax(Document d);
  void Scan(Document d);
}
```

This is a problem. The reason it is a problem is that some implementor of this interface might not need scanning or faxing, just printing. And yet, you are forcing them to implement those extra features: sure, they can all be no-op, but why bother with this?

A typical example would be a good old-fashioned printer that doesn't have any scanning or fax functionality. Implementing the IMachine interface in this situation becomes a real challenge. What's particularly frustrating about this situation is there is no *correct* way of leaving things unimplemented – this is actually a good indicator that interfaces are poorly segregated. I mean, sure, you can throw an exception, and we even have a dedicated exception precisely for this purpose:

```
public class OldFashionedPrinter : IMachine
{
  public void Print(Document d)
  {
    // yep
  }

  public void Fax(Document d)
  {
    throw new System.NotImplementedException();
  }
```

```
public void Scan(Document d)
{
  // left empty
}
}
```

But you are still confusing the user! They can see `OldFashionedPrinter.Fax()` as part of the API, so they can be forgiven for thinking that this type of printer can fax too! So what else can you do? Well, you can just leave the extra methods as no-op (empty), just like the `Scan()` method. This approach violates the *Principle of Least Surprise* (also known as the *Principle of Least Astonishment*, POLA): your users want things to be as predictable as you can possibly make them. And neither a method that throws by default nor a method that does nothing is the most predictable solution – even if you make it explicit in the documentation!

The only option that would categorically work at compile time is the nuclear option of marking all unnecessary methods obsolete:

```
[Obsolete("Not supported", true)]
public void Scan(Document d)
{
  throw new System.NotImplementedException();
}
```

This will prevent compilation if someone does try to use `OldFashionedPrinter.Scan()`. In fact, good IDEs will recognize this ahead of time and will often cross out the method as you call it to indicate that it's not going to work. The only issue with this approach is that it's deeply unidiomatic: the method isn't really obsolete – it's unimplemented. Stop lying to the client!

So what the Interface Segregation Principle suggests you do instead is split up interfaces, so that implementors can pick and choose depending on their needs. Since printing and scanning are different operations (e.g., a scanner cannot print), we define separate interfaces for these:

```
public interface IPrinter
{
  void Print(Document d);
}
```

```
public interface IScanner
{
  void Scan(Document d);
}
```

Then, a printer can implement *just* the required functionality, nothing else:

```
public class Printer : IPrinter
{
  public void Print(Document d)
  {
    // implementation here
  }
}
```

Similarly, if we want to implement a photocopier, we can do so by implementing the IPrinter and IScanner interfaces:

```
public class Photocopier : IPrinter, IScanner
{
  public void Print(Document d) { ... }
  public void Scan(Document d) { ... }
}
```

Now, if we really want a dedicated interface for a multifunction device, we can define it as a combination of the aforementioned interfaces:

```
public interface IMultiFunctionDevice
  : IPrinter, IScanner // also IFax etc.
{
  // nothing here
}
```

And when you make a class for a multifunction device, this is the interface to use. For example, you could use simple delegation to ensure that Machine reuses the functionality provided by a particular IPrinter and IScanner (this is actually a good illustration of the Decorator pattern):

```csharp
public class MultiFunctionMachine : IMultiFunctionDevice
{
  // compose this out of several modules
  private IPrinter printer;
  private IScanner scanner;

  public MultiFunctionMachine(IPrinter printer, IScanner scanner)
  {
    this.printer = printer;
    this.scanner = scanner;
  }

  public void Print(Document d) => printer.Print(d);
  public void Scan(Document d) => scanner.Scan(d);
}
```

Figure 1-2 is a visual illustration of this entire setup.

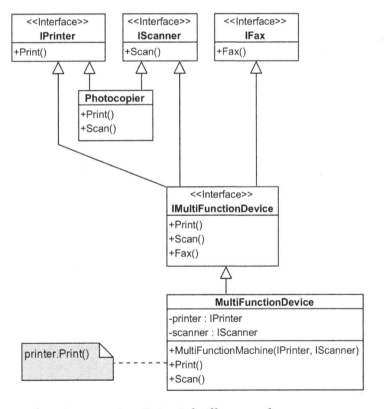

Figure 1-2. *Interface Segregation Principle illustrated*

So, just to recap, the idea here is to split related functionality of a complicated interface into separate interfaces so as to avoid forcing clients to implement functionality that they do not really need. Whenever you find yourself writing a plugin for some complicated application and you're given an interface with 20 confusing methods to implement with various no-ops and `return nulls`, more likely than not the API authors have violated the ISP.

Parameter Object

When we talk about interfaces, we typically talk about the `interface` keyword, but the essence of the ISP can also be applied to a much more local phenomenon: interfaces in the conventional sense, for example, a parameter list exposed by a constructor.

Consider a (completely arbitrary) example of a constructor that takes a large number of parameters. Most of these parameters have defaults, but some do not:

```
public class Foo
{
  public Foo(int a, int b, bool c = false, int d = 42, float e = 1.0f)
  {
    // meaningful code here
  }
}
```

The problem with the interface of the preceding constructor is that it throws a lot into the face of an unsuspecting client. The situation becomes even more comical if the client has to provide arguments a, b, and e because then they'll end up repeating some of the defaults (e.g., for c and d) unnecessarily.

In this situation, the core principle of the ISP (do not throw everything into an interface) also makes sense here, but for different reasons. You need to provide a sensible set of defaults and help the client avoid repeating them.

Any self-respecting IDE offers you the **Parameter Object** refactoring – an ability to take all parameters and put them into a class with all the defaults preserved:

```
public class MyParams
{
  public int a;
  public int b;
  public bool c = false;
```

```
  public int d = 42;
  public float e = 1.0f;

  public MyParams(int a, int b)
  {
    this.a = a;
    this.b = b;
  }
}
```

This parameter object would then be passed into Foo's constructor:

```
public Foo(MyParams myParams)
{
  // meaningful work here
}
```

Notice how MyParams is crafted: it does have a constructor of its own, mandating that you initialize the first two parameters, but it also exposes other parameters for you to initialize arbitrarily if you don't like their default values.

All I'm trying to say is this: principles and patterns don't have to operate at the macro (class) scale – they are also good enough to operate on smaller scales, such as the scale of individual methods.

Dependency Inversion Principle

The original definition of the Dependency Inversion Principle states the following[7]:

A. High-level modules should not depend on low-level modules. Both should depend on abstractions.

What this statement means is that, if you're interested in logging, your reporting component should not depend on a concrete ConsoleLogger, but should instead depend on an ILogger interface. In this case, we are considering the reporting component to be high level (closer to the business domain), whereas logging, being a fundamental concern (kind of like file I/O or threading, but not quite), is considered a low-level module.

---

[7] Robert C. Martin, *Agile Software Development: Principles, Patterns, and Practices* (Prentice Hall, 2003), pp. 127–131.

B. Abstractions should not depend on details. Details should depend on abstractions.

This is, once again, restating that dependencies on interfaces or base classes are better than dependencies on concrete types. Hopefully, the truth of this statement is obvious, because such an approach supports better configurability and testability, especially if you are using a good framework to handle these dependencies for you.

Let's take a look at an example of the DIP in action. Suppose we decide to model a genealogical relationship between people using the following definitions:

```csharp
public enum Relationship
{
  Parent,
  Child,
  Sibling
}

public class Person
{
  public string Name;
  // DoB and other useful properties here
}
```

We create a (low-level) class specifically for storing information about relationships. If we chose to save parent-child relationships in both directions, it would look something like the following:

```csharp
public class Relationships // low-level
{
  public List<(Person,Relationship,Person)> relations = new();

  public void AddParentAndChild(Person parent, Person child)
  {
    relations.Add((parent, Relationship.Parent, child));
    relations.Add((child, Relationship.Child, parent));
  }
}
```

Now, suppose we want to do some research on the relationships we've captured. For example, in order to find all the children of John, we create the following (high-level) class:

```
public class Research
{
  public Research(Relationships relationships)
  {
    // high-level: find all of john's children
    var relations = relationships.Relations;
    foreach (var r in relations
      .Where(x => x.Item1.Name == "John"
               && x.Item2 == Relationship.Parent))
    {
      WriteLine($"John has a child called {r.Item3.Name}");
    }
  }
}
```

The approach illustrated here directly violates the DIP because a high-level module `Research` directly depends on the low- level module `Relationships`. Why is this bad? Because `Research` depends directly on the data storage implementation of `Relationships`: you can see it iterating the list of tuples. What if you wanted to later change the underlying storage of `Relationships`, perhaps by moving it from a list of tuples to a proper database? Well, you couldn't, because you have high-level modules depending on it.

So what do we want? We want our high-level module to depend on an *abstraction*, which, in C# terms, means depending on an interface of some kind. But we don't have an interface yet! No problem, let's create one:

```
public interface IRelationshipBrowser
{
  IEnumerable<Person> FindAllChildrenOf(string name);
}
```

This interface has a single method for finding all children of a particular person by name. We expect that a low-level module such as Relationships would be able to implement this method and thereby keep its implementation details private:

```csharp
public class Relationships : IRelationshipBrowser // low-level
{
  // no longer public!
  private List<(Person,Relationship,Person)> relations = new();

  public IEnumerable<Person> FindAllChildrenOf(string name)
  {
    return relations
      .Where(x => x.Item1.Name == name
                  && x.Item2 == Relationship.Parent)
      .Select(r => r.Item3);
  }
}
```

Now this is something that our Research module can depend upon! We can inject an IRelationshipBrowser into its constructor and perform the research safely, without digging into the low-level module's internals:

```csharp
public Research(IRelationshipBrowser browser)
{
  foreach (var p in browser.FindAllChildrenOf("John"))
  {
    WriteLine($"John has a child called {p.Name}");
  }
}
```

Please note that the DIP isn't the equivalent of dependency *injection* (DI), which is another important topic in its own right. DI can facilitate the application of the DIP by simplifying the representation of dependencies, but those two are separate concepts.

CHAPTER 2

The Functional Perspective

The functional paradigm is supported by both the C# and F# languages. Both languages can claim to be multi-paradigm since they fully support both OOP and functional programming, though F# has more of a "functional-first" mindset with object orientation added for completeness, whereas in C# the integration of functional programming aspects appears to be much more harmonious.

Here we are going to take a very cursory look at functional programming in the C# and F# languages. Some of the material may already be familiar to you; in that case, feel free to skip this part.

Function Basics

First, a note on notation. In this book, I use the words *method* and *function* interchangeably to mean the same thing: a self-contained operation that takes zero or more inputs and has zero or more outputs (return values). I will use the word *method* when working in the C# domain and likewise will use the word *function* when dealing with the functional domain.

In C#, functions are not freestanding: they must be members of some class or other. For example, to define integer addition, you must pack the Add() method into some class (let's call it Ops):

```
struct Ops
{
  public static int Add(int a, int b)
  {
```

© Dmitri Nesteruk 2022
D. Nesteruk, *Design Patterns in .NET 6*, https://doi.org/10.1007/978-1-4842-8245-8_2

```
    return a + b;
  }
}
```

This function is meant to be called as Ops.Add() though you can shorten it to just Add() if you use C#'s import static instruction. Still, this is a particular pain point for the mathematicians because, even if you add global using static System.Math; to your project, you still end up having to use uppercase names for functions like Sin() – not an ideal situation![1]

In F#, the approach is drastically different. The preceding addition function can be defined as

```
let add a b = a + b
```

It may appear as if some magic has happened: we didn't define a class, nor did we specify the data types of arguments. And yet, if you were to look at the C#-equivalent code, you would see something like the following:

```
[CompilationMapping]
public static class Program
{
  [CompilationArgumentCounts(new int[] {1, 1})]
  public static int add(int a, int b)
  {
    return a + b;
  }
}
```

As you may have guessed, the static class Program got its name from the name of the file the code was in (in this case, Program.fs). The types of arguments were chosen as a guesstimate. What if we were to add a call with different argument types?

```
let ac = add "abra" "cadabra"
printfn "%s" ac
```

This code prints "abracadabra," of course, but what's interesting is the code generated... You've guessed it already, haven't you?

---

[1] You could introduce sin() as an alias for Sin(), but unfortunately, aliases cannot be global, so you'll end up having to repeat aliases in every single file that needs them.

```
[CompilationArgumentCounts(new int[] {1, 1})]
public static string add(string a, string b)
{
    return a + b;
}
```

The reason this is possible is called *type inference*: the compiler figures out which types you're actually using in a function and tries to accommodate by constructing a function with corresponding parameters. Sadly, this is not a silver bullet. For example, if you were to subsequently add another call – this time, with integers – it would fail:

```
let n = add 1 2
// Error: This expression was expected to have type 'string' but here has
type 'int'
```

Functional Literals in C#

It's not always convenient to define functions inside classes: sometimes you want to create a function exactly where you need it, that is, in another function. These sorts of functions are called *anonymous* because they are not given persistent names; instead, the function is stored in a delegate.

The old-fashioned, C# 2.0 way of defining anonymous functions is with the use of a delegate keyword, similar to the following:

```
BinaryOperation multiply = delegate(int a, int b) { return a * b; };
int x = multiply(2, 3); // 6
```

Of course, since C# 3.0 we have a much more convenient way of defining the same thing:

```
BinaryOperation multiply = (a, b) => { return a * b; };
```

Notice the disappearance of type information next to a and b: this is type inference at work once again!

Finally, since C# 6 we have expression-bodied members that allow us to omit the return keyword in single-statement evaluations, shortening the definition to the following:

```
BinaryOperation multiply = (a, b) => a * b;
```

Of course, anonymous functions are useless if you don't store them somewhere, and as soon as you're storing something, that something needs a *type*. Luckily, we have types of this too.

Storing Functions in C#

A key feature of functional programming is being able to refer to functions and call them through references. In C#, the simplest way to do this is using delegates.

A *delegate type* is to a function what a class is to an instance. Given our `Add()` function from earlier, we can define a delegate similar to the following:

```
public delegate int BinaryOperation(int a, int b);
```

A delegate doesn't have to live inside a C# class: it can exist at a namespace level. So, in a way, you can treat it as a type declaration. Of course, you can also stick a delegate into a class, in which case you can treat it as a *nested* type declaration.

Having a delegate such as this lets us store a reference to a function in a variable:

```
BinaryOperation op = Ops.Add;
int x = op(2, 3);
```

Compared with instances of a class, there's a note that needs to be made here – not only does a delegate instance know *which* function needs to be called but it also knows the *instance* of the class on which this method should be called. This distinction is critical because it allows us to distinguish, for example, static and non-static functions.

Any other function, which has the same signature, can also be assigned to this delegate, regardless of who is its logical owner. For example, you could define a function called `Subtract()` virtually anywhere and assign it to the delegate. This includes defining it as an ordinary member function:

```
class Program
{
  static int Subtract(int a, int b) => a - b;
  static void Main(string[] args)
  {
      BinaryOperation op = Subtract;
```

```
    int x = op(10, 2); // 8
  }
}
```

However, it can easily be a local (nested) function...

```
static void Main(string[] args)
{
  int Multiply(int a, int b) => a * b;
  BinaryOperation op = Multiply;
  int x = op(10, 2); // 20
}
```

...or even an anonymous delegate or a lambda function:

```
void SomeMethod()
{
  BinaryOperation op = (a, b) => a / b;
  int x = op(10, 2); // 5
}
```

Now, here's the important part. Pay attention: in the majority of cases, *defining your own delegates is not necessary.* Why? Because the .NET Base Class Library (BCL) comes with predefined delegates of up to 16 parameters in length (C# has no variadic templates[2]), which cover most cases that you might be interested in.

The Action delegate represents a function that doesn't return a value (is void). Its generic arguments relate to the types of arguments this function takes. So you can write something like

```
Action doStuff = () => Console.WriteLine("doing stuff!");
doStuff(); // prints "doing stuff!"
```

```
Action<string> printText = x => Console.WriteLine(x);
printText("hello"); // prints "hello"
```

---

[2]Variadic templates are primarily a C++ concept. They allow you to define template (generic) types and methods that take an *arbitrary* number of type arguments and provide (somewhat scary) syntax for iterating the argument type list. .NET generics are implemented differently from C++ templates (their "genericity" is preserved at runtime), so variadics in .NET are not possible.

The generic arguments of Action are needed to specify parameter types. If a function takes no parameters, just use a nongeneric Action.

If your function does need to return a value, then you can use a predefined delegate Func<T1, T2, ..., TR>. This is always generic, where TR has the type of the return value. In our case, we could have defined a binary operation as

```
Func<int, int, int> mul = Multiply;
// or
Func<int, int, int> div = (a, b) => a / b;
```

Together, Action and Func cover all the realistic needs you might encounter for a delegate. Since C# 10, these delegates can also be deduced into "natural delegate types." In other words, you can write

```
var div = (int a, int b) => a / b;
```

And after compiling, div will be of type Func<int, int, int> because, absent type information, the compiler will go off looking for a compatible Action/Func and, assuming it finds one, will set the variable's type accordingly.

Functional Literals in F#

In F#, the process of defining a function is a lot more harmonized. For example, there is no real distinction between the syntax for defining a variable and that for defining a method in the global scope:

```
let add a b = a + b

[<EntryPoint>]
let main argv =
  let z = add
  let result = z 1 2 // 3
  0
```

However, the decompiled results of this code are too frightening to show here. What is important to realize is that F# *does*, in fact, automatically map your function to a type without any extra hints. But instead of mapping it to a Func delegate, it maps it to its own type called FSharpFunc.

In order to understand the reason for FSharpFunc's existence, we need to understand something called *currying*. Currying (nothing to do with Indian food) is an entirely different approach from the way functions are defined and called. Remember when our F# function add a b got turned into a C#-equivalent int add(int a, int b)? Well, let me show you a very similar situation where this will *not* happen:

```
let printValues a b =
  printf "a = %i; b = %i" a b
```

As you may have guessed, all this code does is print the two integers passed in. But what does this *compile* to? Well, without showing extra levels of gore, the compiler generates, among other things, a class inheriting from FSharpFunc<int, Unit> (Unit can be seen as F#'s equivalent of void) that also happens to have another FSharpFunc<int, Unit> as an invocable member. Why?!

To simplify things, your printValues call actually got turned into something like

```
let printValues a =
  let printValues@10-1 b =
    printf "a = %i; b = %i" a b
  return printValues@10-1
```

So, in C# terms, instead of making a function callable as printValues(a,b), we made a function callable as printValues(a)(b).

What's the advantage of this? Well, let's come back to our add function:

```
let add a b = a + b
```

We can now use this function to define a new function called addFive that adds 5 to a given number. This function can be defined as follows:

```
let addFive x = add 5 x
```

We can now call it as

```
let z = addFive 5 // z = 10
```

Having this definition forces the compile to express the invocation of any call of add x y as being equivalent to add(x) (y). But add(x) (without the y) is already prepackaged as a standalone FSharpFunc<int,int> that itself yields a function that takes a y and adds it to the result. Therefore, the implementation of addFive can reuse this function without spawning any further objects!

And now we come back to the question of why F# uses FSharpFunc instead of Func. The answer is…inheritance! Since an invocation of arguments involves not just a single function call but an entire chain, a really useful way of organizing this chain of invocations is by using good old-fashioned inheritance.

Composition

F# has special syntax for calling several functions one after another. In C#, if you need to take the value x and apply to it functions g and then f, you would simply write it as f(g(x)). In F#, the possibilities are more interesting.

Let us actually take a look at how these functions could be defined and used. We are going to consider the successive application of two functions, one that adds 5 to a number and another that doubles it:

```
let addFive x = x + 5
let timesTwo x = x * 2

printfn "%i" (addFive (timesTwo 3)) // 11
```

If you think about it, the number 3 goes through a pipeline of operations: first, it is fed to timesTwo and then to addFive. This notion of a pipeline is represented in code through the F# forward pipe and backward pipe operators, which can be used to implement these operations as follows:

```
printfn "%i" (3 |> timesTwo |> addFive)
printfn "%i" (addFive <| (timesTwo <| 3))
```

Notice that while the forward operator |> example is very clean, the backward operator <| is much less so because extra brackets are required due to associativity rules.

We might want to define a new function that applies timesTwo followed by addFive to any argument. Of course, you could simply define it as

```
let timesTwoAddFive x =
  x |> timesTwo |> addFive
```

However, F# also defines function composition operators >> (forward) and << (backward) for composing several functions into a single function. Naturally, their arguments must match:

```
let timesTwoAddFive = timesTwo >> addFive
printfn "%i" timesTwoAddFive 3 // 11
```

Functional-Related Language Features

While not central to the discussion of functional programming, certain features often go with it hand in hand. This includes the following:

- Tail recursion helps with defining algorithms in a recursive fashion.

- Discriminated unions allow very quick definitions of related types with primitive storage mechanics. Sadly, this feature breaks the OCP because it's impossible to extend a discriminated union without changing its original definition.

- Pattern matching expands the domain of if statements with an ability to match against templates. This is omnipresent in F# (for lists, record types, and others) and is now appearing in C# too.

- Functional lists are a unique feature (entirely unrelated to List<T>), leveraging pattern matching and tail recursion.

These features are synergetic with the functional programming paradigm and can help the implementation of some of the patterns described in this book.

PART II

Creational Patterns

In a "managed" language such as C#, the process of creating a new object is simple: just new it up and forget about it. Now, with the proliferation of dependency injection, another question is whether creating objects manually is still acceptable, or should we instead defer the creation of all key aspects of our infrastructure to specialized constructs such as factories (more on them in just a moment!) or Inversion of Control containers?

Whichever option you choose, creation of objects can still be a chore, especially if the construction process is complicated or needs to abide by special rules. So that's where creational patterns come in: they are common approaches related to the creation of objects in less-than-trivial situations.

Just in case you're rusty on the ways an object can be constructed in C#, let's recap the main approaches:

- Invocation of new creates an object on the managed heap. The object doesn't need to be destroyed explicitly because the Garbage Collector (GC) will take care of it for us.

- Stack allocation with `stackalloc` allocates memory on the stack rather than the heap. Stack-allocated objects only exist in the scope they were created and get cleaned up auto when they go out of scope. This construct can only be used with value types.

- You can allocate unmanaged (native) memory with `Marshal.AllocHGlobal` and `CoTaskMemAlloc` and must explicitly free it with `Marshal.FreeHGlobal` and `CoTaskMemFree`. This is primarily needed for interoperation with unmanaged code.

Needless to say, some managed component might be working with unmanaged memory behind the scenes. This is one of the main reasons for the existence of the `IDisposable` interface. This interface has a single method, `Dispose()`, that can contain cleanup logic. If you are working with an object that implements `IDisposable`, it might make sense to wrap its use in a `using` statement (we now also have `using var`) so that its cleanup code gets executed as soon as the object is no longer needed.

CHAPTER 3

Builder

The Builder pattern is concerned with the creation of *complicated* objects, that is, objects that cannot be built up in a single-line constructor call. These types of objects may themselves be composed of other objects and might involve less-than-obvious logic, necessitating a separate component specifically dedicated to object construction.

I suppose it's worth noting beforehand that, while the Builder is concerned with *complicated* objects, we'll be taking a look at a rather trivial example. This is done purely for the purposes of space optimization, so that the complexity of the domain logic doesn't interfere with your ability to appreciate the actual implementation of the pattern.

Scenario

Let's imagine that we are building a component that renders web pages. A page might consist of just a single paragraph (let's forget all the typical HTML trappings for now), and to generate it, you'd probably write something like the following:

```
var hello = "hello";
var sb = new StringBuilder();
sb.Append("<p>");
sb.Append(hello);
sb.Append("</p>");
WriteLine(sb);
```

This is some serious overengineering, Java style, but it is a good illustration of one builder that we've already got in the .NET Framework: the `StringBuilder`! `StringBuilder` is, of course, a separate component that is used for memory-efficient string concatenation. It has utility methods such as `AppendLine()` so you can append both the text and a line break (as in `Enrivonment.NewLine`). But the real benefit of `StringBuilder` is that, unlike string concatenation that results in lots of temporary strings, it just allocates a buffer and fills it up with text that is being appended.

© Dmitri Nesteruk 2022
D. Nesteruk, *Design Patterns in .NET 6*, https://doi.org/10.1007/978-1-4842-8245-8_3

So how about we try to output a simple unordered (bulleted) list with two items containing the words *hello* and *world*? A very simplistic implementation might look as follows:

```
var words = new[] { "hello", "world" };
sb.Append("<ul>");
foreach (var word in words)
{
  sb.AppendFormat("<li>{0}</li>", word);
}
sb.Append("</ul>");
WriteLine(sb);
```

This does in fact give us what we want, but the approach is not very flexible. How would we change this from a bulleted list to a numbered list? How can we add another item to the list *after* the list has been created? Clearly, in this rigid scheme of ours, this is not easy once the StringBuilder has been initialized.

We might, therefore, go the OOP route and define an HtmlElement record class to store information about each HTML tag:

```
public record HtmlElement(string Name, string Text)
{
  public string Name = Name;
  public string Text = Text;
  private readonly Lazy<List<HtmlElement>> elements = new();
  public List<HtmlElement> Elements => elements.Value;
  private const int indentSize = 2;

  public HtmlElement() : this("", "") { }
}
```

This class models a single HTML tag that has a name and can also contain either text or a number of children, which are themselves HtmlElements. The key functionality here is the ToString() implementation. Since HtmlElement can be infinitely nested, ToString() needs to be able to handle this recursive nature. But since there is no way to alter the method signature to add an additional parameter, we simply implement it as...

```
public override string ToString() => ToStringImpl(0);
```

...with the actual implementation hidden in a private method:

```
private string ToStringImpl(int indent)
{
  var sb = new StringBuilder();
  var i = new string(' ', indentSize * indent);
  sb.Append($"{i}<{Name}>\n");
  if (!string.IsNullOrWhiteSpace(Text))
  {
    sb.Append(new string(' ', indentSize * (indent + 1)));
    sb.Append(Text);
    sb.Append('\n');
  }

  foreach (var e in Elements)
    sb.Append(e.ToStringImpl(indent + 1));

    sb.Append($"{i}</{Name}>\n");
    return sb.ToString();
}
```

With this approach, we can now create our list in a more sensible fashion:

```
var words = new[] { "hello", "world" };
var tag = new HtmlElement("ul", null);
foreach (var word in words)
  tag.Elements.Add(new HtmlElement("li", word));
WriteLine(tag); // calls tag.ToString()
```

This works fine and gives us a more controllable, OOP-driven representation of a list of items. It also greatly simplifies other operations, such as the removal of entries. But the process of building up each HtmlElement is not very convenient, especially if that element has children or some special requirements. Consequently, we turn to the Builder pattern.

Simple Builder

The Builder pattern simply tries to outsource the piecewise construction of an object into a separate class. Our first attempt might yield something like this:

```
class HtmlBuilder
{
  protected readonly string rootName;
  protected HtmlElement root = new HtmlElement();

  public HtmlBuilder(string rootName)
  {
    this.rootName = rootName;
    root.Name = rootName;
  }

  public void AddChild(string childName, string childText)
  {
    var e = new HtmlElement(childName, childText);
    root.Elements.Add(e);
  }

  public override string ToString() => root.ToString();
}
```

This is a dedicated component for building up an HTML element. The constructor of the builder takes a rootName, which is the name of the root element that's being built: this can be "ul" if we are building an unordered list, "p" if we're making a paragraph, and so on. Internally, we store the root as an HtmlElement and assign its Name in the constructor. But we also keep hold of the rootName so we can reset the builder later on if we want to.

The AddChild() method is the method that's intended to be used to add additional children to the current element, each child being specified as a name-text pair. It can be used as follows:

```
var builder = new HtmlBuilder("ul");
builder.AddChild("li", "hello");
builder.AddChild("li", "world");
WriteLine(builder.ToString());
```

You'll notice that, at the moment, the AddChild() method is void-returning. There are many things we could use the return value for, but one of the most common uses of the return value is to help us build a fluent interface.

Fluent Builder

Let's change our definition of AddChild() to the following:

```
public HtmlBuilder AddChild(string childName, string childText)
{
  var e = new HtmlElement(childName, childText);
  root.Elements.Add(e);
  return this;
}
```

By returning a reference to the builder itself, the builder calls can now be chained. This is what's called a *fluent interface*:

```
var builder = new HtmlBuilder("ul");
builder.AddChild("li", "hello")
        .AddChild("li", "world");
WriteLine(builder.ToString());
```

The "one simple trick" of returning this allows us to build interfaces where several operations can be crammed into one statement. Note that StringBuilder itself also exposes a fluent interface. Fluent interfaces are generally nice, but making decorators that use them (e.g., using an automated tool such as ReSharper or Rider) can be a problem – we'll encounter this later.

Static Initialization

As soon as we start working with fluent interfaces, we have a possibility of invoking the entire building process in a single line of code. The only annoyance is that, given that we have to invoke the constructor, the end result is not as pretty as it could be:

```
var b = new HtmlBuilder("ul")
  .AddChild("li", "hello").AddChild("li", "world");
```

We can avoid the new part altogether by introducing a very simple static Init() method that simply sends the arguments to the constructor:

```
public static HtmlBuilder Init(string rootName)
{
  return new HtmlBuilder(rootName);
}
```

This simple factory method (see Chapter 4) lets us write slightly cleaner code:

```
var b = HtmlBuilder.Init("ul")
  .AddChild("li", "hello").AddChild("li", "world");
```

An advantage of this approach is that you can have different Init() methods with different names – a rather niche feature for a builder. Yes, you can have a factory method with a polymorphic return, but this implies that you have a family of related builders – also something that's rather rare. But to be honest, the only advantage seems to be in being able to avoid the new keyword.

Communicating Intent

We have a dedicated builder implemented for an HTML element, but how will the users of our classes know how to use it? One idea is to simply *force* them to use the builder whenever they are constructing an object. Here's what you need to do:

```
class HtmlElement
{
  protected string Name, Text;
  protected List<HtmlElement> Elements = new();
  protected const int indentSize = 2;

  // hide the constructors!
  protected HtmlElement() {}
  protected HtmlElement(string name, string text)
  {
    Name = name;
    Text = text;
  }
```

```
// factory method
public static HtmlBuilder Create(string name) => new HtmlBuilder(name);
}
```

Our approach is two-pronged. First, we have hidden all constructors, so they are no longer available. I recommend that if you need to hide things, you make them `protected` rather than `private` just in case you decide to subclass later on.

Second, we have also hidden the implementation details of the builder itself, something we haven't done previously. We have, however, created a factory method (this is a design pattern we shall discuss later) for creating a builder right out of the `HtmlElement`. And it's a static method too! Here's how one would go about using it:

```
var builder = HtmlElement.Create("ul");
builder.AddChild("li", "hello")
  .AddChild("li", "world");
WriteLine(builder);
```

In the preceding example, we are *forcing* the client to use the static `Create()` method because, well, there's really no other way to construct an `HtmlElement` – after all, all the constructors are `protected`. So the client creates an `HtmlBuilder` and is then forced to interact with it in the construction of an object. The last line of the listing simply prints the object being constructed.

But let's not forget that our ultimate goal is to build an `HtmlElement`, and so far we have no way of getting to it! So the icing on the cake can be an implementation of `implicit operator HtmlElement` on the builder to yield the final value:

```
// the element we're building
protected HtmlElement root = new HtmlElement();

// support for implicit casts
public static implicit operator HtmlElement(HtmlBuilder builder)
{
  return builder.root;
}
```

The addition of the operator allows us to write the following:

```
HtmlElement root = HtmlElement
  .Create("ul")
  .AddChildFluent("li", "hello")
  .AddChildFluent("li", "world");
WriteLine(root);
```

Regrettably, there is no way of explicitly telling other users to use the API in this manner. Hopefully, the restriction on constructors coupled with the presence of the static `Create()` method encourages the user to use the builder, but in addition to the operator, it might make sense to also add a corresponding `Build()` function to `HtmlBuilder` itself:

```
public HtmlElement Build() => root;
```

Nested Builder and Immutability

Consider a situation where you want the constructed objects to be immutable. For example, you want to ensure that the children of an `HtmlElement` constructed by an `HtmlBuilder` cannot be modified after the builder is done.

How can we enforce it? At the moment, it is impossible. After all, the builder needs access to a mutable interface. However, we can entangle the two together by making the builder a nested type in the constructed object:

```
public record HtmlElement(...)
{
  ...
  public static HtmlBuilder Create(string name) => new(name);
  // and then
  public class HtmlBuilder
  {
    ...
  }
}
```

This allows for interesting opportunities. First, the publicly exposed set of nested elements can now be defined as

```
private readonly Lazy<List<HtmlElement>> elements = new();
// note the type below:
public IReadOnlyList<HtmlElement> Elements => elements.Value;
```

So we're now returning an IReadOnlyList. All that remains is to adjust the AddChildXxx() methods to now use the private elements instead, that is:

```
public HtmlBuilder AddChildFluent(string childName, string childText)
{
  var e = new HtmlElement(childName, childText);
  root.elements.Value.Add(e);
  //              ↑↑↑↑↑↑
  return this;
}
```

And that's it!

Now, of course, whether or not something like this is okay to do is a philosophical discussion. If you are designing both the object and the builder from the outset, it might be argued that this approach is fine, besides obviously breaking the SRP by entangling two classes together.

If, however, you are doing this post hoc by breaking the OCP as well as public API surface (by making a switch from constructors to enforced builders midstream), this, in my mind, is a more egregious offense and requires careful deliberation.

Composite Builder

Let us continue the discussion of the Builder pattern with an example where multiple builders are used to build up a single object. This scenario is relevant to situations where the building process is so complicated that the builder itself becomes subject to the Single Responsibility Principle and needs to be fragmented into smaller parts.

Let's say we decide to record some information about a person:

```
public class Person
{
  // address
  public string StreetAddress, Postcode, City;

  // employment info
  public string CompanyName, Position;
  public int AnnualIncome;
}
```

There are two aspects to `Person`: their address and employment information. What if we want to have separate builders for each – how can we provide the most convenient API? To do this, we'll construct a composite builder. This construction is not trivial, so pay attention: even though we want two separate builders for job and address information, we'll spawn no fewer than *three* distinct classes.

We'll call the first class `PersonBuilder`:

```
public class PersonBuilder
{
  // the object we're going to build
  protected Person person; // this is a reference!

  public PersonBuilder() => person = new Person();
  protected PersonBuilder(Person person) => this.person = person;

  public PersonAddressBuilder Lives => new PersonAddressBuilder(person);
  public PersonJobBuilder Works => new PersonJobBuilder(person);

  public static implicit operator Person(PersonBuilder pb)
  {
    return pb.person;
  }
}
```

This is *much* more complicated than our simple builder earlier, so let's discuss each member in turn:

- The reference `person` is a reference to the object that's being built. This field is marked `protected`, and this is done deliberately for the sub-builders. It's worth noting that this approach only works for reference types – if `person` were a `struct`, we would encounter unnecessary duplication.

- `Lives` and `Works` are properties returning builder facets: those sub-builders that initialize the address and employment information separately.

- `operator Person` is a trick that we've used before.

One very important point to note is the constructors: instead of just initializing the `person` reference with a `new Person()` everywhere, we only do so in the public, parameterless constructor. There is another constructor that takes a reference and saves it. This constructor is designed to be used by inheritors and not by the client. That's why it is protected. The reason things are set up this way is so that a `Person` is instantiated only once per use of the builder, even if the sub-builders are used.

Now, let's take a look at the implementation of a sub-builder class:

```
public class PersonAddressBuilder : PersonBuilder
{
  public PersonAddressBuilder(Person person) : base(person)
  {
    this.person = person;
  }

  public PersonAddressBuilder At(string streetAddress)
  {
    person.StreetAddress = streetAddress;
    return this;
  }

  public PersonAddressBuilder WithPostcode(string postcode)
  {
    person.Postcode = postcode;
```

```
    return this;
  }

  public PersonAddressBuilder In(string city)
  {
    person.City = city;
    return this;
  }
};
```

As you can see, `PersonAddressBuilder` provides a fluent interface for building up a person's address. Note that it actually *inherits* from `PersonBuilder` (meaning it has acquired the `Lives` and `Works` properties). It has a constructor that takes and stores a reference to the object that's being constructed, so when you use these sub-builders, you are always working with just a single instance of `Person` – you are not accidentally spawning multiple instances. It is *critical* that the base constructor is called – if it is not, the sub-builder will call the parameterless constructor automatically, causing the unnecessary instantiation of additional `Person` instances.

As you can guess, `PersonJobBuilder` is implemented in identical fashion, so I'll omit it here.

And now, the moment you've been waiting for – an example of these builders in action:

```
var pb = new PersonBuilder();
Person person = pb
  .Lives
    .At("123 London Road")
    .In("London")
    .WithPostcode("SW12BC")
  .Works
    .At("Fabrikam")
    .AsA("Engineer")
    .Earning(123000);

WriteLine(person);
// StreetAddress: 123 London Road, Postcode: SW12BC, City: London,
// CompanyName: Fabrikam, Position: Engineer, AnnualIncome: 123000
```

Can you see what's happening here? We make a builder and then use the `Lives`
property to get us a `PersonAddressBuilder,` but once we're done initializing the address
information, we simply call `Works` and switch to using a `PersonJobBuilder` instead. And
just in case you need a visual illustration of what we just did, it's rather uncomplicated.

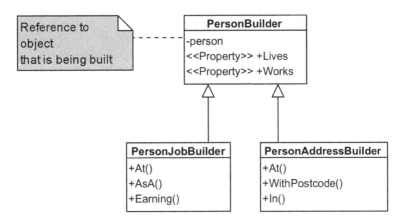

Figure 3-1. *Class diagram for a composite builder*

When we're done with the building process, we use the same implicit conversion
trick as before to get the object being built up as a `Person`. Alternatively, you can invoke
`Build()` to get the same result.

There's one fairly obvious downside to this approach: it's not extensible. Generally
speaking, it's a bad idea for a base class to be aware of its own subclasses, yet this
is precisely what's happening here – `PersonBuilder` is aware of its own children
by exposing them through special APIs. If you wanted to have an additional sub-
builder (say, a `PersonEarningsBuilder`), you would have to break the OCP and edit
`PersonBuilder` directly; you cannot simply subclass it to add an interface member.

Builder Marker Interfaces

As we mentioned previously, marker interfaces are used to communicate some extra
information about types without necessarily adding anything to the type's API. So
consider the marker interface for a builder:

```
interface IBuilder<T>
{
  T Build();
}
```

This interface is almost useless because you expect builders to implement `Build()` already. It's a convenient way of indicating that the type is used to build something. The choice of the interface also enforces the SRP in a strange way: since you cannot overload methods by return type, attempting to implement two builder interfaces on one type forces you to implement them explicitly, that is:

```
class SomeBuilder : IBuilder<Foo>, IBuilder<Bar>
{
  Bar IBuilder<Bar>.Build() { ... }
  Foo IBuilder<Foo>.Build() { ... }
}
```

This is something we generally want to avoid.

In a similar vein, if we want to indicate that a type is buildable, we could introduce an interface such as

```
interface IBuildableUsing<T>
{
  T New { get; }
}
```

If we want to be pedantic, we can go for an even stronger version that enforces T being an `IBuilder`:

```
interface IBuildableUsing<out TBuilder, TSubject>
  where TBuilder : IBuilder<TSubject>
{
  TBuilder New { get; }
}
```

If we decide to similarly define `IBuildableUsing`, we now have to put no fewer than two constraints on types: one on the builder and another on the subject being built:

```
interface IBuildableUsing<out TBuilder, TSubject>
  where TBuilder : IBuilder<TSubject>
  where TSubject : IBuildableUsing<IBuilder<TSubject>, TSubject>
{
  TBuilder New { get; }
}
```

Again, this is not something we can overload, so we cannot easily specify that a type has two different alternative builders.

And sure, we can go even further, producing abstract classes such as `Builder<T>` that would instantiate the target object (subject to a `new()` constraint) and a `BuildableUsing<T>` class that would default-construct a builder and return it through a property getter.

In my opinion, the examples here (especially the ones with generic constraints) are overengineered, especially considering that these interfaces, by themselves, add very little benefit to the application while increasing complexity.

Stepwise Builder (Wizard)

The Builder examples we have seen so far all allow us to define the elements of the constructed object in any order we want. There are situations, however, when the builder is order-sensitive. In other words, the order in which things are configured actually matters. Thus, what we need is some kind of stepwise builder that enforces configuration order. We often see such builders in UI construction – they are often called *wizards*, for some reason.

Why do we need to enforce order? One situation where this may be relevant is where only certain configurations are valid. Here is a very trivial scenario:

- A builder can construct a car that is a sedan or a crossover.

- A sedan can have wheels in the 15"–17" range, whereas a crossover can have wheels from 17" to 20".

Notice that the second build step is only actionable if the first build step has been completed. Adding wheels to a car where the car type is unknown (because nobody called the prior build step) is a scenario we simply cannot process, because we cannot apply validation *post hoc*: it has to happen in the right build step. Thus, builder method invocation order is critical.

This scenario has three steps (choose type, choose wheel size, build car) and so implies three different builder methods, and all of them need to return distinct types in order to allow the order to be followed. And we are certainly not going to have three different builders in order to achieve this!

So what's the solution to this problem? Why, we've met it before – it's the Interface Segregation Principle (ISP)! Each builder step needs to constrain the *interface* of the object returned from its step.

A simple model of a car is as follows:

```
public enum CarType { Sedan, Crossover };
public class Car
{
  public CarType Type;
  public int WheelSize;
}
```

The interfaces that allow us to guide the user step-by-step through the car configuration are the following:

```
public interface ISpecifyCarType
{
  public ISpecifyWheelSize OfType(CarType type);
} //                    ↓
  //                    ↓
public interface ISpecifyWheelSize
{
  public IBuildCar WithWheels(int size);
} //                    ↓
  //                    ↓
public interface IBuildCar
{
  public Car Build();
}
```

I've added arrows to show how the control flow keeps switching types.

Now, we need a starting point for the builder, which we'll call `CarBuilder`. Here we'll adopt an approach of completely hiding the builder *implementation* behind a private class:

```
public class CarBuilder
{
  public static ISpecifyCarType Create()
```

```
  {
    return new Impl();
  }

  interface ISpecifyCarType { ... }
  // other interfaces here

  private class Impl :
    ISpecifyCarType,
    ISpecifyWheelSize,
    IBuildCar
  {
    private Car car = new Car();

    // soon
  }
}
```

Take a moment to read through this code listing. It starts simply with a static Create() method, but what it returns is an instance of a private class whose name doesn't really matter – all it matters is this private class implements all the required interfaces.

Furthermore, you'll notice that we use composition instead of aggregation for the interfaces: since the interfaces make sense *only* for the builder, it makes sense to have them within the builder class. Nested types are not convenient when you need to use their type names, but here we plan on never seeing them being explicit, so we may as well hide them somewhat from the client – they are still public, of course.

Now, it is in this Impl class that all of the builder methods are implemented:

```
private class Impl :
  ISpecifyCarType,
  ISpecifyWheelSize,
  IBuildCar
{
  private readonly Car car = new();
```

```
public ISpecifyWheelSize OfType(CarType type)
{
  car.Type = type;
  return this;
}

public IBuildCar WithWheels(int size)
{
  switch (car.Type)
  {
    case CarType.Crossover when size < 17 || size > 20:
    case CarType.Sedan when size < 15 || size > 17:
      throw new ArgumentException($"Wrong size of wheels for {car.
      Type}.");
  }
  car.WheelSize = size;
  return this;
}

public Car Build()
{
  return car;
}
}
```

So now the game is up, and you hopefully have realized just how a stepwise builder is created. What we do is provide a constrained fluent interface: yes, we do return this, but typed to several interfaces, one after another.

The end result is you can write something like

```
var car = CarBuilder.Create() // ISpecifyCarType
  .OfType(CarType.Crossover)   // ISpecifyWheelSize
  .WithWheels(18)              // IBuildCar
  .Build();
```

I have added comments to the preceding listing to show the return types of the different methods. Note that this builder allows only a *single* build order: the client *must* specify the car type and *then* the wheel size, and then and only then are they allowed to build the car. They have no way of accessing the Impl builder so as to interfere with this order. See Figure 3-2 for a visual illustration of our step-by-step builder.

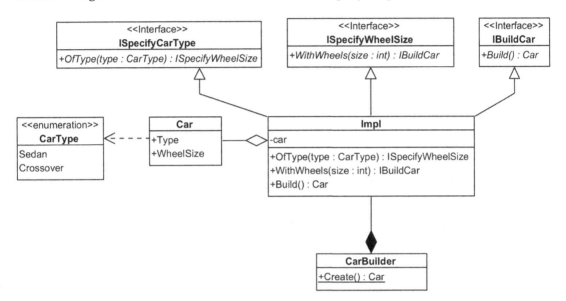

Figure 3-2. *Stepwise builder class diagram*

As always, if we wanted Car to have private fields only set from the builder, we could introduce CarBuilder as a private nested class – had we done this, the use of the Impl class would have become unnecessary because the only reason we've introduced an inner class in the first place is to have an implementation that's private. What I mean is that...

```
public class Car
{
  // private constructor
  private Car(){}

  private CarType Type;
  // other private fields here, then...
```

```
public static ISpecifyCarType Create()
{
  return new CarBuilder();
}

private class CarBuilder :
  ISpecifyCarType,
  ISpecifyWheelSize,
  IBuildCar
{
  // as before
}
}
```

...is an equally viable alternative provided you are prepared to tightly couple the car and its builder. The advantage here is you can hide Car members and even disallow its direct creation with a constructor.

Builder Parameter

As I have demonstrated, the only way to coerce the client to use a builder rather than constructing the object directly is to make the object's constructors inaccessible. There are situations, however, when you want to explicitly force the user to interact with the builder from the outset, possibly concealing even the object they're actually building.

For example, suppose you have an API for sending emails, where each email is described internally like this:

```
public class Email
{
  public string From, To, Subject, Body;
  // other members here
}
```

Note that I said *internally* here – you have no desire to let the user interact with this class directly, perhaps because there is some additional service information stored in it. Keeping it public is fine though, provided you expose no API that allows the client to send an Email directly. Some parts of the email (e.g., the Subject) are optional, so the object doesn't have to be fully specified.

You decide to implement a fluent builder that people will use for constructing an Email behind the scenes. It may appear as follows:

```
public class EmailBuilder
{
  private readonly Email email;
  public EmailBuilder(Email email) => this.email = email;

  public EmailBuilder From(string from)
  {
    email.From = from;
    return this;
  }

  // other fluent members here
}
```

Now, to coerce the client to use only the builder for sending emails, you can implement a MailService as follows:

```
public class MailService
{
  public class EmailBuilder { ... }

  private void SendEmailInternal(Email email) {}

  public void SendEmail(Action<EmailBuilder> builder)
  {
    var email = new Email();
    builder(new EmailBuilder(email));
    SendEmailInternal(email);
  }
}
```

As you can see, the SendEmail() method that clients are meant to use takes a function, not just a set of parameters or a prepackaged object. This function takes an EmailBuilder and then is expected to use the builder to construct the body of the message. Once that is done, we use the internal mechanics of MailService to process a fully initialized Email.

You'll notice there's a clever bit of subterfuge here: instead of storing a reference to an email internally, the builder gets that reference in the constructor argument. The reason we implement it this way is so that EmailBuilder wouldn't have to expose an Email publicly anywhere in its API.

Here's what the use of this API looks like from the client's perspective:

```
var ms = new MailService();
ms.SendEmail(email => email.From("foo@bar.com")
                           .To("bar@baz.com")
                           .Body("Hello, how are you?"));
```

Long story short, the Builder Parameter approach forces the consumer of your API to use a builder, whether they like it or not. This Action trick that we employ ensures that the client has a way of receiving an already-initialized builder object.

Builder Extension with Recursive Generics

One interesting problem that doesn't just affect the fluent builder but *any* class with a fluent interface is the problem of inheritance. Is it possible (and realistic) for a fluent builder to inherit from another fluent builder? It is, but it's not easy.

Here is the problem. Suppose you start out with the following (very trivial) object that you want to build up:

```
public class Person
{
  public string Name;
  public string Position;
}
```

You make a base class Builder that facilitates the construction of Person objects:

```
public abstract class PersonBuilder
{
  protected Person person = new Person();
  public Person Build()
  {
    return person;
  }
}
```

This is followed by a dedicated class for specifying the Person's name:

```
public class PersonInfoBuilder : PersonBuilder
{
  public PersonInfoBuilder Called(string name)
  {
    person.Name = name;
    return this;
  }
}
```

This works, and there is absolutely no issue with it. But now, suppose we decide to subclass PersonInfoBuilder so as to also specify employment information. You might write something like this:

```
public class PersonJobBuilder : PersonInfoBuilder
{
  public PersonJobBuilder WorksAsA(string position)
  {
    person.Position = position;
    return this;
  }
}
```

Sadly, we've now broken the fluent interface and rendered the entire setup unusable:

```
var me = Person.New
  .Called("Dmitri")  // returns PersonInfoBuilder
  .WorksAsA("Quant") // will not compile
  .Build();
```

Why won't the preceding code compile? It's simple: `Called()` returns `this`, which is an object of type `PersonInfoBuilder`; that object simply doesn't have the `WorksAsA()` method!

You might think the situation is hopeless, but it's not: you can design your fluent APIs with inheritance in mind, but it's going to be a bit tricky. Let's take a look at what's involved by redesigning the `PersonInfoBuilder` class. Here is its new incarnation:

```
public class PersonInfoBuilder<SELF> : PersonBuilder
  where SELF : PersonInfoBuilder<SELF>
{
  public SELF Called(string name)
  {
    person.Name = name;
    return (SELF) this;
  }
}
```

If you're not familiar with recursive generics, this code may seem rather overwhelming, so let's discuss what we actually did and why.

Firstly, we essentially introduced a new generic argument, `SELF`. What's more curious is that this `SELF` is specified to be an inheritor of `PersonInfoBuilder<SELF>`; in other words, the generic argument of the class is required to inherit from this exact class. This may seem like madness, but is actually a very popular trick for doing CRTP-style inheritance in C#.[1] Essentially, we are enforcing an inheritance chain: we are saying that `Foo<Bar>` is only an acceptable specialization if `Foo` derives from `Bar`, and all other cases should fail the `where` constraint.

The biggest problem in fluent interface inheritance is being able to return a `this` reference that is typed to the class you're currently in, even if you are calling a fluent interface member of a *base* class.[2] The only way to efficiently propagate this is by having a generic parameter (the `SELF`) that permeates the entire inheritance hierarchy.

To appreciate this, we need to look at `PersonJobBuilder` too:

---

[1] The CRTP – Curiously Recurring Template Pattern – is a popular C++ pattern that looks like this: `class Foo<T> : T`. In other words, you inherit from a generic parameter, something that's impossible in C#.

[2] In our example, the top-level class of the hierarchy is not generic. Had we made it generic such that it, too, received the `SELF` argument, we could use its constructor to cache a value of `(SELF)` `this` in a protected member. This would make the casts in the builder methods redundant.

```csharp
public class PersonJobBuilder<SELF>
  : PersonInfoBuilder<PersonJobBuilder<SELF>>
  where SELF : PersonJobBuilder<SELF>
{
  public SELF WorksAsA(string position)
  {
    person.Position = position;
    return (SELF) this;
  }
}
```

Look at its base class! It's not just an ordinary PersonInfoBuilder as before. Instead, it's a PersonInfoBuilder<PersonJobBuilder<SELF>>! So when we inherit from a PersonInfoBuilder, we set its SELF to PersonJobBuilder<SELF> so that all of its fluent interfaces return the correct type, *not* just the type of the owning class.

Does this make sense? If not, take your time and look through the source code once again. Here, let's test your understanding: Suppose I introduce another member called DateOfBirth and a corresponding PersonDateOfBirthBuilder. What class would it inherit from?

If you answered…

```csharp
PersonInfoBuilder<PersonJobBuilder<PersonBirthDateBuilder<SELF>>>
```

…then you are wrong, but I cannot blame you for trying. Think about it: PersonJobBuilder is *already* a PersonInfoBuilder, so that information doesn't need to be restated explicitly as part of the inheritance type list. Instead, you would define the builder as follows:

```csharp
public class PersonBirthDateBuilder<SELF>
  : PersonJobBuilder<PersonBirthDateBuilder<SELF>>
  where SELF : PersonBirthDateBuilder<SELF>
{
  public SELF Born(DateTime dateOfBirth)
  {
    person.DateOfBirth = dateOfBirth;
    return (SELF)this;
  }
}
```

The final question we have is this: how do we actually construct such a builder, considering that it *always* takes a generic argument? Well, I'm afraid you now need a new *type*, not just a variable. So, for example, the implementation of Person.New (the property that starts off the construction process) can be as follows:

```
public class Person
{
  public class Builder : PersonJobBuilder<Builder>
  {
    internal Builder() {}
  }

  public static Builder New => new Builder();

  // other members omitted
}
```

This is probably the most annoying implementation detail: the fact that you need to have a nongeneric inheritor of a recursive generic type in order to use it.

That said, putting everything together, you can now use the builder, leveraging all methods in the inheritance chain:

```
var builder = Person.New
  .Called("Natasha")
  .WorksAsA("Doctor")
  .Born(new DateTime(1981, 1, 1));
```

Lazy Functional Builder

The previous example of using recursive generics requires a lot of work. A fair question to ask is: should inheritance have been used to extend the builders? After all, we could have used extension methods instead.

If we adopt a functional approach, the implementation becomes a lot simpler, without the need for recursive generics. Let's once again build up a Person class defined as follows:

```
public class Person
{
  public string Name, Position;
}
```

This time round, we'll define a *lazy* builder that only constructs the object when its `Build()` method is called. Until that time, it will simply keep a list of `Actions` that need to be performed when an object is built:

```
public sealed class PersonBuilder
{
  private readonly List<Func<Person, Person>> actions = new ();

  public PersonBuilder Do(Action<Person> action)
    => AddAction(action);

  public Person Build()
    => actions.Aggregate(new Person(), (p, f) => f(p));

  private PersonBuilder AddAction(Action<Person> action)
  {
    actions.Add(p => { action(p); return p; });
    return this;
  }
}
```

The idea is simple: instead of having a mutable "object under construction" that is modified as soon as any builder method is invoked, we simply store a list of actions that need to be applied upon an initialized object whenever someone calls `Build()`. But there are additional complications in our implementation.

The first complication is that the action taken upon the person, while taken as an `Action<T>` parameter, is actually stored as a `Func<T,T>`. The motivation behind this is that by providing this fluent interface, we're allowing for the `Aggregate()` call inside `Build()` to work correctly. Of course, we could have used a good old-fashioned `ForEach()` instead.

The second complication is that, in order to allow OCP-conformant extensibility, we really don't want to expose `actions` as a public member, since this would allow far too many operations (e.g., arbitrary removal) on the list that we don't necessarily want exposed to whoever extends this builder in the future. Instead, we publicly expose only a single operation, Do(), that allows you to specify an action to be performed on the object under construction. That action is then added to the overall set of actions.

Under this paradigm, we can now give this builder a concrete method for specifying a Person's name:

```
public PersonBuilder Called(string name)
  => Do(p => p.Name = name);
```

But now, thanks to the way the builder is structured, we can use extension methods instead of inheritance to give the builder additional functionality, such as an ability to specify a person's position:

```
public static class PersonBuilderExtensions
{
  public static PersonBuilder WorksAs
    (this PersonBuilder builder, string position)
    => builder.Do(p => p.Position = position);
}
```

With this approach, there are no inheritance issues and no recursive magic. Any time we want additional behaviors, we simply add them as extension methods, preserving adherence to the OCP.

And here is how you would use this setup:

```
var person = new PersonBuilder()
  .Called("Dmitri")
  .WorksAs("Programmer")
  .Build();
```

This functional approach can be made into a generic base class that can be reused for building different objects. The only issue is that you'll have to propagate the derived type into the base class, which, once again, requires recursive generics.

You would define the base FunctionalBuilder as...

```
public abstract class FunctionalBuilder<TSubject, TSelf>
  where TSelf: FunctionalBuilder<TSubject, TSelf>
  where TSubject : new()
```

```
{
  private readonly List<Func<TSubject, TSubject>> actions = new();

  public TSelf Do(Action<TSubject> action)
    => AddAction(action);

  private TSelf AddAction(Action<TSubject> action)
  {
    actions.Add(p => { action(p); return p; });
    return (TSelf) this;
  }

  public TSubject Build()
    => actions.Aggregate(new TSubject(), (p, f) => f(p));
}
```

...with PersonBuilder now simplifying to...

```
public sealed class PersonBuilder
  : FunctionalBuilder<Person, PersonBuilder>
{
  public PersonBuilder Called(string name)
    => Do(p => p.Name = name);
}
```

...and the PersonBuilderExtensions class remaining as it was. With this approach, you could easily reuse FunctionalBuilder as a base class for other functional builders in your application. Notice that, under the functional paradigm, we're still sticking to the idea that the derived builders are all sealed and extended through the use of extension methods.

Builder-Decorator

Suppose you're into code generation and you want to extend StringBuilder in order to offer additional utility methods such as supporting indentation or scopes or whatever code generation functionality makes sense. It would be nice to simply inherit from

StringBuilder, but it's sealed for security reasons. Also, since you might want to store the current indentation level (say, to provide Indent()/Unindent() methods), you cannot simply go ahead and use extension methods, since those are stateless.[3]

So the solution is to create a brand-new class that aggregates a StringBuilder but also stores and exposes the same members as StringBuilder did and a few more. This is the Decorator pattern that you'll meet later in the book.

From the outset, the class can look as follows:

```
public class CodeBuilder
{
  private StringBuilder builder = new StringBuilder();
  private int indentLevel = 0;

  public CodeBuilder Indent()
  {
    indentLevel++;
    return this;
  }
}
```

As you can see, we have both the "underlying" StringBuilder and some additional members related to the extended functionality. What we need to do now is expose the members of StringBuilder as members of CodeBuilder, delegating the calls. StringBuilder has a very large API, so doing this by hand is unreasonable: instead, what you would do is use code generation (e.g., ReSharper/Rider's *Delegated Members* generator) to automatically create the necessary API.

This operation can be applied to every single member of StringBuilder and will generate the following signatures:

```
public class CodeBuilder
{
  public StringBuilder Append(string value)
```

---

[3] Strictly speaking, it *is* possible to store state in extension methods, albeit in a very roundabout way. Essentially, what you'd do is have your extension class keep a static member of type ConditionalWeakTable and then modify the entries in this dictionary to map an object to its set of properties (e.g., a Dictionary<string, object>). Plenty of fiddling is required here, both in terms of working with weak references (we don't want this store to extend the lifetime of the original object, right?) and the boxing and unboxing that comes with storing a bunch of objects.

```
  {
    return builder.Append(value);
  }

  public StringBuilder AppendLine()
  {
    return builder.AppendLine();
  }
  // other generated members omitted
}
```

This might seem great at first glance, but in actual fact, the implementation is incorrect. Remember, StringBuilder exposes a fluent API in order to be able to write things like

```
myBuilder.Append("Hello").AppendLine(" World");
```

In other words, it provides a fluent interface. But our decorator does not! For example, it won't let us write myBuilder.Append("x").Indent() because the result of Append(), as generated by ReSharper/Rider, is a StringBuilder that doesn't have an Indent() member. That's right – ReSharper does not know that we want a proper fluent interface. What you want is the fluent calls in CodeBuilder to appear as

```
public class CodeBuilder
{
  public CodeBuilder Append(char value, int repeatCount)
  {
    builder.Append(value, repeatCount);
    return this; // return a CodeBuilder, not a StringBuilder!
  }
  ...
}
```

This is something that you'd need to fix by hand or possibly through regular expressions. This modification, when applied to every single call that's delegated to StringBuilder, would allow us to chain StringBuilder's calls together with our unique, CodeBuilder-specific ones.

Scoping Builder Method

As part of implementing a `CodeBuilder`, we may wish to generate code that has scopes, like this:

```
class Foo
{
  // inside the scope
}
```

Inside the scope created by curly braces, the indentation level is increased; it is decreased when we leave the scope. How can we implement this?

One possibility is that our builder can implement a scoping method, that is, a method that takes a function that is then executed by the builder with pre- and post-actions applied:

```
public CodeBuilder Scope(Action<CodeBuilder> builder)
{
  AppendLine("{");
  indentLevel++;
  builder(this);
  indentLevel--;
  return AppendLine("}");
}
```

We would use the scoping builder method as

```
var cb = new CodeBuilder();
cb.AppendLine("class Foo")
  .Scope(b =>
  {
    b.AppendLine("int bar;");
  });
```

This way, a scope in your code is reflected by the scope generated by the code itself. Whether or not you actually need the scoping method to take this in the call is up to you – we could equally have captured the original cb object. The reason I have it here is because, sometimes, the object passed into the `Action` is a *completely different* object that operates according to different rules. It may define special rules, be an inheritor of the original object, have its own pre-/postprocessing steps, and so on. Writing code this way is better because you can refactor your solution to start using this substitute object.

Of course, that's not the only way we can set a value temporarily within a given scope. One approach would be to create some Scope class inheriting from IDisposable, whose constructor increments the indentation level, while the destructor decrements it. Our approach is a little neater.

DSL Construction in F#

Many programming languages (such as Groovy, Kotlin, or F#) try to throw in a language feature that will simplify the process of creating domain-specific languages (DSLs), that is, small languages that help describe a particular problem domain. Many applications of such embedded DSLs are used to implement the Builder pattern. For example, if you want to build an HMTL page, you don't have to fiddle with classes and methods directly; instead, you can write something that very much approaches HTML right in your code!

The way this is made possible in F# is using list comprehensions: the ability to define lists without any explicit calls to builder methods. For example, if you wanted to support HTML paragraphs and images, you could define the following builder functions:

```
let p args =
  let allArgs = args |> String.concat "\n"
  ["<p>"; allArgs; "</p>"] |> String.concat "\n"

let img url = "<img src=\"" + url + "\"/>"
```

Notice that whereas the img tag only has a single textual parameter, the <p> tag accepts a sequence of args, allowing it to contain any number of inner HTML elements, including ordinary plain text. We could therefore construct a paragraph containing both text and an image:

```
let html =
  p [
    "Check out this picture";
    img "pokemon.com/pikachu.png"
  ]
printfn "%s" html
```

This results in the following output:

```
<p>
Check out this picture
<img src="pokemon.com/pikachu.png"/>
</p>
```

This approach is used in web frameworks such as WebSharper. There are many variations of this approach, including the use of record types (letting people use curly braces instead of lists), custom operators for specifying plain text, and more.[4]

It's important to note that this approach is only convenient when we are working with an immutable, append-only structure. Once you start dealing with mutable objects (e.g., using a DSL to construct a definition for a Microsoft project document), you end up falling back into OOP. Sure, the end-result DSL syntax is still very convenient to use, but the plumbing required to make it work is anything but pretty.

Summary

The goal of the Builder pattern is to define a component dedicated entirely to piecewise construction of a complicated object or set of objects. We have observed the following key characteristics of a builder:

- Builders can have a fluent interface that is usable for complicated construction using a single invocation chain. To support this, builder functions should return `this`.

- To force the user of the API to use a builder, we can make the target class constructors inaccessible and then define a static `Create()` method that returns an instance of the builder. (The naming is up to you. You can call it `Make()`, `New()`, or something else.)

- A builder can be coerced to the object itself by defining the appropriate implicit conversion operator.

---

[4] For an example, see Tomas Petricek's snippet for an F#-based HTML-constructing DSL at `http://fssnip.net/hf`

- You can force the client to use a builder by specifying it as part of a parameter function. This way you can hide the object that's being built entirely.

- A single builder interface can expose multiple sub-builders. Through clever use of inheritance and fluent interfaces, one can jump from one builder to another with ease.

- Inheritance of fluent interfaces (not just for builders) is possible through recursive generics.

Just to reiterate something that I've already mentioned, the use of the Builder pattern makes sense when the construction of the object is a *nontrivial* process. Simple objects that are unambiguously constructed from a limited number of sensibly named constructor parameters should probably use a constructor (or dependency injection) without necessitating a builder as such.

CHAPTER 4

Factories

I had a problem and tried to use Java. Now I have a ProblemFactory.

—*Old Java joke*

This chapter covers two GoF patterns: *Factory Method* and *Abstract Factory*. These patterns are closely related, so we'll discuss them together. The truth, though, is that the real design pattern is called *Factory* and that both Factory Method and Abstract Factory are simply variations that are important, but certainly not as important as the main thing.

Scenario

Let's begin with a motivating example. Suppose you want to store information about a Point in Cartesian (X-Y) space. So you go ahead and implement something like this:

```
public class Point
{
  private double x, y;

  public Point(double x, double y)
  {
    this.x = x;
    this.y = y;
  }
}
```

So far, so good. But now, you also want to initialize the point from *polar* coordinates instead. You need another constructor with the following signature:

© Dmitri Nesteruk 2022
D. Nesteruk, *Design Patterns in .NET 6*, https://doi.org/10.1007/978-1-4842-8245-8_4

```
Point(float r, float theta)
{
  x = r * Math.Cos(theta);
  y = r * Math.Sin(theta);
}
```

Unfortunately, you've already got a constructor with two floats, so you cannot have another one.[1] What do you do? One approach is to introduce an enumeration:

```
public enum CoordinateSystem
{
  Cartesian,
  Polar
}
```

And then add another parameter to the point constructor:

```
public Point(double a,
  double b, // names do not communicate intent
  CoordinateSystem cs = CoordinateSystem.Cartesian)
{
  switch (cs)
  {
    case CoordinateSystem.Polar:
      x = a * Math.Cos(b);
      y = a * Math.Sin(b);
      break;
    default:
      x = a;
      y = b;
      break;
  }
}
```

---

[1] Some programming languages, most notably Objective-C and Swift, do allow overloading of functions that only differ by parameter names. Unfortunately, this idea results in a viral propagation of parameter names in all calls. I still prefer positional parameters, most of the time.

Notice how the names of the first two arguments were changed to a and b: we can no longer afford telling the user which coordinate system those values should come from. This is a clear loss of expressivity when compared with using x, y, rho, and theta to communicate intent.

Overall, our constructor design is usable, but ugly. In particular, in order to add some third coordinate system, for example, you would need to

- Give CoordinateSystem a new enumeration value.

- Change the constructor to support the new coordinate system.

There must be a better way of doing this.

Factory Method

The trouble with the constructor is that its name always matches the type. This means we cannot communicate any extra information in it, unlike in an ordinary method. Also, given the name is always the same, we cannot have two overloads, one taking x,y and another taking r,theta.

So what can we do? Well, how about making the constructor protected[2] and then exposing some static functions for creating new points?

```
public class Point
{
  protected Point(double x, double y)
  {
    this.x = x;
    this.y = y;
  }

  public static Point NewCartesianPoint(double x, double y)
  {
    return new Point(x, y);
  }
```

---

[2] Whenever you want to prevent a client from accessing something, I always recommend you make it protected rather than private because then you make the class inheritance-friendly.

```csharp
public static Point NewPolarPoint(double rho, double theta)
{
  return new Point(rho*Math.Cos(theta), rho*Math.Sin(theta));
}

// other members omitted
}
```

Each of these static functions is called a factory method. All it does is create a `Point` and return it, the advantages being that both the name of the method and the names of the arguments clearly communicate what kind of coordinates are required.

Now, to create a point, you simply write

```csharp
var point = Point.NewPolarPoint(5, Math.PI / 4);
```

From this line of code, we can clearly surmise that we are creating a new point with polar coordinates $r = 5$ and $\theta = \pi/4$.

Asynchronous Factory Method

When we talk about constructors, we always assume that the body of the constructor is synchronous. A constructor always returns the type of the constructed object – it cannot return a `Task` or `Task<T>`. Therefore, it cannot be asynchronous. And yet, there are situations where you do want the object to be initialized in an asynchronous fashion.

There are (at least) two ways this can be handled. The first is *by convention*: we simply agree that any asynchronously initialized type has a method called, say, `InitAsync()`:

```csharp
public class Foo
{
  private async Task InitAsync()
  {
    await Task.Delay(1000);
  }
}
```

The assumption here is that the client would recognize this member and will remember to call it, as in the following:

```
var foo = new Foo();
await foo.InitAsync();
```

But this is very optimistic. A second and better approach is to hide the constructor (make it `protected`) and then create a `static` factory method that both creates an instance of Foo and initializes it. We can even give it a fluent interface so that the resulting object is ready to use:

```
public class Foo
{
  protected Foo() { /* init here */ }

  public static Task<Foo> CreateAsync()
  {
    var result = new Foo();
    return result.InitAsync();
  }
}
```

This can now be used as

```
var foo = await Foo.CreateAsync();
```

Naturally, if you need constructor arguments, you can add them to the constructor and forward them from the factory method.

Factory

Just like with Builder, we can take all the Point-creating functions out of Point into a separate class that we call a *factory*. It's actually very simple:

```
class PointFactory
{
  public static Point NewCartesianPoint(float x, float y)
  {
    return new Point(x, y); // needs to be public
  }
  // same for NewPolarPoint
}
```

It's worth noting that the Point constructor can no longer be private or protected because it needs to be externally accessible. Unlike C++, there is no friend keyword for us to use; we'll resort to a different trick later on.

But for now, that's it – we have a dedicated class specifically designed for creating Point instances, to be used as follows:

```
var myPoint = PointFactory.NewCartesian(3, 4);
```

Inner Factory

An inner factory is simply a factory that is an inner (nested) class within the type it creates. The reason inner factories exist is because a nested class can access the outer class' private/protected members and, conversely, an outer class can access an inner class' private/protected members. This means that our Point class can also be defined as follows:

```
public class Point
{
  // typical members here

  // note the constructor is again private
  private Point(double x, double y) { ... }

  public static class Factory
  {
    public static Point NewCartesianPoint(double x, double y)
    {
      return new Point(x, y); // using a private constructor
    }
    // similar for NewPolarPoint()
  }
}
```

Okay, so what's going on here? Well, we've stuck the factory right into the class the factory creates. This is convenient if a factory only works with one single type and not so convenient if a factory relies on several types (and pretty much impossible if it needs their private members too).

With this approach, we can now write

```
var point = Point.Factory.NewCartesianPoint(2, 3);
```

You might find this approach familiar because several parts of the .NET Framework use this approach to expose factories. For example, the TPL lets you spin up new tasks with `Task.Factory.StartNew()`.

Physical Separation

If you don't like the idea of having the entire definition of the `Factory` being placed into your `Point.cs` file, you can use the `partial` keyword because, guess what, it works on inner classes too. First, in `Point.cs`, you would modify the `Point` type to now read

```
public partial class Point { ... }
```

Then, simply make a new file (e.g., `Point.Factory.cs`) and, inside it, define another part of `Point`, that is:

```
public partial class Point
{
  public static class Factory
  {
    // as before
  }
}
```

That's it! You've now physically separated the factory from the type itself, even though logically they are still entwined since one contains the other.

Abstract Factory

So far, we've been looking at the construction of a single object. Sometimes, you might be involved in the creation of families of objects. This is actually a pretty *rare* case, so unlike Factory Method and the plain old Factory pattern, Abstract Factory is a pattern that only shows up in complicated systems. We need to talk about it, regardless, primarily for historical reasons.

The scenario we're going to take a look at here is a scenario that is shown by many sources all over the Web, so I hope you'll forgive the repetition. We'll consider a hierarchy of geometrical shapes that we want to draw. We'll consider only shapes that have lines joining at right angles:

```
public interface IShape
{
  void Draw();
}

// these two are needed for IoC
public interface ISquare {}
public interface IRectangle {}

public class Square : ISquare
{
  public void Draw() => Console.WriteLine("Basic square");
}

public class Rectangle : IRectangle
{
  public void Draw() => Console.WriteLine("Basic rectangle");
}
```

Both Square and Rectangle, which transitively implement the IShape interface, form a kind of family: they are simple geometric shapes drawn using straight lines connected at right angles. We can now imagine another parallel reality where right angles are considered aesthetically displeasing and where both squares and rectangles would have their corners rounded:

```
public class RoundedSquare : ISquare
{
  public void Draw() => Console.WriteLine("Rounded square");
}

public class RoundedRectangle : IRectangle
{
  public void Draw() => Console.WriteLine("Rounded rectangle");
}
```

You'll notice that the two hierarchies are related conceptually, but there's no code element to indicate that they are part of the same thing. We could introduce such an element in a number of ways, one being a simple enumeration with all the possible shapes that the system supports:

```
public enum Shape
{
  Square,
  Rectangle
}
```

So we now have two *families* of objects: a family of basic shapes and a family of rounded shapes. With that in mind, we can create a factory for basic shapes...

```
public class BasicShapeFactory : ShapeFactory
{
  public override IShape Create(Shape shape)
  {
    switch (shape)
    {
      case Shape.Square:
        return new Square();
      case Shape.Rectangle:
        return new Rectangle();
      default:
        throw new ArgumentOutOfRangeException(
          nameof(shape), shape, null);
    }
  }
}
```

...and a similar RoundedShapeFactory for rounded shapes. Since the methods of these two factories would be identical, they can both inherit from an abstract factory defined as follows:

```
public abstract class ShapeFactory
{
  public abstract IShape Create(Shape shape);
}
```

What we've ended up with is a situation where a hierarchy of shapes got a corresponding hierarchy of factories. We can now create a method that will yield a particular type of factory on the basis of whether shape rounding is actually required:

```
public static ShapeFactory GetFactory(bool rounded)
{
  if (rounded)
    return new RoundedShapeFactory();
  else
    return new BasicShapeFactory();
}
```

And that's it! We now have a configurable way of instantiating not just individual objects, but entire families of objects:

```
var basic = GetFactory(false);
var basicRectangle = basic.Create(Shape.Rectangle);
basicRectangle.Draw(); // Basic rectangle

var roundedSquare = GetFactory(true).Create(Shape.Square); roundedSquare.
Draw(); // Rounded square
```

Naturally, the kind of manual configuration that we've done here could easily be done using an Inversion of Control (IoC) container – you simply define whether requests for a ShapeFactory should yield instances of BasicShapeFactory, RoundedShapeFactory, or some other factory type. In fact, unlike this GetFactory() method, the use of an IoC container will not suffer from a (trivial) OCP violation since no code other than the container configuration would have to be rewritten if a new ShapeFactory was to be introduced.

There's an additional thing that has to be said about the relationship between the Shape enum and the IShape inheritors. Strictly speaking, though our example works, there's no real enforcement that the enum members correspond one-to-one to the entire set of possible hierarchies. You could introduce such validations at compile time, but to derive the set of enum members (via T4/Roslyn, perhaps?), you would probably have to introduce additional IShape-implementing abstract classes (e.g., BasicShape and RoundedShape) so you have clear delineation between the two different hierarchies. It's up to you to decide whether or not this approach makes sense in your particular case.

Delegate Factories in IoC

One problem that we encounter when we work with dependency injection and IoC containers is that, sometimes, you have an object that has a bunch of services it depends on (that can be injected) but also has some constructor arguments that you need.

For example, given a service such as...

```
public class Service
{
  public string DoSomething(int value)
  {
    return $"I have {value}";
  }
}
```

...imagine a domain object that depends on this service, but also has a constructor argument that needs to be provided and is subsequently used in the dependent service:

```
public class DomainObject
{
  private Service service;
  private int value;

  public DomainObject(Service service, int value)
  {
    this.service = service;
    this.value = value;
  }

  public override string ToString()
  {
    return service.DoSomething(value);
  }
}
```

How would you configure your DI container (e.g., Autofac) to construct an instance of DomainObject that injects the service and also specifies the value of 42 for the value? Well, there's a brute-force approach, but it's rather ugly:

```
var cb = new ContainerBuilder();
cb.RegisterType<Service>();
cb.RegisterType<DomainObject>();

using var container = cb.Build();
var dobj = container.Resolve<DomainObject>(
  new PositionalParameter(1, 42));
Console.WriteLine(dobj); // I have 42
```

This works, but this code is brittle and not refactoring-friendly. What if the position of the parameter value changes? This would invalidate the Resolve() step. And, yes, we can try getting the parameter by name, but then again, the ability to refactor (e.g., rename) the constructor will suffer.

Luckily, there is a solution for this problem, and it's called a delegate factory. A delegate factory is, quite simply, a delegate that initializes an object, but it only requires you to pass the parameters that are not injected automatically. For example, a delegate factory for our domain object is as simple as

```
public class DomainObject
{
  public delegate DomainObject Factory(int value);
  // other members here
}
```

Now, when you use the DomainObject in your IoC container, instead of resolving the object itself, you resolve the factory!

```
var factory = container.Resolve<DomainObject.Factory>();
var dobj2 = factory(42);
Console.WriteLine(dobj2); // I have 42
```

The registration steps remain exactly the same. What happens behind the scenes is this: The IoC container initializes the delegate to construct an instance of an object that makes use of both the dependent services and the values provided in the delegate. Then, when you resolve it, the delegate is fully initialized and is ready to use!

Object Tracking and Bulk Replacements

Up to now, we've primarily looked at factories that could all be made static without loss of generality. After all, most factories do not have any state, and it's not obvious how a factory having state would benefit the client.

Perhaps the most obvious example is configurable factories, where some presets are defined before any factory methods are invoked. This takes us close to the Prototype Factory design pattern (see Chapter 5).

Another useful feature is when a factory can keep track of the objects it has constructed and can make adjustments to objects after they've been put to use. Even if the factory does not offer any construction-specific functionality, this ability has benefits because it allows us to, at the very least, keep track of the objects in the system and, furthermore, lets us perform modifications on constructed objects if they are needed.

Object Tracking

One advantage of objects constructed through a factory is that every instance of an object can be tracked. Given a model such as the following...

```csharp
public interface ITheme
{
  string TextColor { get; }
  string BgrColor { get; }
}

class LightTheme : ITheme
{
  public string TextColor => "black";
  public string BgrColor => "white";
}

class DarkTheme : ITheme
{
  public string TextColor => "white";
  public string BgrColor => "dark gray";
}
```

...we can easily construct a factory that keeps track of the objects it has created:

```
public class TrackingThemeFactory
{
  private readonly List<WeakReference<ITheme>> themes = new();

  public ITheme CreateTheme(bool dark)
  {
    ITheme theme = dark ? new DarkTheme() : new LightTheme();
    themes.Add(new  WeakReference<ITheme>(theme));
    return theme;
  }

  public string Info
  {
    get
    {
      // pretty-print what's in themes
    }
  }
}
```

This lets you get arbitrary info about the objects that the factory has created, for example:

```
var factory = new TrackingThemeFactory();
var theme = factory.CreateTheme(true);
var theme2 = factory.CreateTheme(false);
Console.WriteLine(factory.Info);
// Dark theme
// Light theme
```

This by itself is already useful because you can get all sorts of diagnostic data without using a profiler. You can collect information about how many objects are created and the way they are created. You can also collect statistics about the parameter use and, of course, perform caching if necessary.

But all these operations are read-only: the factory does not try to affect the objects it has given out. There are, however, situations where a factory may wish to adjust objects post hoc (think of factory recalls in the real world).

Bulk Modifications

You can also perform bulk modifications: for example, if you decide that LightTheme should use dark-gray text color instead of black, you can simply iterate the set of references, go through each one, and modify it or even overwrite its entire object state.

What you *cannot* do is replace each instance with an entirely different instance for every object that has been made by the factory. It would be cool to be able to replace LightTheme by DarkTheme application-wide, but WeakReference does not help here.

If you want to perform this kind of bulk replacement, you'll need double indirection – a kind of WeakReference<Ref<T>> with Ref<T> defined as[3]

```
public class Ref<T> where T : class
{
  public T Value;
  public Ref(T value) { Value = value; }
}
```

Now, a bulk replacement factory can keep a list of weak references of Ref<ITheme> objects and, in its factory method, would return a Ref<ITheme> instead of an ordinary theme:

```
public class ReplaceableThemeFactory
{
  private readonly List<WeakReference<Ref<ITheme>>> themes
    = new();

  private ITheme createThemeImpl(bool dark)
  {
    return dark ? new DarkTheme() : new LightTheme();
  }
```

---

[3] A viable alternative could be to instead define a WeakRef<T> class that would inherit directly from WeakReference<T>.

```csharp
public Ref<ITheme> CreateTheme(bool dark)
{
  var r = new Ref<ITheme>(createThemeImpl(dark));
  themes.Add(new(r));
  return r;
}
}
```

Given this implementation, we can now replace every returned instance of ITheme with a different one:

```csharp
public void ReplaceTheme(bool dark)
{
  foreach (var wr in themes)
  {
    if (wr.TryGetTarget(out var reference))
    {
      reference.Value = createThemeImpl(dark);
    }
  }
}
```

In real-world terms, you can think of this functionality as a factory recall: if a car factory finds that cars sold up to now have a defective part, it collects your car and replaces the part, for free. The same principle is applied here:

```csharp
var factory2 = new ReplaceableThemeFactory();
var magicTheme = factory2.CreateTheme(true);
Console.WriteLine(magicTheme.Value.BgrColor); // dark gray
factory2.ReplaceTheme(false);
Console.WriteLine(magicTheme.Value.BgrColor); // white
```

Lucky for us, there are no safety issues here. If there is an ongoing operation on the old variable, that operation can continue as before while we update the new value. The Garbage Collector (GC) will take care of lifetimes, correctly retiring old values when there isn't anyone referencing them.

There is one problem with this example: there's really nothing preventing people from unwrapping a Ref<T>, getting its Value, and storing it independently, in which case bulk replacement will of course not work. How can we solve this? We can build a transparent proxy[4] (see Chapter 13 for a general description of the Proxy pattern). We already have one of the building blocks of an indirection proxy in our Ref<T> class, so now all we have to do is make a new class that also implements the ITheme interface:

```
public class ThemeRef : Ref<ITheme>, ITheme
{
  public ThemeRef(ITheme value) : base(value) {}

  public string TextColor => Value.TextColor;
  public string BgrColor => Value.BgrColor;
}
```

With this modification, things become a lot simpler. Our factory now keeps a List <WeakReference<ThemeRef>>, and the factory method simplifies to

```
public ITheme CreateTheme(bool dark)
{
  var r = new ThemeRef(createThemeImpl(dark));
  themes.Add(new(r));
  return r;
}
```

Notice the return value – it's a genuine ITheme that the client can use straight away without unpacking. They do not have direct access to the underlying reference:

```
Console.WriteLine(magicTheme.BgrColor); // dark gray
factory2.ReplaceTheme(false);
Console.WriteLine(magicTheme.BgrColor); // white
```

Now, if you keep Ref<T> publicly accessible, the client could cast to it and get at the Value. If you really want to prevent this, my suggestion would be to move Ref<T> into either your factory or a designated factory base class, make it private, and make Value private, and then you'd have more protection against clients messing with your designs. Mind you, the persistent ones can still get to the value using reflection.

---

[4] This has nothing to do with TransparentProxy in System.Runtime.Remoting.

Another argument can be that Ref<T> is simply unnecessary. It's not polymorphic, so if you wanted your factory to manage disjoint classes of objects, you would still introduce a marker interface by having Ref<T> implement some IRef interface.

Functional Factory

Under the purely functional paradigm, the Factory pattern is of limited use, since F# prefers to work with concrete types whenever possible, using functions and functional composition to express variability in implementation.

If you wanted to go with interfaces (which F# allows), then, given the following definition…

```
type ICountryInfo =
  abstract member Capital : string

type Country =
  | USA
  | UK
```

…you could define a factory function that, for a given country, yields a properly initialized ICountryInfo object:

```
let make country =
  match country with
  | USA -> { new ICountryInfo with
              member x.Capital = "Washington" }
  | UK -> { new ICountryInfo with
              member x.Capital = "London" }
```

Suppose you want to be able to create a country by specifying its name as a string. In this case, in addition to having a freestanding function that gives you the right Country type, you can have a static factory method very similar to the ones we have in the OOP world:

```
type Country =
  | USA
  | UK
with
```

```
static member Create = function
    | "USA" | "America" -> USA
    | "UK" | "England" -> UK
    | _ -> failwith "No such country"
let usa = Country.Create "America"
```

Naturally, the Abstract Factory approach is similarly implementable using functional composition instead of inheritance.

Summary

Let's recap the terminology:

- A *factory method* is a class member that creates instances of some object. It typically replaces a constructor and is static. Asynchronous factory methods are awaitable (`Task`-returning) factory methods.

- A *factory* is typically a separate class that knows how to construct objects, though if you pass a function (as in `Func<T>` or similar) that constructs objects, this argument is also called a factory.

- A *nested factory* (aka *inner factory*) lives inside the object it creates. This allows us to hide all of the object's constructors and ensure that the object can *only* be created with a factory.

- An *abstract factory* is, as its name suggests, an abstract class that can be inherited by concrete classes that offer a family of types. Abstract factories are rare in the wild.

- A *delegate factory* is a delegate that is initialized by an IoC container to create an object using the provided parameters, excluding those parameters directly initialized through constructor injection.

Factory is different from Builder in that, with Factory, you typically create an object in one go (i.e., a single statement), whereas with Builder, you construct the object piecewise – either through several statements or, possibly, in a single statement if the builder supports a fluent interface.

A factory has several critical advantages over a constructor call, namely:

- A factory can say *no*, meaning that instead of actually returning an object, it can return, for example, a `null` or `None` of some `Option<T>` type.

- Naming is better and unconstrained, unlike constructor name.

- A single factory can make objects of many different types.

- A factory can exhibit polymorphic behavior, instantiating a class and returning it through a reference to its base class or interface.

- A factory can implement caching and other storage optimizations; it is also a natural choice for approaches such as pooling or the Singleton pattern.

- A factory can change its behavior at runtime; `new` is expected to always yield a new instance.

CHAPTER 5

Prototype

Think about something you use every day, like a car or a mobile phone. Chances are it wasn't designed from scratch; instead, the manufacturer chose an *existing* design, made some improvements, made it visually distinctive from the old design (so people could show off), and started selling it, eventually retiring the old product. It's a natural state of affairs, and in the software world, we get a similar situation: sometimes, instead of creating an entire object from scratch (the Factory and Builder patterns can help here), you want to take a preconstructed object and either use a copy of it (which is easy) or, alternatively, customize it a little.

And this leads us to the idea of having a prototype: a model object that we can make copies of. We can customize these copies and then use them. The challenge of the Prototype pattern is really the copying part; everything else is easy.

Deep vs. Shallow Copying

Suppose we define a class `Person` as...

```
public class Person
{
  public readonly string Name;
  public readonly Address Address;

  public Person(string name, Address address) { ... }
}
```

...with the `Address` defined as

```
public class Address
{
  public readonly string StreetName;
```

© Dmitri Nesteruk 2022
D. Nesteruk, *Design Patterns in .NET 6*, https://doi.org/10.1007/978-1-4842-8245-8_5

```
  public int HouseNumber;

  public Address(string streetName, int houseNumber) { ... }
}
```

Assume John Smith and Jane Smith are neighbors. It should be possible to construct John, then just copy him, and change the name and house number, right? Well, using the assignment operator (=) certainly won't help:

```
var john = new Person(
  "John Smith",
  new Address("London Road", 123));

var jane = john;
jane.Name = "Jane Smith"; // John's name changed!
jane.Address.HouseNumber = 321; // John's address changed!
```

This does not work because now john and jane refer to the same object, so all changes to jane affect john too. This is what is known as a *shallow copy* – it is called shallow because all it does is copy the memory in john to jane, without going any deeper and copying the nested structures recursively. This is a fast operation (a raw memory copy), but it means the two objects are now sharing references, which is not what we want.

What we want instead, of course, is for jane to become a new, independent object, whose modifications do not affect john in any way. This requires us to make a *deep copy* – a recursive copy where each member of john is replicated in memory. Doing this by hand means we have to follow different rules for different data types – we'll discuss them soon enough.

ICloneable Is Bad

The .NET Framework comes with an interface called ICloneable. This interface has a single method, Clone(), but this method is *ill-specified*: the documentation does not say whether this should be a shallow copy or a deep copy, which is a problem because the clients could have different expectations on how it actually works. Also, the name of the method, Clone, does not really help here since we don't know exactly what cloning does. The typical implementation of ICloneable for a type (say, Person) is something like this:

```csharp
public class Person : ICloneable
{
  // members as before
  public Person Clone()
  {
    return (Person)MemberwiseClone();
  }
}
```

The method Object.MemberwiseClone() is a protected method of Object, so it's automatically inherited by every single reference type. It creates a *shallow copy* of the object. Essentially, it makes a new object and then copies every non-static field as is. If the field is a value type, the copy happens by value, but if the field is a reference type, the reference will be copied, rather than the entire object being referenced.

In other words, if you were to implement it on Address and Person in our example, you'd hit the following problem:

```csharp
var john = new Person(
  "John Smith",
  new Address("London Road", 123));

var jane = john.Clone();
jane.Name = "Jane Smith"; // John's name DID NOT change (good!)
jane.Address.HouseNumber = 321; // John's address changed :(
```

This helped, but not a lot. Even though the name was now assigned correctly, john and jane now share an Address reference – it was simply copied over, so they both point to the same Address. So shallow copy is not for us: we want *deep copying*, that is, recursive copying of all object's members and the construction of shiny new counterpart objects, each initialized with identical data.

It's worth noting that, in spite of the fact that ICloneable is not recommended, plenty of classes in the BCL do in fact implement it. Furthermore, it is OK to call Clone() on those types provided a shallow copy is what you want.

Deep Copying via Copy Construction

One of the simplest code constructs you can use for deep copying is *copy construction*. A copy constructor is an artifact straight from the C++ world – a constructor that takes another instance of the type we're in and copies that type into the current object, for example...

```
public Address(Address other)
{
  StreetAddress = other.StreetAddress;
  City = other.City;
  Country = other.Country;
}
```

...and similarly:

```
public Person(Person other)
{
  Name = other.Name;
  Address = new Address(other.Address); // uses a copy constructor here
}
```

This allows us to perform a deep copy of john to jane:

```
var john = new Person(
  "John Smith",
  new Address("London Road", 123));

var jane = new Person(john); // copy constructor!
jane.Name = "Jane Smith";
jane.Address.HouseNumber = 321; // john is still at 123
```

Now, the copy constructor is pretty good in that it provides a unified copying interface, but it is of little help if the client is unable to discover it. At least, when the developer sees some IDeepCopyable interface with a DeepCopy() method, they know what they are getting; discoverability of a copy constructor, on the other hand, is suspect.

Another problem with this approach is that it's very intrusive: it requires that every single class in the composition chain implement a copy constructor and will likely malfunction if any class doesn't do it correctly. As such, it's a very challenging approach to use on preexisting data structures, as you'd be violating the OCP on a massive scale if you wanted to support this post hoc.

Finally, it's worth noting that, in the BCL, copy constructors typically provide *shallow* copy operations. This is a problem because, by doing deep copying in our constructors, we may be violating the Principle of Least Surprise.

Note on Record Classes

In creating record classes, the C# team had an excellent opportunity to provide some out-of-the-box deep copying support…and they blew it! Long story sort, record classes only provide shallow copying out of the box.[1]

The way they do it is not very intuitive, either. Behind the scenes, a record type generates lots of members, one of them being <Clone>$() – yeah, with the weird symbols. It's not meant to be called directly, but it *is* meant to be called in with statements such as

```
var john = new Person("John", "123 London Road");
var jane = john with { Name = "Jane" };
```

The Clone method uses, drumroll please…a synthesized protected copy constructor! And, regrettably, the copy constructor does shallow copying, just like all those BCL collection types.

None of this really helps us with our copying troubles.

Deep Copying with a Special Interface

If you want to have an interface specifically to indicate that your objects support the notion of deep copying, I recommend you be explicit about it,[2] that is:

```
public interface IDeepCopyable<out T>
{
  T DeepCopy();
}
```

---

[1] Record structs, being value types, provide deep copying out of the box, provided they are themselves composed exclusively of value types.

[2] Sometimes you'll see people call this interface as ICloneable<T>. I do not like this approach because if you're making your own interface, you want to be as specific as you can. *Cloning* is a very vague concept, whereas *deep copying* is clearly defined.

where T is the type of object to clone. Here is an example implementation:

```
public class Person : IDeepCopyable<Person>
{
  public string[] Names;
  public Address Address;

  public Person DeepCopy()
  {
    var copy = new Person();
    copy.Names = Names.Clone(); // string[] is not IDeepCopyable
    copy.Address = Address.DeepCopy(); // Address is IDeepCopyable
    return copy;
  }
  // other members here
}
```

This has two benefits compared with ICloneable:

- It is explicit in its intent: it talks specifically about deep copying.

- It is strongly typed, whereas ICloneable returns an object that you are expected to cast.

You'll notice that, in the implementation of DeepCopy(), we adopt different strategies depending on whether or not the members are themselves IDeepCopyable. If they are, things are fairly straightforward. If they are not, we need to use an appropriate deep copy mechanic for the given type. For example, for an array of trivially copyable types such as string, you can simply call Clone().

Deep Copying and Inheritance

Suppose we decide to inherit from Person and make an Employee class with a single salary field:

```
public class Employee : Person
{
  public int Salary;

  public Employee(string[] names, Address address, int salary)
```

```
  : base(names, address)
{
  Salary = salary;
}
}
```

We now have an odd situation: Employee, by virtue of inheriting from Person, implements IDeepCopyable<Person>. Without intervention, this can lead to odd behavior:

```
var john = new Employee(
  new []{"John", "Smith"},
  new Address("London Road", 123),
  100000);
Person copy = john.DeepCopy();
Console.WriteLine(copy is Employee); // False
```

To get the desired behavior, we need to do the following:

- Mark the DeepCopy() method as virtual in the base class.

- Implement IDeepCopyable<Employee>.

- Perform deep copying in the overridden DeepCopy() method:

  ```
  public override Employee DeepCopy()
  {
    return new Employee(
      (string[]) Names.Clone(),
      Address.DeepCopy(),
      Salary);
  }
  ```

This entire approach hinges on one very important assumption: all classes in the hierarchy have fully initializing constructors (or public members), and the implementor isn't bothered by having to pass these arguments around. In a large enough hierarchy, this could become a real problem, so much so that it would make more sense for each element in the hierarchy to do its part.

In order to construct an implementation of this approach that would actually scale, we shall redefine the IDeepCopyable interface to the following:

```
public interface IDeepCopyable<T> where T : new()
{
  void CopyTo(T target);

  public T DeepCopy()
  {
    T t = new T();
    CopyTo(t);
    return t;
  }
}
```

There are now two methods in the interface:

- The CopyTo() method that copies the concepts of the class into the variable provided.

- The default-implemented DeepCopy() method that creates an empty object (subject to the new() constraint) and calls CopyTo() to copy data into it.

With this implementation, T can no longer be an out parameter, which means we lose return-type covariance in DeepCopy() but what we gain is not having to type it out for every single type.

Now, here is how you would implement this class for Person (I omit implementation for Address)…

```
public class Person : IDeepCopyable<Person>
{
  public string[] Names;
  public Address Address;
  // other members as before
  public void CopyTo(Person target)
  {
```

```
    target.Names = (string[]) Names.Clone();
    target.Address = Address.DeepCopy(); // <-- extension method call
  }
}
```

...and similarly for Employee:

```
public class Employee : Person, IDeepCopyable<Employee>
{
  public int Salary;
  public void CopyTo(Employee target)
  {
    base.CopyTo(target); // <-- extension method call on base class
    target.Salary = Salary;
  }
}
```

In both previous listings, we call DeepCopy(), but it most certainly is not an interface member – remember, with default interface implementations, you need to cast the variable to the interface type. So where is this cast happening? The answer is we've had to define an additional extension method for this to work:

```
public static T DeepCopy<T>(this IDeepCopyable<T> item)
  where T : new()
{
  return item.DeepCopy();
}
```

But that's not all! This extension method may work within the CopyTo() bodies, but you're still not able to write code like this:

```
var john = new Employee();
var copy = john.DeepCopy(); // will not compile
```

Don't be sad, because this problem highlights something very powerful: our john variable can be deep copied not just into Employee, but it can also be partially copied into Person (and any other class up the hierarchy):

```
var john = new Employee();
Person p = john.DeepCopy<Person>();
Employee e = john.DeepCopy<Employee>();
```

Now, if you want to ensure that, by default, an object of type T gets copied into an object also of type T without explicit generic definitions, you can add yet another extension method:

```
public static T DeepCopy<T>(this T person)
  where T : Person, new()
{
  return ((IDeepCopyable<T>) person).DeepCopy();
}
```

So now we finally see an explicit cast! And with this, our example is complete. Here is how one would use this functionality:

```
var john = new Employee();
john.Names = new[] {"John", "Doe"};
john.Address = new Address {
  HouseNumber = 123, StreetName = "London Road"
};
john.Salary = 321000;
var copy = john.DeepCopy(); // of type Employee
```

Of course, there are other approaches to this problem, including the use of recursive generics, but with the default interface member, we keep things reasonably clean and usable.

Deep Copying Guidelines

It would be great if .NET had a uniform way of deep copying an object regardless of its type. Sadly, this is far from reality, which is why we must discuss ways of deep copying objects. We've seen some approaches already in the preceding implementations, but now we need to cover the entire spectrum of different data types.

Trivially Copyable Types

First of all, let me introduce the concept of *trivially copyable* types. A trivially copyable type is

- A primitive type (`bool`, `int`, etc.)

- A string

- A value type (`struct`) composed solely of trivially copyable types

Trivially copyable types are easy to deep copy because all you need is an assignment (=) operator:

```
var dt = DateTime.UtcNow; // DateTime is a struct
var copy = dt; // deep copy
```

Notice that `string` is also a trivially copyable type. Even though strings are reference types, they have value semantics, so there is no risk of two classes sharing a mutable reference to a single string.

It's important to note that if you have a reference type composed exclusively of trivially copyable members, then deep and shallow copying are the same. This means you can use shallow copying mechanisms such as `MemberwiseClone()` with impunity.

Arrays

Let us consider the following class that we want to copy:

```
public class Person
{
  public string [] Names;
  public Address [] Addresses;
}
```

There are, as in all collections, two cases here. If an array is composed of a trivially copyable type, we can copy it by value using its own `Clone()` method – yes, that's the "evil" method from `ICloneable` that performs a shallow copy.

It's important to remember that since `ICloneable` does not have a generic `ICloneable<T>` counterpart, the return value of `Clone()` needs to be cast into the correct array. We'll see it in just a moment.

Now, if an array is composed of types that are not trivially copyable, we need to create a brand-new array where each member is deep copied. You can do this using

- The static `Array.ConvertAll()` method

- The `ToArray()` LINQ extension method

Consequently, a deep copy method for `Person` would appear as follows:

```
public Person DeepCopy()
{
  var copy = new Person();
  copy.Names = (string[]) Names.Clone();
  copy.Addresses = Array.ConvertAll(Addresses, a => a.DeepCopy());
  return copy;
}
```

Common Collection Types

When it comes to common collection types, such as `List`, `Dictionary`, and others, shallow copying is implemented in the copy constructor. This means that a collection such as `List<int>` can be copied like this:

```
List<int> items = new(){1, 2, 3};
List<int> replica = new(items); // copy constructor
```

When it comes to collections containing types that are not trivially copyable, there are many choices. For example, just like arrays, `List<T>` has a method called `ConvertAll()`. A `Dictionary`, on the other hand, can be copied using the LINQ `ToDictionary()` method:

```
var people = new Dictionary<string, Address>
{
  ["John"] = new(38, "London Road"),
  ["Jane"] = new(72, "Jane Street")
};
var peopleCopies = people.ToDictionary(
  x => x.Key,
  x => x.Value.DeepCopy());
```

As for other collections, it depends on what you're working with. For example, one-dimensional collections quite often support the LINQ Select() operator, which can be useful to perform a "double hop" where you

- Materialize a temporary IEnumerable with deep copied values from original.

- Use an IEnumerable-taking shallow copy constructor in the requisite type.

Here's an example of what I mean:

```
var addresses = new HashSet<Address>{
  new(38, "London Road"),
  new(72, "Jane Street")
};
var replicas = new HashSet<Address>(
  addresses.Select(a => a.DeepCopy()));
```

MemberwiseClone Is Not Terrible

While implementing ICloneable or just having a member called Clone() is probably a bad idea, exposing a MemberwiseClone() call is okay provided you know what you're doing – creating a complete memory copy of an existing object. This is 100% acceptable in cases where all members of your object are trivially copyable types: in such classes, shallow and deep copy operations are one and the same, which means that by performing a memberwise copy, you are, in fact, performing deep copying.

A direct implementation of this may appear as follows:

```
public class Person
{
  public Person DeepCopy()
  {
    return (Person)MemberwiseClone();
  }
}
```

For an object without any parents, you can introduce an abstract base class to expose this functionality:

```
public abstract class TriviallyCopyable<T>
  : IDeepCopyable<T>
{
  public T DeepCopy()
  {
    return (T) MemberwiseClone();
  }
}
```

For a record type, the synthesized Clone() method works through a copy constructor but, in essence, does pretty much the same thing. The cloning name is mangled, but you can expose it like this:

```
public record Person
{
  public Person DeepCopy()
  {
    return this with {};
    // or
    return new Person(this);
  }
}
```

Summary

Let us summarize the key aspects of deep copying of objects:

- A *trivially copyable type* is a primitive type, a string, or a struct that only contains trivially copyable members.

- For trivially copyable types, deep and shallow copy are the same, since they're effectively "by value."

- For a reference type that contains only trivially copyable members, deep and shallow copying are the same, which means that

  - In your own types of such a nature, you can use `MemberwiseClone()`; just don't implement `ICloneable`.

  - In common collection types, you can typically use their copy constructor.

  - Record types can expose a copy constructor, or you can use the `with` keyword.

- For a reference type that contains non-trivially copyable members, you need to ensure you are copying things correctly, that is, performing deep copying where relevant.

Serialization

We need to thank the designers of C# for the fact that most objects in C#, whether they be primitive types or collections, are "trivially serializable" – by default, you are able to take a class and save it to a file or to memory without adding extra code to the class (well, maybe an attribute or two, at most) or having to fiddle with reflection.

Why is this relevant to the problem at hand? Because if you can serialize something to a file or to memory, you can then deserialize it, preserving all the information, including all the dependent objects. Isn't this convenient? For example, you could define an extension method (this is formally known as a Behavioral Mixin) for in-memory cloning using binary serialization:

```
public static T DeepCopy<T>(this T self)
{
  if (!typeof(T).IsSerializable)
    throw new ArgumentException("Type must be serializable", nameof(self));
  if (ReferenceEquals(self, null)) return default;

var stream = new MemoryStream();
BinaryFormatter formatter = new BinaryFormatter(); formatter.
Serialize(stream, self);
stream.Seek(0, SeekOrigin.Begin);
return (T) formatter.Deserialize(stream);
}
```

This code simply takes an object of *any* type T, performs binary serialization into memory, and then deserializes from that memory, thereby gaining a deep copy of the original object.

This approach is fairly universal and will let you easily clone your objects:

```
var foo = new Foo { Stuff = 42, Whatever = new Bar { Baz = "abc"} };
var foo2 = foo.DeepCopy();
foo2.Whatever.Baz = "xyz"; // works fine
```

There is just one catch: binary serialization requires every class to be marked with [Serializable]; otherwise, the serializer simply throws an exception (not a good thing). So, if we wanted to use this approach on an existing set of classes, including those *not* marked as [Serializable], we might go with a different approach that doesn't require the aforementioned attribute. For example, you could use XML serialization instead:

```
public static T DeepCopyXml<T>(this T self)
{
  using var ms = new MemoryStream()
  XmlSerializer s = new XmlSerializer(typeof(T));
  s.Serialize(ms, self);
  ms.Position = 0;
  return (T) s.Deserialize(ms);
}
```

You can use any serializer you want. The only requirement is that it knows how to traverse every single element in the object graph. Most serializers are smart enough to go over things that shouldn't be serialized (like read-only properties), but sometimes they need a little help in order to make sense of trickier structures. For example, the XML serializer will not serialize an IDictionary, so if you are using a dictionary in your class, you'd need to mark it as [XmlIgnore] and create a Property Surrogate that we discuss in Chapter 7.

Prototype Factory

If you have predefined objects that you want to replicate, where do you actually store them? A static field of some class? Perhaps. In fact, suppose our company has both main and auxiliary offices. Now we could try to declare some static variables, for example:

```
static Person main = new Person(null,
  new Address("123 East Dr", "London", 0));
static Person aux = new Person(null,
  new Address("123B East Dr", "London", 0));
```

We could stick these members into Person so as to provide a hint that, when you need a person working at a main office, just clone main and, similarly for the auxiliary office, one can clone aux. But this is far from intuitive: what if we want to prohibit the creation of Person instances working anywhere other than these two offices? And, from the SRP perspective, it would also make sense to keep the set of possible addresses separate.

This is where a prototype factory comes into play. Just like an ordinary factory, it can store these static members and provide convenience methods for creating new employees:

```
public class EmployeeFactory
{
  private static Person main =
    new Person(null, new Address("123 East Dr", "London", 0));
  private static Person aux =
    new Person(null, new Address("123B East Dr", "London", 0));

  public static Person NewMainOfficeEmployee(string name, int suite) =>
    NewEmployee(main, name, suite);

  public static Person NewAuxOfficeEmployee(string name, int suite) =>
    NewEmployee(aux, name, suite);

  private static Person NewEmployee(Person proto, string name, int suite)
  {
    var copy = proto.DeepCopy();
    copy.Name = name;
    copy.Address.Suite = suite;
    return copy;
  }
}
```

Notice how, following the DRY principle, we don't call DeepCopy() in more than one location: all the different NewXxxEmployee() methods simply forward their arguments to one private NewEmployee() method, passing it the prototype to use when constructing a new object.

The preceding prototype factory can now be used as

```
var john = EmployeeFactory.NewMainOfficeEmployee("John Doe", 100);
var jane = EmployeeFactory.NewAuxOfficeEmployee("Jane Smith", 123);
```

Naturally, this implementation assumes that the constructors of Person are accessible; if you want to keep them private/protected, you'll need to implement the Inner Factory approach as outlined in Chapter 4.

Source Generators

The latest advances in the C# language introduce the concept of source generators. These are assemblies similar to Roslyn analyzer assemblies that can be used to dynamically generate code behind the scenes and add it to the existing projects, with features such as code completion available as soon as an edit is made.

While computationally expensive and requiring lots of caching tricks to ensure regeneration doesn't happen too often, source generators have been adopted by creators of various serialization frameworks to ensure that, instead of using reflection at runtime, serialization code is generated at compile time. This gives significant performance advantages.

You can benefit from source generators in two ways. The first is that you can use existing serialization frameworks to encode data, in which case you get better performance, but also traceability in that you can examine the generated source code if any issues occur. The second option is to write your own source generators for serialization and similar operations.

Summary

The Prototype design pattern embodies the notion of *deep* copying of objects so that, instead of doing full initialization each time, you can take a premade object, copy it, fiddle it a little bit, and then use it independently of the original.

There are really only two ways of implementing the Prototype pattern. They are as follows:

- Write code that correctly duplicates your object, that is, performs a deep copy. This can be done in a copy constructor, or you can define an appropriately named method, possibly with a corresponding interface (but *not* ICloneable).

- Write code for the support of serialization/deserialization and then use this mechanism to implement cloning as serialization immediately followed by deserialization. This carries the extra computational cost; its significance depends on how often you need to do the copying. The advantage of this approach is that you can get away without significantly modifying existing structures. It's also much safer, because you're less likely to forget to clone a member properly.

Don't forget that, for value types, the cloning problem doesn't really exist: if you want to clone a struct, just assign it to a new variable. Also, strings are immutable, so you can use the assignment operator = on them without worrying that subsequent modification will affect more objects than it should.

CHAPTER 6

Singleton

> When discussing which patterns to drop, we found that we still love them all. (Not really – I'm in favor of dropping Singleton. Its use is almost always a design smell.)
>
> —*Erich Gamma*

Singleton is by far the most hated design pattern in the (rather limited) history of design patterns. Just stating that fact, however, doesn't mean you shouldn't use Singleton: a toilet brush is not the most pleasant device either, but sometimes it is simply necessary.

The Singleton design pattern grew out of a very simple idea that you should only have one instance of a particular component in your application. For example, a component that loads a database into memory and offers a read-only interface is a prime candidate for a singleton since it really doesn't make sense to waste memory storing several identical datasets. In fact, your application might have constraints such that two or more instances of the database simply won't fit into memory or will result in such a lack of memory as to cause the program to malfunction.

Singleton by Convention

The naïve approach to this problem is to simply agree that we are not going to instantiate this object more than once, that is:

```
public class Database
{
  /// <summary>
  /// Please do not create more than one instance.
  /// </summary>
  public Database() {}
};
```

© Dmitri Nesteruk 2022
D. Nesteruk, *Design Patterns in .NET 6*, https://doi.org/10.1007/978-1-4842-8245-8_6

The problem with this approach, apart from the fact that your developer colleagues might simply ignore the advice, is that objects can be created in stealthy ways where the call to the constructor isn't immediately obvious. This can be anything – a call through reflection, creation in a factory (e.g., `Activator.CreateInstance`), or injection of the type by an IoC container.

The most obvious idea that comes to mind is to offer a single, static global object:

```
public static class Globals
{
  public static Database Database = new Database();
}
```

However, this really doesn't do much in terms of safety: clients are not in any way prevented from constructing additional `Databases` as they see fit. And how will the client find the `Globals` class?

Classic Implementation

So now that we know what the problem is, how can we prevent all clients from making more than one instance of an object? We can, for example, put a static counter right in the constructor and throw an exception if the value is ever incremented:

```
public class Database
{
  private static int instanceCount = 0;
  public Database()
  {
    if (++instanceCount > 1)
      throw new InvalidOperationException("Cannot make >1 database!");
  }
};
```

This is a particularly hostile approach to solving this problem: even though it prevents the creation of more than one instance by throwing an exception, it fails to *communicate* the fact that we don't want anyone calling the constructor more than once. Even if you adorn it with plenty of XML documentation, I guarantee there will still be some poor soul trying to call this more than once in some nondeterministic setting. Probably in production too!

The only way to prevent explicit construction of a `Database` is to make its constructor inaccessible (private/protected) and introduce a property or method to return the one and only instance:

```
public class Database
{
  private Database() { ... }
  public static Database Instance { get; } = new();
}
```

Note how we removed the possibility of directly creating `Database` instances by hiding the constructor. Of course, you can use reflection to access private members, so construction of this class isn't quite impossible, but it does require extra hoops to jump through, and hopefully this is enough to prevent most people trying to invoke the constructor directly.

By declaring the instance as `static`, we removed any possibility of controlling the lifetime of the database: it now lives as long as the program does. This choice is forced upon all clients, even those who need the `Database` to be short-lived.

Lazy Loading and Thread Safety

The implementation shown in the previous section happens to be thread-safe. After all, static constructors are guaranteed to run only once per AppDomain, before any instances of the class are created or any static members accessed.

But what if you don't want initialization in the static constructor? What if, instead, you want to initialize the singleton (i.e., call its constructor) only when the object is first accessed? In this case, you can use `Lazy<T>`[1]:

```
public class MyDatabase
{
  private MyDatabase()
  {
    Console.WriteLine("Initializing  database");
```

---

[1] Note that, similar to C#, F# has the `lazy` keyword. The only difference is that F# has a somewhat more concise syntax: writing `lazy(x + y())` automatically constructs a `Lazy<'T>` behind the scenes.

```
  }
  private static Lazy<MyDatabase> instance =
    new ();

  public static MyDatabase Instance => instance.Value;
}
```

This is also a thread-safe approach because the objects Lazy<T> creates are thread-safe by default. In a multi-threaded setting, the first thread to access the Value property of a Lazy<T> is the one that initializes it for all subsequent accesses on all threads.

Reusable Base Class

Seeing how every singleton will have more or less the same contents (e.g., a static lazy variable and an exposed public static property), why not turn it into a base class? In a simple case, this is entirely possible! Consider the following base class:

```
public abstract class Singleton<T> where T : Singleton<T>
{
  private static readonly Lazy<T> Lazy =
    new Lazy<T>(() => Activator.CreateInstance(typeof(T), true) as T);

  public static T Instance => Lazy.Value;
}
```

The only thing we need to use this class is a derived class that has a single nonpublic parameterless constructor, for example:

```
class MyDatabase : Singleton<MyDatabase>
{
  private MyDatabase() { /* load data here */ }
}
```

The only downside to this implementation is the fact that the constructor call is not statically checked. Sadly, this isn't something we can do anything about: while we can certainly add a new() constraint to Singleton<T>'s type parameter, this would force the singleton's constructor to be public.

The Trouble with Singleton

Let us now consider a concrete example of a singleton. Suppose that our database contains a list of capital cities and their populations. The interface that our singleton database is going to conform to is

```
public interface IDatabase
{
  int GetPopulation(string name);
}
```

We have a single method that gives us the population of a given city. Now, let us suppose that this interface is adopted by a concrete implementation called SingletonDatabase that implements the singleton the same way as we've done before:

```
public class SingletonDatabase : IDatabase
{
  private Dictionary<string, int> capitals;

  private SingletonDatabase()
  {
    WriteLine("Initializing database");

    capitals = File.ReadAllLines(
      Path.Combine(
        new  FileInfo(typeof(IDatabase).Assembly.Location).DirectoryName,
          "capitals.txt")
      )
      .Batch(2) // from MoreLINQ
      .ToDictionary(
        list => list.ElementAt(0).Trim(),
        list => int.Parse(list.ElementAt(1)));
  }

  public int GetPopulation(string name)
  {
    return capitals[name];
  }
}
```

```
  private static Lazy<SingletonDatabase> instance =
    new Lazy<SingletonDatabase>(() =>
    {
      return new SingletonDatabase();
    });

  public static IDatabase Instance => instance.Value;
}
```

The constructor of the database reads the names and populations of various capitals from a text file and stores them in a `Dictionary<>`. The `GetPopulation()` method is used as an accessor to get the population of a given city.

As we noted before, the real problem with singletons like the preceding one is their use in other components. Here's what I mean – suppose that, on the basis of the preceding singleton, we build a component for calculating the sum total population of several different cities:

```
public class SingletonRecordFinder
{
  public int TotalPopulation(IEnumerable<string> names)
  {
    int result = 0;
    foreach (var name in names)
      result += SingletonDatabase.Instance.GetPopulation(name);
    return result;
  }
}
```

The trouble is that `SingletonRecordFinder` is now firmly dependent on `SingletonDatabase`. This presents an issue for testing – if we want to check that `SingletonRecordFinder` works correctly, we need to use data from the actual database, that is:

```
[Test]
public void SingletonTotalPopulationTest()
{
  // testing on a live database
  var rf = new SingletonRecordFinder();
```

```
var names = new[] {"Seoul", "Mexico City"};
int tp = rf.TotalPopulation(names);
Assert.That(tp, Is.EqualTo(17500000 + 17400000));
}
```

This is a terrible unit test. It tries to read a live database (something that you typically don't want to do too often), but it's also very fragile, because it depends on the concrete values in the database. What if the population of Seoul changes (as a result of North Korea opening its borders, perhaps)? Then the test will break. But of course, many people run tests on continuous integration systems that are isolated from live databases, so that fact makes the approach even more dubious.

This test is also bad for ideological reasons. Remember, we want a *unit* test where the unit we're testing is the SingletonRecordFinder. However, the test we wrote is not a unit test but an *integration* test because the record finder uses SingletonDatabase, so in effect we're testing both systems at the same time. Nothing wrong with that if an integration test is what you wanted, but we would really prefer to test the record finder in isolation.

So we know we don't want to use an actual database in a test. Can we replace the database with some dummy component that we can control from within our tests? Well, in our current design, this is impossible, and it is precisely this inflexibility that is Singleton's downfall.

So what can we do? Well, for one, we need to stop depending on SingletonDatabase explicitly. Since all we need is something implementing the Database interface, we can create a new ConfigurableRecordFinder that lets us configure where the data comes from:

```
public class ConfigurableRecordFinder
{
  private IDatabase database;

  public ConfigurableRecordFinder(IDatabase database)
  {
    this.database = database;
  }
```

```csharp
  public int GetTotalPopulation(IEnumerable<string> names)
  {
    int result = 0;
    foreach (var name in names)
      result += database.GetPopulation(name);
    return result;
  }
}
```

We now use the database reference instead of using the singleton explicitly. This lets us make a dummy database specifically for testing the record finder:

```csharp
public class DummyDatabase : IDatabase
{
  public int GetPopulation(string name)
  {
    return new Dictionary<string, int>
    {
      ["alpha"] = 1,
      ["beta"] = 2,
      ["gamma"] = 3
    }[name];
  }
}
```

And now, we can rewrite our unit test to take advantage of this DummyDatabase:

```csharp
[Test]
public void DependentTotalPopulationTest()
{
  var db = new DummyDatabase();
  var rf = new ConfigurableRecordFinder(db);
  Assert.That(
    rf.GetTotalPopulation(new[]{"alpha",  "gamma"}),
    Is.EqualTo(4));
}
```

This test is more robust because if data changes in the actual database, we won't have to adjust our unit test values – the dummy data stays the same. Also, it opens interesting possibilities. We can now run tests against an empty database or, say, a database whose size is greater than the available RAM. You get the idea.

Per-Thread Singleton

We've talked about thread safety in relation to the construction of the singleton, but what about thread safety with respect to a singleton's own operations? It might be the case that, instead of one singleton shared between all threads in an application, you need one singleton to exist per thread.

The construction of the per-thread singleton is identical to that which we've already seen before, except that Lazy<T> is replaced by ThreadLocal<T> – it also provides lazy initialization semantics, but on a thread-local basis:

```
public sealed class PerThreadSingleton
{
  private static ThreadLocal<PerThreadSingleton> threadInstance
    = new(() => new PerThreadSingleton());

  public int Id;

  private PerThreadSingleton()
  {
    Id = Thread.CurrentThread.ManagedThreadId;
  }

  public static PerThreadSingleton Instance => threadInstance.Value;
}
```

My listing preserves the thread id for illustration purposes: you don't need to keep it if you don't want to. Now, to verify we're really getting one instance per thread, we can run something like

```
var t1 = Task.Factory.StartNew(() =>
{
  Console.WriteLine("t1: " + PerThreadSingleton.Instance.Id);
});
```

```
var t2 = Task.Factory.StartNew(() =>
{
  Console.WriteLine("t2: " + PerThreadSingleton.Instance.Id);
  Console.WriteLine("t2 again: " + PerThreadSingleton.Instance.Id);
});
Task.WaitAll(t1, t2);
```

This gives the output

```
t2: 5
t1: 4
t2 again: 5
```

Thread-local singletons solve peculiar problems. For example, say you've got a dependency graph similar to the following:

```
    Needs      needs
A ------> B ------> C

    needs
A ------> C
```

Now, you spawn off 20 threads, which all use A. The component A needs C twice: directly and also indirectly through B. Now, if C is stateful and mutated in each thread, you cannot have one global `CSingleton`, but what you *can* do is create per-thread singletons. That way, an operation A will use the same instance of C both by itself and indirectly through B.

And, of course, an added benefit is that within a thread-local singleton, you don't have to worry about thread safety, so you can use, say, a `Dictionary` instead of `ConcurrentDictionary`.

Ambient Context

Say you're making building plans. You need to add walls to the ground floor of a house. Those walls will have different positions, but the wall height for the entire floor will probably remain the same.

You can keep typing in the same value into dozens of method calls, but you don't want to. Nor do you want to declare a variable and pass that instead. You want to have some sort of global setting for wall height, the requirements being that

1. You can set a wall height, and it will be used as the default value.

2. *But* sometimes you want to do a few walls with a different height and then revert to the previous value.

3. *And* sometimes you want to specify the exact height via the API.

The height of the wall in this scenario is part of an *ambient context*: a set of states that are meaningful to a certain set of operations being undertaken at a particular point in time.

You can pass in an ambient context as an injected parameter into dozens of APIs, but this involves having lots of parameters and probably lots of delegate factories too! The only way to avoid this is to create a static construct addressable from within every point within the application.

Let's start defining the ambient context class:

```
public sealed class BuildingContext : IDisposable
{
  // make this inaccessible

  private BuildingContext() {}

  public int Height { get; private set; }
```

As you can see, our ambient context class

*   Is `sealed`: typically it makes very little sense to support inheritance of ambient contexts.

*   Has a private constructor, so it cannot be instantiated directly.

*   Has a property for the height of the walls we plan to build.

*   Implements `IDisposable` – we'll see why in a moment.

Moving on, we see some interesting members:

```
private static readonly Stack<BuildingContext> stack = new();

static BuildingContext() { stack.Push(new BuildingContext()); }
```

Our ambient context statically stores several instances in a Stack<T>. Why? Take a look at Requirement 2 from our earlier list. Sometimes we want to build several walls (e.g., a chimney) at a height drastically different from the currently used height. How do we do this? We create a new state and push it on the stack. When we're done, we pop the stack and return to the old value.

Speaking of which, here is how one would do this:

```
public static IDisposable WithHeight(int height)
{
  var copy = Current.DeepCopy();
  copy.Height = height;
  stack.Push(copy);
  return copy;
}
```

This method is just a helper piece of API that you can wrap in a using statement. It creates a deep copy[2] of the current context, changes a particular value, pushes it onto the stack, and also returns it as an IDisposable, so we can call Dispose() when we're done using it.

Now, given that we have a stack of states, the current ambient context is simply whatever exists on top of the stack. Notice our previously defined static constructor ensures that there's always at least one state there:

```
public static BuildingContext Current => stack.Peek();
```

And, finally, the mystery of why we use the IDisposable interface: calling Dispose() pops the state off the stack, making sure that there's at least one state always available:

```
public void Dispose()
{
  if (stack.Count > 1) stack.Pop();
  }
}
```

---

[2] See Chapter 5 for examples of how to implement deep copying.

I will omit most of the plumbing required for this demo to work (see the source code for details), but I want to show you how you would handle Requirement 3 – an ability to override the ambient context value if needed. A Wall class with an optionally ambient height could be defined as

```
public class Wall
{
  public Point Start;
  public Point End;
  public int Height;

  public Wall(Point start, Point end, int? height = null)
  {
    Start = start;
    End = end;
    Height = height ?? BuildingContext.Current.Height;
  }
}
```

Thus, you can either provide your own value (in which case, height will be non-null) or let the class take it from the ambient context.

The use of the ambient context would appear as follows:

```
using (BuildingContext.WithHeight(2000))
{
  building.Walls.Add(new Wall(
    new Point(0, 1000), new Point(1000, 1000)));
  using (BuildingContext.WithHeight(1000))
  {
    building.Walls.Add(new Wall(
      new Point(1000, 2000), new Point(2000, 3000)));
  }
  building.Walls.Add(new Wall(
    new Point(0, 1000), new Point(1000, 1000)));
}
```

Something worth noting is that an ambient context, in our case, is not a singleton but is *singleton-like* in that, even though many instances may exist in the stack, only one instance, exposed through the `Current` property, is ever returned at any given time. Furthermore, if you wanted to construct several buildings in parallel, you could simply change the stack from `static` to `ThreadLocal` while most of the code would remain the same.

It goes without saying that an ambient context introduces quite a bit of coupling into many classes. On the other hand, unlike the "canonical" singleton that we've seen in earlier parts of this chapter, an ambient context is actually *good* for testability: it is designed to be "mutable" (in the `Stack` sense), so you can write unit tests on the basis of its states – provided, of course, that it doesn't rely on external states (such as reading from a database), which it really shouldn't be, since an ambient context is typically just a container for states (and possibly strategies) that need to be taken within some finite lifetime. Furthermore, note the provision for value overrides (Requirement 3) allows us to bypass the ambient context entirely, should we need to.

Uses in the .NET Framework

The Ambient Context pattern is used in many places in the .NET Framework:

- `CultureInfo` stores the current culture and allows you to switch the culture of an application deliberately, rather than accepting defaults taken from the operating system.

- `ActivationContext,` which contains an `ApplicationIdentity` and provides access to the application manifest.

- `ExecutionContext` and `SynchronizationContext`.

- `TransactionScope`, used for SQL transactions.

- `HttpContext` encapsulates HTTP-specific information about a request.

Many other ambient contexts are used in the BCL and various frameworks such as ASP.NET.

Singletons and Inversion of Control

The approach of explicitly making a component a singleton is distinctly invasive, and if you make a decision to stop treating the component as a singleton later on, the changes required may end up being very expensive to implement. An alternative solution is to adopt a convention where, instead of directly enforcing the lifetime of a class, this is outsourced to an Inversion of Control (IoC) container.

Here's what defining a singleton component looks like when using the Autofac dependency injection framework:

```
var builder = new ContainerBuilder();
builder.RegisterType<Database>().SingleInstance(); // <-- singleton!
builder.RegisterType<RecordFinder>();

var container = builder.Build();
var finder = container.Resolve<RecordFinder>();
var finder2 = container.Resolve<RecordFinder>();
// finder and finder2 refer to the same database!
```

The key here is that `Database` is defined in the container as `SingletInstance()`, which makes it a thread-safe singleton. Thus, when it is injected into any number of `RecordFinder` types, the same instance will be injected everywhere.

Many people believe that using a singleton in a DI container is the only socially acceptable use of a singleton. At least, with this approach, if you need to replace a singleton object with something else, you can do it in one central place: the container configuration code. An added benefit is that you won't have to implement any singleton logic yourself, which prevents possible errors. Oh, and did I mention that all container operations in Autofac are thread-safe?

In actual fact, one thing IoC containers highlight is the fact that a singleton is only a unique case of lifetime management (one object per lifetime of entire application). Different lifetimes are possible – you can have one object per thread, one object per web request, and so on. You can also have *pooling* – situations where the number of live object instances can be between 0 and X, whatever X happens to be.

Monostate

The Monostate pattern, also known as the Borg pattern,[3] is a variation on the Singleton pattern. It is a class that *behaves* like a singleton while appearing as an ordinary class.

For example, suppose you are modeling a company structure, and a company typically has only one CEO. What you can do is define the following class:

```
public class ChiefExecutiveOfficer
{
  private static string name;
  private static int age;

  public string Name
  {
    get => name;
    set => name = value;
  }

  public int Age
  {
    get => age;
    set => age = value;
  }
}
```

Can you see what's happening here? The class appears as an ordinary class with getters and setters, but they actually work on `static` data!

This might seem like a really neat trick: you let people instantiate `ChiefExecutiveOfficer` as many times as they want, but all the instances refer to the same data. However, how are users supposed to know this? A user will happily instantiate two CEOs, assign them different `id`s, and will be very surprised when both of them are identical!

---

[3] In the *Star Trek* television series, the Borg is a fictional race of partially robotic beings that are assimilated into a single collective. The Borg collective has no individuals: everyone shares a single consciousness, that is, every drone within the collective has access to the same data.

The Monostate approach works to some degree and has a couple of advantages. For example, it is easy to inherit, it can leverage polymorphism, and its lifetime is reasonably well-defined (but then again, you might not always wish it so). Its greatest advantage is that you can take an existing object that's already used throughout the system and patch it up to behave in a Monostate way, and provided your system works fine with the non-plurality of object instances, you've got yourself a singleton-like implementation with no extra code needing to be rewritten.

But that's all that Monostate really is: a Band-Aid when you want one component to become a singleton throughout the entire codebase without any large-scale changes. This pattern is not meant for production, as it can cause too much confusion. If you need centralized control over things, a DI container is your best bet.

Multiton

Multiton, like its name suggests, is a pattern that, instead of forcing us to have just one instance, gets us to have a finite number of named instances of some particular component. For example, suppose we have two subsystems – the main one and another for backup:

```
enum Subsystem
{
  Main,
  Backup
}
```

If only a single printer is meant to exist for every subsystem, we can define the Printer class as follows:

```
class Printer
{
  private Printer() { }

  public static Printer Get(Subsystem ss)
  {
    if (instances.ContainsKey(ss))
      return instances[ss];
```

```
    var instance = new Printer();
    instances[ss] = instance;
    return instance;
  }

  private static Dictionary<Subsystem, Printer> instances = new ();
}
```

As before, we've hidden the constructor and made an accessor method that lazily constructs and returns a printer corresponding to the required subsystem. This implementation is, of course, not thread-safe, but that can be easily corrected via the use of, say, a `ConcurrentDictionary`.

Notice also that our implementation has the same problems as the singleton in terms of direct dependencies. If your code relies on `Printer.Get(Subsystem.Main)`, how would you substitute the result with a different implementation? Well, just as with the database example we looked at, the best solution would be to extract some `IPrinter` interface and to depend on that instead.

Summary

Singletons are not completely evil, but when used carelessly, they'll mess up the testability and refactorability of your application. If you really must use a singleton, try avoiding using it directly (as in writing `SomeComponent.Instance.Foo`) and instead keep specifying it as a dependency (e.g., a constructor argument) where all dependencies are satisfied from a single location in your application (ideally, an Inversion of Control container). Relying on abstractions (interfaces/abstract classes) conforms with the DIP and is generally a good idea if you want to perform a substitution later on.

Finally, it's worth mentioning that the Singleton pattern is, traditionally, just one expression of a concept of a "lifetime" of a particular component, suggesting that just one instance exists from the moment it is required (assuming it is lazy) until the instance is garbage-collected or the program terminates. As we have seen, other lifetime expressions (such as per-thread objects) are also possible. A competent DI framework provides much finer control over the lifetime of components than any handwritten singleton ever could.

PART III

Structural Patterns

As the name suggests, structural patterns are all about setting up the structure of your application so as to improve SOLID conformance as well as general usability and maintainability of your code.

When it comes to determining the structure of an object, we can apply these fairly well-known methods:

- *Inheritance*: An object automagically acquires all members' base class or classes. To allow instantiation, the object must implement every abstract member from its parent; if it does not, it is abstract and cannot be created (but you can inherit from it).

- *Composition*: Generally implies that the child cannot exist without the parent. This is typically implemented with nested classes. For example, a class `Car` can have a nested class `Wheel`. Ever since the introduction of default interface methods, interfaces themselves can also contain classes.

- *Aggregation*: An object can contain another object, but that object can also exist independently. Think of a `Car` having a `driver` field or property.

Nowadays, both composition and aggregation are treated in an identical fashion. If you have a `Person` class with a field of type `Address`, you have a choice as to whether `Address` is an external type or a nested type. In either case, provided it's `public`, you can refer to it as either `Address` or `Person.Address`.

I would argue that using the word *composition* when we really mean aggregation has become so commonplace that we may as well use them in interchangeable fashion. Here's some proof: when we talk about IoC containers, we speak of a *composition root*. But wait. Doesn't the IoC container control the lifetime of each object individually? It does, and so we're using the word *composition* when we really mean aggregation.

There are, fundamentally, three ways in which data structures can be defined in C#:

- *Statically*, when you simply write the classes and they get compiled. This is the most common case out there.

- *Via code generation*. This happens when structures get created from T4 templates or databases or some user scripts (source generators, custom tools). Plenty of code gets generated behind the scenes when you edit UI, for example, in a WinForms or WPF application.

- *Dynamically*, that is, at runtime. This is the most sophisticated option. Advanced libraries are capable of constructing data structures and compiling them into executable code right at the moment when the application is executing.

It's worth noting that many data structures are created implicitly behind the scenes by the compiler. This includes things like `ValueTuples`, classes for anonymous types, as well as state machines in charge of orchestrating enumerators (`yield` functionality) or asynchronous (`async`/`await`) operations.

In F#, the amount of data structures (and corresponding allocations) created behind the scenes is *huge*, as is the complexity of those data structures. For example, any sort of currying operations generate deep inheritance hierarchies. Or, let's say, you decide to pass an operator such as (`+`) as a parameter to a function – in this case, an entire `struct` will be created purely for the purpose of housing a method that would in turn call this operator. And it would be very naive to think that all such allocations are automatically inlined during JIT compilation!

CHAPTER 7

Adapter

I used to travel quite a lot, and quite often only when you arrive in a new country you remember that their sockets are different and you didn't prepare for this. This is why airport travel shops carry travel adapters and also why some hotels (the better ones) have at least one outlet of a nonlocal type just in case a customer has forgotten to get an adapter, but needs to, say, work on their laptop without interruption.

A travel adapter that lets me plug a European plug into a UK or USA socket[1] is very good analogy to what's going on with the Adapter pattern in the software world: we are given an interface, but we want a different one, and building an adapter over the interface is what gets us to where we want to be.

Scenario

Suppose you're working with a library that's great at drawing pixels. You, on the other hand, work with geometric objects – lines, rectangles, that sort of thing. You want to keep working with those objects but also need the rendering, so you need to *adapt* your vector geometry to pixel-based representation.

Let us begin by defining the (rather simple) domain objects of our example:

```
public class Point
{
  public int X, Y;
  // other members omitted
}

public class Line
```

---

[1] Just in case you're European like me and want to complain that everyone should be using European plugs and sockets: *no*, the UK plug design is technically better and safer, so if we did want just one standard, the UK one would be the one to go for.

© Dmitri Nesteruk 2022
D. Nesteruk, *Design Patterns in .NET 6*, https://doi.org/10.1007/978-1-4842-8245-8_7

```
{
  public Point Start, End;
  // other members omitted
}
```

A typical vector object is likely to be defined by a collection of Line objects. Thus, we can make a class that would simply inherit from Collection<Line>:

```
public abstract class VectorObject : Collection<Line> {}
```

So, this way, if you want to define, say, a Rectangle, you can simply inherit from this type, and there's no need to define additional storage:

```
public class VectorRectangle : VectorObject
{
  public VectorRectangle(int x, int y, int width, int height)
  {
    Add(new Line(new Point(x,y), new Point(x+width, y) ));
    Add(new Line(new Point(x+width,y), new Point(x+width, y+height) ));
    Add(new Line(new Point(x,y), new Point(x, y+height) ));
    Add(new Line(new Point(x,y+height), new Point(x+width, y+height) ));
  }
}
```

Now, here's the setup. Suppose we want to draw lines on-screen. Rectangles, even! Unfortunately, we cannot, because the only interface for drawing is literally this:

```
// the interface we have
public static void DrawPoint(Point p)
{
  bitmap.SetPixel(p.X, p.Y, Color.Black);
}
```

I'm using the Bitmap class here for illustration, but the actual implementation doesn't matter. Let's just take this at face value: we only have an API for drawing pixels. That's it.

Adapter

All right, so let's suppose we want to draw a couple of rectangles:

```
private static readonly List<VectorObject> vectorObjects
  = new()
{
  new VectorRectangle(1, 1, 10, 10),
  new VectorRectangle(3, 3, 6, 6)
};
```

In order to draw these objects, we need to convert every one of them from a series of lines into a rather large number of points, because the only interface that we have for drawing is a DrawPoint() method. For this, we make a separate class that will store the points and expose them as a collection. That's right – this is our Adapter pattern!

```
public class LineToPointAdapter : Collection<Point>
{
  private static int count = 0;

  public LineToPointAdapter(Line line)
  {
    WriteLine($"{++count}: Generating points for line"
      + $" [{line.Start.X},{line.Start.Y}]-"
      + $"[{line.End.X},{line.End.Y}] (no caching)");

    int left = Math.Min(line.Start.X, line.End.X);
    int right = Math.Max(line.Start.X, line.End.X);
    int top = Math.Min(line.Start.Y, line.End.Y);
    int bottom = Math.Max(line.Start.Y, line.End.Y);

    if (right - left == 0)
    {
      for (int y = top; y <= bottom; ++y)
      {
        Add(new Point(left, y));
      }
    } else if (line.End.Y - line.Start.Y == 0)
    {
```

```
    for (int x = left; x <= right; ++x)
    {
      Add(new Point(x, top));
    }
  }
}
}
```

This code is simplified: we only handle perfectly vertical or horizontal lines and ignore everything else. The conversion from a line to a number of points happens right in the constructor, so our adapter is *eager*. Don't worry. We'll make it lazy toward the end of this chapter.

We can now use this adapter to actually render some objects. We take the two rectangles from earlier and simply render them like this:

```
private static void DrawPoints()
{
  foreach (var vo in vectorObjects)
  {
    foreach (var line in vo)
    {
      var adapter = new LineToPointAdapter(line);
      adapter.ForEach(DrawPoint);
    }
  }
}
```

Beautiful! All we do is, for every vector object, get each of its lines, construct a LineToPointAdapter for that line, and then iterate the set of points produced by the adapter, feeding them to DrawPoint(). And it works! (Trust me it does.)

Adapter Temporaries

There's a major problem with our code, though: DrawPoints() gets called on literally every screen refresh that we might need, which means the same data for same line objects gets regenerated by the adapter, like a zillion times. What can we do about it?

Well, on one hand, we can make some lazy-loading method, for example:

```
private static List<Point> points = new ();
private static bool prepared = false;

private static void Prepare()
{
  if (prepared) return;
  foreach (var vo in vectorObjects)
  {
    foreach (var line in vo)
    {
      var adapter = new LineToPointAdapter(line);
      adapter.ForEach(p => points.Add(p));
    }
  }
  prepared = true;
}
```

And then the implementation of `DrawPoints()` simplifies to

```
private static void DrawPointsLazy()
{
  Prepare();
  points.ForEach(DrawPoint);
}
```

But let's suppose, for a moment, that the original set of `vectorObjects` can change. Saving those points forever makes no sense then, but we still want to avoid the incessant regeneration of potentially repeating data. How do we deal with this? With caching, of course!

First of all, to avoid regeneration, we need unique ways of identifying lines, which transitively means we need unique ways of identifying points. ReSharper/Rider's **Equality Members generator** to the rescue[2]:

---

[2] The implementation of `GetHashCode()` is likely to be different depending on the .NET Framework being used. For example, in .NET 6, the `Combine()` method from `System.Runtime.HashCode` is likely to be used instead.

```csharp
public class Point
{
  // other members here

  protected bool Equals(Point other) { ... }
  public override bool Equals(object obj) { ... }

  public override int GetHashCode()
  {
    unchecked { return (X * 397) ^ Y; }
  }
}

public class Line
{
  // other members here

  protected bool Equals(Line other) { ... }
  public override bool Equals(object obj) { ... }

  public override int GetHashCode()
  {
    unchecked
    {
      return ((Start != null ? Start.GetHashCode() : 0) * 397)
        ^ (End != null ? End.GetHashCode() : 0);
    }
  }
}
```

As you can see, ReSharper (or Rider, if you prefer that IDE) has generated different implementations of Equals() as well as GetHashCode(). The latter is more important because it allows us to uniquely (to some degree) identify an object by its hash code without performing a direct comparison. Now, we can build a new LineToPointCachingAdapter such that it caches the points and regenerates them only when necessary, that is, when their hashes differ. The implementation is almost the same except for the following nuances.

First, the adapter now has a static cache of points that correspond to particular lines:

```
static Dictionary<int, List<Point>> cache = new();
```

The type int here is precisely the type returned from GetHashCode(). Now, when processing a Line in the constructor, we first check whether or not the line is already cached. If it is, we don't need to do anything:

```
hash = line.GetHashCode();
if (cache.ContainsKey(hash)) return; // we already have it
```

Notice that we actually *store* the hash of the current adapter in its non-static field. This allows us to store and use adapters that correspond to individual lines. Alternatively, we could make the entire adapter static.

The full implementation of the constructor is as before, except that instead of calling Add() for the generated points, we simply add them to the cache:

```
public LineToPointAdapter(Line line)
{
  hash = line.GetHashCode();
  if (cache.ContainsKey(hash)) return; // we already have it

  List<Point> points = new();

  // points are added to the 'points' member as before, then...

  cache.Add(hash, points);
}
```

Lastly, we need to implement IEnumerable<Point>. This is easy: we use the hash field to reach into the cache and yield the right set of points:

```
public IEnumerator<Point> GetEnumerator()
{
  return cache[hash].GetEnumerator();
}
```

Yay! Thanks to hash functions and caching, we've drastically cut down on the number of conversions being made. The only issue with this implementation is that, in a long-running program, the cache can accumulate a huge number of unnecessary point collections. How would you clean it up? One idea would be to set up a timer to wipe the entire cache at regular intervals. See if you can come up with other possible solutions to this problem.

The Problem with Hashing

One reason we implemented the adapter the way we did is that our current implementation is robust with respect to changes in objects. If any aspect of a Rectangle changes, the adapter will calculate a different hash value and will regenerate the appropriate set of points.

This is effectively done by *polling*: any time an adapted dataset is required, we take the target object and recalculate its hash. The assumption is always that the hash can be calculated quickly and that hash collisions – situations where two different objects have identical hashes – are unlikely. Let's remind ourselves of how Point hashes are calculated:

```
public override int GetHashCode()
{
  unchecked
  {
    return (X * 397) ^ Y;
  }
}
```

The truth is the hash function for a Point is a pretty bad hash function and will give us lots of collisions. For example, points (0,0) and (1, 397) will give the same hash value of 0, which means, in turn, that two lines with these Start points and an identical End point will end up overwriting each other's generated set of points with incorrect data, inevitably causing problems.

How would you solve this issue? Well, you could pick a prime number N that is larger than 397. That way, if you can guarantee that your values are less than this larger N, you won't have any collisions. Alternatively, you could go for a more robust hashing function. In the case of a Point, assuming positive X and Y, this could be as simple as

```
public int GetHashCode()
{
  return (X << 32) | Y;
}
```

This hash code calculation is robust provided that a coordinate value fits inside 16 bits and is positive – which is very likely if, for example, we're talking about screen coordinates. There are plenty of sophisticated functions out there (Cantor pairing function, Szudzik function, etc.) that are able to handle situations at the boundaries of the range of numbers.

The point I'm trying to make here is that the calculation of hashing functions is a slippery slope: the code generated by IDEs might not be as robust as you think. What can we do to avoid all of this? Why, we can hold a reference to the adaptee, rather than the hash, in our cache. It's as simple as

```
public class LineToPointAdapter : IEnumerable<Point>
{
  static Dictionary<Line, List<Point>> cache = ();
  private Line line;

  public LineToPointAdapter(Line line)
  {
    if (cache.ContainsKey(line)) return; // we already have it
    this.line = line;

    // as before

    cache.Add(line, points);
  }

  public IEnumerator<Point> GetEnumerator()
  {
    return cache[line].GetEnumerator();
  }
}
```

What's the difference? Well, the difference is that, when searching through the dictionary, *both* GetHashCode() and Equals() are used to find the right item. As a result, collisions can still occur, but they won't mess up the final value. This approach does have its downsides though: for example, the lifetime of lines is now bound to the adapter because it has strong references to them.

This approach of holding on to the reference gives us an additional benefit: laziness. Instead of calculating everything in the constructor, we can split the preparation of points into a separate function that only gets invoked when adapter points are iterated:

```
public class LineToPointAdapter : IEnumerable<Point>
{
  ...
  private void Prepare()
  {
    if (cache.ContainsKey(line)) return; // we already have it
    // rest of code as before
  }

  public IEnumerator<Point> GetEnumerator()
  {
    Prepare();
    return cache[line].GetEnumerator();
  }
}
```

Property Adapter (Surrogate)

One very common application of the Adapter design pattern is to get your class to provide additional properties that serve only one purpose: to take existing fields or properties and expose them in some useful way, quite often as projections to a different data type. And while it often makes sense to do this in a separate class (e.g., when building a ViewModel), sometimes you're forced to do this right in the class where the original data is kept.

Consider the following example: if you have an IDictionary member in your class, you cannot use an XmlSerializer because Microsoft didn't implement this functionality "due to schedule constraints." Consequently, if you want a serializable dictionary, you have two options: you either go online and search for a `SerializableDictionary` implementation, or alternatively, you build a property adapter (or surrogate), which exposes the dictionary in a way that's easy to serialize.

For example, suppose you need to serialize the following property:

```
public Dictionary<string, string> Capitals { get; set; }
```

To make it happen, you would first of all mark the property with [XmlIgnore]. You would then construct another property of a type that *can* be serialized, such as an array of tuples:

```
public (string, string)[] CapitalsSerializable
{
  get
  {
    return Capitals.Keys.Select(country =>
      (country, Capitals[country])).ToArray();
  }
  set
  {
    Capitals = value.ToDictionary(x => x.Item1, x => x.Item2);
  }
}
```

I have made very careful choice of types for serialization here:

- The overall type of the variable is an array. If you made this a List, the serializer would never call the setter and would instead try to use the getter and then Add() to that getter – we definitely don't want that.

- We are using a ValueTuple instead of an ordinary Tuple. Conventional tuples cannot be serialized because they do not have parameterless constructors, whereas ValueTuples don't have this problem.

In case you're wondering, here's how a serialized class would look in XML:

```xml
<?xml version="1.0" encoding="utf-16"?>
<CountryStats   xmlns:xsi="http://www.w3.org/2001/XMLSchema-instance"
  xmlns:xsd="http://www.w3.org/2001/XMLSchema">
  <CapitalsSerializable>
    <ValueTupleOfStringString>
      <Item1>France</Item1>
      <Item2>Paris</Item2>
    </ValueTupleOfStringString>
  </CapitalsSerializable>
</CountryStats>
```

The adapter presented here is quite different from what you might expect because the API we're trying to adapt the class to is *implicit* – serialization mechanics are concealed by the serializer we're using, so the only way to know about this issue is through trial and error.[3]

This example is a bit ambiguous with respect to SOLID principles: On the one hand, we're separating out the serialization concern. On the other hand, should this really be part of the class itself? It would be a lot neater if we could decorate the member with some [SerializeThisDictionary] attribute and have the conversion process handled elsewhere. Alas, such are the limitations of the way serialization is implemented in .NET.

Generic Value Adapter

In C++, unlike in C#, generic arguments don't have to be types: they can be literals instead. For example, you can write template <int n> class X {} and then instantiate a class of type X<42>. There are cases where this sort of functionality is necessary in C#, and even though the language does not allow the use of values in generic arguments, we can build adapters that help us adapt values to generic types.

---

[3] You really want to use third-party serialization components if you can. The support for both binary and XML serialization in .NET is very patchy and has lots of unpleasant caveats. If you were to take a JSON serializer such as Json.NET, none of the problems described previously would be an issue.

The idea behind this is very simple, so to make it interesting, I'm going to throw in an added bonus: not only are we going to work with the Generic Value Adapter pattern but we'll also make use of some advanced generic magic just to spice things up.

First, here's the scenario I propose. Say you're working in a mathematical or graphics domain and you want to have (geometric) vectors of different sizes and use different data types. For example, you want Vector2i to be a vector with two integer values, whereas a Vector3f would be a three-dimensional vector with floating-point values.

What we really want is to have a class Vector<T, D> (T = type, D = dimensions) that would be defined as…

```csharp
public class Vector<T, D>
{
  protected T[] data;

  public Vector()
  {
    data = new T[D]; // impossible
  }
}
```

…and then instantiated it as

```csharp
var v = new Vector<int, 2>(); // impossible
```

Both the constructor initialization and the instantiation are impossible in C#. The solution to this problem is not pretty: we basically wrap literals like 2, 3, and so on inside classes. To do this, first of all, we define an interface for returning an integer:

```csharp
public interface IInteger
{
  int Value { get; }
}
```

And now this interface can be implemented by concrete structures (no reason to use classes here)[4] that would yield values of 2, 3, and so on. To make it a bit neater to use, I'll put all of those inside a class that would act as an enum-like entity:

---

[4]Sadly, it is impossible to declare these classes as ref structs for two reasons. They cannot implement interfaces, and furthermore, they cannot be used as type arguments.

```
public static class Dimensions
{
  public readonly struct Two : IInteger
  {
    public int Value => 2;
  }

  public readonly struct Three : IInteger
  {
    public int Value => 3;
  }
}
```

So now we can finally define a working Vector<T, D> class that would initialize the data correctly:

```
public class Vector<T, D>
  where D : IInteger, new()
{
  protected T[] data;

  public Vector()
  {
    data = new T[new D().Value];
  }
}
```

This approach may be convoluted, but it does, in fact, work. We require that D is an IInteger that also has a default constructor, and when it comes to initializing the data storage, we spin up an instance of D and take its value.

To make use of this new class, you'd write something like the following:

```
var v = new Vector<int, Dimensions.Two>();
```

Alternatively, you could make things reusable by defining inheriting types, for example:

```
public class Vector2i : Vector<int, Dimensions.Two> {}
// and then
var v = new Vector2i();
```

So that's it. We are done with the discussion of the Generic Value Adapter pattern as such. As I'm sure you can appreciate, the idea is both trivial and, unfortunately, ugly at the same time. Imagine having to make Dimensions.Three, Dimensions.Four, and so on! Maybe some code generation can help here, though.

Now, it would be grossly unfair of me to abandon this example and just let you fend for yourself from this point on, so let's discuss a few ideas on how to get this example to production status. Even though these ideas are not central to design patterns, an attempt to get this Vector fully functional brings up one of the tricky aspects of C# – namely, recursive generics.

Let's start with the obvious things: we want to somehow access and modify data in the vector as if it were an array. A simple approach would be to simply expose an indexer:

```
public class Vector<T, D>
  where D : IInteger, new()
{
  // ... other members omitted
  public T this[int index]
  {
    get => data[index];
    set => data[index] = value;
  }
}
```

Similarly, if you decide to inherit, you can create additional getters and setters for having named coordinates:

```
public class Vector2i : Vector<int, Dimensions.Two>
{
  public int X
  {
    get => data[0];
    set => data[0] = value;
  }
  // similarly for Y
}
```

You could, theoretically, stick predictable properties such as X,Y,Z into the base class, too, but that would be a bit confusing because then you could have a one-dimensional vector with an exposed Z coordinate that would simply throw an exception when accessed.

Anyways, with this all set, you can now initialize a vector as follows:

```
var v = new Vector2i();
v[0] = 123; // using an indexer
v.Y = 456;  // using a property
```

Of course, it would really be nice if we could somehow initialize data in the constructor. Thanks to the params keyword, our base Vector can have a constructor taking an arbitrary number of arguments. We just need to make sure that the data being initialized is of the right size:

```
public Vector(params T[] values)
{
  var requiredSize = new D().Value;
  data = new T[requiredSize];

  var providedSize = values.Length;

  for (int i = 0; i < Math.Min(requiredSize, providedSize); ++i)
  data[i] = values[i];
}
```

Now we can initialize a vector using a constructor; we cannot really initialize the derived Vector2i this way, though, not until we create a forwarding constructor:

```
public class Vector2i : Vector<int, Dimensions.Two>
{
  public Vector2i() {}
  public Vector2i(params int[] values) : base(values) {}
}
```

So now we can finally make a new Vector2i(2, 3), and everything will compile. This is actually one of the two possible approaches to instantiating these vectors, the other involving the use of a factory method. But, before we get there, let's first of all consider one problem that will throw a fairly big spanner in the works.

Here's what I want to be able to write:

```
var v = new Vector2i(1, 2);
var vv = new Vector2i(3, 2);
var result = v + vv;
```

Now, this is a sad story. We cannot go into our Vector<T, D> and give it an operator +. Why not? Well, because T is not constrained to numerics. It could be a Guid or something, and the operation to add two GUIDs is undefined. There is no way for us to tell C# to constrain T to numeric types (other languages, such as Rust, have solved this problem), so the only way we can get this all to work is to create more types derived from Vector – types such as VectorOfInt, VectorOfFloat, and so on:

```
public class VectorOfInt<D> : Vector<int, D>
  where D : IInteger, new()
{
  public VectorOfInt() {}

  public VectorOfInt(params int[] values) : base(values) {}

  public static VectorOfInt<D> operator +
    (VectorOfInt<D> lhs, VectorOfInt<D> rhs)
  {
    var result = new VectorOfInt<D>();
    var dim = new D().Value;
    for (int i = 0; i < dim; i++)
    {
      result[i] = lhs[i] + rhs[i];
    }

    return result;
  }
}
```

As you can see from this listing, we've had to replicate the constructor API of `Vector`, but we managed to provide a good `operator +` implementation that adds the two vectors together. Now all we need to do is modify our `Vector2i`, and we're good to go:

```
public class Vector2i : VectorOfInt<Dimensions.Two>
{
  public Vector2i(params int[] values) : base(values)
  {
  }
}
```

Notice something interesting: we removed the parameterless constructor because it's no longer required, as it's now contained in `VectorOfInt`. However, we still have to keep the `params` constructor so we can initialize a `Vector2i` instance.

Here's a final complication that we can consider. Suppose you're not really interested in doing this constructor propagation all over the place. Say you decide that, instead of constructors, all derived classes (`VectorOfInt`, `VectorOfFloat`, `Vector2i`, etc.) will have *no* constructors in their bodies. Instead, we decide that the creation of all these types will be handled by a single `Vector<T, D>.Create()` factory method. How can we get this done?

This situation is not simple and calls for the use of recursive generics. Why? Because the static `Vector.Create()` method needs to return the right type. If I call `Vector3f.Create()`, I expect a `Vector3f` to be returned, not a `Vector<float, Dimensions.Three>` and not `VectorOfFloat<Dimensions.Three>` either.

This means that we need to make several modifications. First, `Vector` now gets a new generic parameter `TSelf` referring to the class deriving from it:

```
public abstract class Vector<TSelf, T, D>
  where D : IInteger, new()
  where TSelf : Vector<TSelf, T, D>, new()
{
  // ...
}
```

As you can see, TSelf is constrained to be an inheritor of Vector<TSelf, T, D>. Now, any derived type (say, VectorOfFloat) needs to be changed to

```
public class VectorOfFloat<TSelf, D>
  : Vector<TSelf, float, D>
  where D : IInteger, new()
  where TSelf : Vector<TSelf, float, D>, new()
{
  // wow, such empty!
}
```

Notice that this class no longer has any forwarding constructors, since we plan on using a factory method. Similarly, you'd have to modify any class that derives from VectorOfFloat, for example:

```
public class Vector3f
  : VectorOfFloat<Vector3f, Dimensions.Three>
{
  // empty again
}
```

Notice how the TSelf gets propagated up the hierarchy: first, Vector3f travels up to VectorOfFloat and then up to Vector. This way, we can be sure that Vector knows that its factory method needs to return a Vector3f. Oh, and speaking of the factory method, we can finally write it!

```
public static TSelf Create(params T[] values)
{
  var result = new TSelf();
  var requiredSize = new D().Value;
  result.data = new T[requiredSize];

  var providedSize = values.Length;

  for (int i = 0; i < Math.Min(requiredSize, providedSize); ++i)
   result.data[i] = values[i];

  return result;
}
```

This is where TSelf comes in handy – it is the return type of our factory method. Now, whichever derived class you create, making an instance of this class is as simple as writing

```
var coord = Vector3f.Create(3.5f, 2.2f, 1);
```

And there you have it! Naturally, the type of the preceding coord is a Vector3f – no need for casts or any other magic. This is the kind of functionality recursive generics allow you to have. Figure 7-1 is an illustration of our entire scenario.

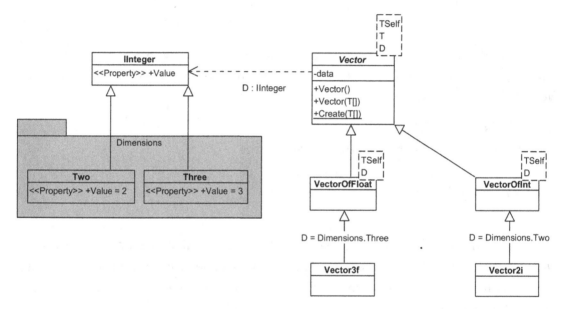

Figure 7-1. *Generic value adapter class diagram*

Adapter in Dependency Injection

There are certain advanced adapter scenarios that are handled nicely by dependency injection frameworks such as Autofac. The approach here is, admittedly, somewhat different from the "adapt component X to interface Y" that is discussed in the rest of the chapter.

Consider a scenario where your application has a bunch of commands that you want to invoke. Each command is able to execute itself, and that's about it:

```
public interface ICommand
{
  void Execute();
}
```

```
public class SaveCommand : ICommand
{
  public void Execute()
  {
    Console.WriteLine("Saving current file");
  }
}

public class OpenCommand : ICommand
{
  public void Execute()
  {
    Console.WriteLine("Opening a file");
  }
}
```

Now, in your editor, you want to create a bunch of buttons. Each button, when pressed, executes the corresponding command. We can represent the button as follows:

```
public class Button
{
  private ICommand command;
  private string name;

  public Button(ICommand command, string name)
  {
    this.command = command;
    this.name = name;
  }

  public void Click() { command.Execute(); }

  public void PrintMe()
  {
    Console.WriteLine($"I am a button called {name}");
  }
}
```

So here is a challenge: how do you make an editor that has a single button created for each of the commands registered in the system? We can begin by defining it as follows:

```
public class Editor
{
  public IEnumerable<Button> Buttons { get; }

  public Editor(IEnumerable<Button> buttons)
  {
    Buttons = buttons;
  }
}
```

We can set up a dependency injection container with all the possible commands. We can also add a bit of metadata to each command, storing its name:

```
var b = new ContainerBuilder();
b.RegisterType<OpenCommand>()
  .As<ICommand>()
  .WithMetadata("Name", "Open");
b.RegisterType<SaveCommand>()
  .As<ICommand>()
  .WithMetadata("Name", "Save");
```

We can register an adapter inside the DI container that will construct a Button for each registered command and, furthermore, will take the metadata Name value from each command and pass it as the second constructor argument:

```
b.RegisterAdapter<Meta<ICommand>, Button>(cmd =>
  new Button(cmd.Value, (string)cmd.Metadata["Name"]));
```

Now we register the Editor itself and build the container. When we resolve the editor, its constructor will receive an IEnumerable<Button> with one button per registered command:

```
b.RegisterType<Editor>();

using var c = b.Build();
var editor = c.Resolve<Editor>();
foreach (var btn in editor.Buttons)
```

```
  btn.PrintMe();
```
// I am a button called Open
// I am a button called Save

So, as you can see, while this is not an adapter in the classic sense, it allows us to enforce one-to-one correspondence between a set of types conforming to some criteria and a set of instances related to those types.

Bidirectional Adapter

A bidirectional adapter adapts the interface both ways. This means that, one way or another, two components can interact with one another both ways through an intermediary.

The most common example is a numeric text field on a form. A text field, by definition, works with text. But if you bind it to an integer variable, you need to perform conversions: when the user enters input, you need to check it's actually an integer and assign it to the variable; when the user changes the variable behind the scenes, you need to turn it into a string to actually show on-screen.

In the WPF framework, we have the IValueConverter interface designed for this exact purpose:

```csharp
public interface IValueConverter
{
  object Convert(object value, Type targetType, object parameter,
  CultureInfo culture);
  object ConvertBack(object value, Type targetType, object parameter,
  CultureInfo culture);
}
```

The implementation of, say, a string-to-int converter could be something like

```csharp
public class IntToString : IValueConverter
{
  public object Convert(object value, Type targetType, object parameter,
  CultureInfo culture)
  {
    return value.ToString();
  }
```

```
public object ConvertBack(object value, Type targetType, object
parameter, CultureInfo culture)
{
  return int.TryParse((string)value, out int ret) ? ret : 0;
}
}
```

WPF also has an IMultiValueConverter to convert multiple values to/from a particular type. Both interfaces take input values as objects, that is, they are weakly typed. If I needed such a converter in my application, I would most likely go for something like an IValueConverter<TFrom, TTo> interface and use those type parameters in the methods.

Adapters in the .NET Framework

There are many uses of the Adapter pattern in the .NET Framework, including the following:

- ADO.NET providers living in System.Data, such as SqlCommand, adapt an OOP-defined database command or query to be executed using SQL. Each ADO.NET provider is an adapter for a particular database type.

- Database data adapters – types that inherit from DbDataAdapter – perform a similar, higher-level operation. Internally, they represent a set of data commands and a connection to a particular data source (a database, typically), their goal being to populate a DataSet and update the data source.

- LINQ providers are also adapters, each adapting some underlying storage technology to be usable through LINQ operators (Select, Where, etc.). Expression trees exist with the central purpose of translating conventional C# lambda functions into other query languages and mechanisms such as SQL.

- Stream adapters (e.g., `TextReader`, `StreamWriter`) adapt a stream to read a particular type of data (binary, text) into a particular type of object. For example, a `StringWriter` writes into a buffer held by a `StringBuilder`.

- WPF uses the `IValueConverter` interface to allow scenarios such as a text field being bound to a numeric value. Unlike most of the adapters here, this one is *bidirectional*, meaning that the interface is adapted in both directions: changes to a numeric field/property get turned into text displayed in the control and, conversely, text entered into the control gets parsed and converted into a numeric value.

- Interop-related entities in C# represent the Adapter pattern. For example, that dummy P/Invoke type that you write allows you to adapt a C/C++ library to your C# needs. Same goes for Runtime Callable Wrappers (RCWs), which allow managed classes and COM components to interact despite their obvious interface differences.

Summary

Adapter is a very simple concept: it allows you to adapt the interface you have to the interface you need. The only real issue with adapters is that, in the process of adaptation, you sometimes end up generating temporary data so as to satisfy requirements related to representation of data in a form palatable for the target API. And when this happens, we turn to caching: ensuring that new data is only generated when necessary. If we are implementing caching with a special key, we need to ensure that collisions are either impossible or handled appropriately. If we are using the object itself as the underlying key, the presence of both `GetHashCode()` and `Equals()` solves this problem for us.

As an additional optimization, we can ensure that the adapter doesn't generate the temporaries immediately, but instead only generates them when they are actually required. Further optimizations are possible but are domain-specific: for example, in our case lines can be parts of other lines, which would let us to further save on the number of `Point` objects created.

CHAPTER 8

Bridge

One very common situation that occurs when designing software is the so-called *state space explosion* where the number of related entities required to represent all possible states "explodes" in a Cartesian product fashion. For example, if you have circles and squares of different colors, you might end up with classes such as `RedSquare`, `BlueSquare`, `RedCircle`, `BlueCircle`, etc. Clearly, nobody wants that.

What we do instead is we connect things together, and there are different ways of doing that. For example, if object color is simply a trait, we create an `enum`. But if color has mutable fields, properties, or behaviors, we cannot restrict ourselves to an `enum`: if we do, we'll have plenty of `if`/`switch` statements in unrelated classes. Again, it's not something that we want.

The Bridge pattern essentially connects constituent aspects of an object using, ahem, references. Not very exciting, is it? Well, I can offer some excitement toward the end of our exploration, but we first need to take a look at a conventional implementation of the pattern.

Conventional Bridge

Let's imagine that we are interested in drawing different kinds of shapes on the screen. Suppose that we have a variety of shapes (circle, square, etc.) and also different APIs for rendering these (say, raster vs. vector rendering).

We want to create objects that specify both the type of shape and the rendering mechanism the shape should use for rendering. How can we do this? Well, on the one hand, we can define an infinite bunch of classes (`RasterSquare`, `VectorCircle`, etc.) and provide an implementation for each. Or we could somehow get each shape to refer to which renderer it's using.

© Dmitri Nesteruk 2022

D. Nesteruk, *Design Patterns in .NET 6*, https://doi.org/10.1007/978-1-4842-8245-8_8

Let's begin by defining an IRenderer. This interface will determine how different shapes are rendered by whatever mechanism is required[1]:

```
public interface IRenderer
{
  void RenderCircle(float radius);
  // RenderSquare, RenderTriangle, etc.
}
```

And, on the other side, we can define an abstract class (not an interface) for our shape hierarchy. Why an abstract class? Because we want to keep a reference to the renderer:

```
public abstract class Shape
{
  protected IRenderer renderer;

  // a bridge between the shape that's being drawn an
  // the component which actually draws it
  public Shape(IRenderer renderer)
  {
    this.renderer = renderer;
  }

  public abstract void Draw();
  public abstract void Resize(float factor);
}
```

This may seem counterintuitive, so let's take a pause and ask ourselves: what are we trying to guard against, exactly? Well, we're trying to handle two situations: when new renderers get added and when new shapes get added to the system. We don't want either of these to spawn *multiple* changes. So here are the two situations:

---

[1] I am being sly here by using a calling convention. This is done purely for illustration purposes. If every rendered shape is neither parent nor child of another shape, you can simplify this by making a series of similarly named overloads, that is, Render(Circle c), Render(Square s), and so on. The choice is up to you.

- If a new shape gets added, all it has to do is inherit Shape and implement its members (say there are M different ones). Each renderer then has to implement just one new member (RenderXxx). So if there are M different renderers, the total number of operations required for a new shape is M+N.

- If a new renderer gets added, all it has to do is implement M different members, one for every shape.

As you can see, we either implement M members or M+N members. At no point do we get an M×N situation, which is what the pattern actively tries to avoid. Another added benefit is that renderers always know how to render all the shapes available in the system because each shape Xxx has a Draw() method that explicitly calls RenderXxx().

So here is the implementation of the Circle:

```
public class Circle : Shape
{
  private float radius;

  public Circle(IRenderer renderer, float radius) : base(renderer)
  {
    this.radius = radius;
  }

  public override void Draw()
  {
    renderer.RenderCircle(radius);
  }

  public override void Resize(float factor)
  {
    radius *= factor;
  }
}
```

And here is a sample implementation of one of the renderers:

```
public class VectorRenderer : IRenderer
{
  public void RenderCircle(float radius)
  {
    WriteLine($"Drawing a circle of radius {radius}");
  }
}
```

Notice that the Draw() method simply uses the bridge: it calls the corresponding renderer's drawing implementation for this particular object. The entire arrangement is illustrated in Figure 8-1.

In order to use this setup, you have to instantiate both an IRenderer and the shape. This can be done directly:

```
var raster = new RasterRenderer();
var vector = new VectorRenderer();
var circle = new Circle(vector, 5);
circle.Draw(); // Drawing a circle of radius 5
circle.Resize(2);
circle.Draw(); // Drawing a circle of radius 10
```

Or, if you are using a dependency injection framework, you can define a default renderer to be used throughout the application. This way, all constructed instances of a Circle will be preinitialized with a renderer that is centrally defined. Here is an example that uses the Autofac container:

```
var cb = new ContainerBuilder();
cb.RegisterType<VectorRenderer>().As<IRenderer>();
cb.Register((c, p) => new Circle(c.Resolve<IRenderer>(),
  p.Positional<float>(0)));
using (var c = cb.Build())
{
  var circle = c.Resolve<Circle>(
    new PositionalParameter(0, 5.0f)
  );
```

```
  circle.Draw();
  circle.Resize(2);
  circle.Draw();
}
```

This specifies that, by default, a new VectorRenderer instance should be provided when someone asks for an IRenderer. Furthermore, since shapes take an additional parameter (their size, presumably), we specify that such a parameter must be provided. There are alternatives to this approach, such as defining a default value (e.g., zero) or creating a delegate factory (see Chapter 4) and resolving that instead.

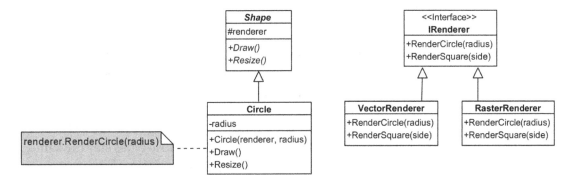

***Figure 8-1.** Bridge class diagram*

Dynamic Prototyping Bridge

You may have noticed that the bridge is nothing more than the application of the Dependency Inversion Principle, where you connect two distinct hierarchies together through a common parameter. So now we are going to take a look at a more sophisticated example involving something called Dynamic Prototyping.

Dynamic Prototyping is a technique for editing .NET programs *while they are running*. You have already experienced this as the "Edit & Continue" feature in Visual Studio. The idea of Dynamic Prototyping is to allow the user to make immediate changes to the program that's currently running by editing and runtime-compiling the program's source code.

How does it work? Well, imagine you are sticking to "one class per file" approach and you know in advance that your DI container can satisfy *all* dependencies of a given class. What you can do in this case is as follows:

- Allow the user to edit the source code of this class. This works best if there is one-to-one correspondence between the class and the file. Most modern IDEs try to enforce this approach.

- After you edit and save the new source code, you use the C# compiler to compile just that class and get an in-memory implementation of the new type. You basically get a System.Type. You could, if you wanted, just instantiate that new type and use it to update some reference, or...

- You change the registration options in the DI container so that your new type is now a replacement for the original type. This naturally requires that you are using abstractions of some kind.

The last point needs explaining. If you have a concrete type Foo.Bar and you build a brand-new, in-memory type Foo.Bar, then, even if the APIs of those types stay the same, those types are *incompatible*. You cannot assign a reference to the old Bar with the new one. The only way to use them interchangeably is via dynamic or reflection, and both of those are niche cases.

Let me illustrate how the entire process works. Suppose you have a Log class being used by a Payroll class. Using hypothetical dependency injection, you could define it as

```
// Log.cs
public class Log
{
  void Info(string msg) { ... }
}

// Payroll.cs
public class Payroll
{
  [Service]
  public Log Log { get; set; }
}
```

Notice that I'm defining the Log as an injected property, not via constructor injection. Now, to make a dynamic bridge, you would introduce an interface, that is:

```
// ILog.cs
public interface ILog
{
  void Info(string msg);
}

// Log.cs
public class Log : ILog { /* as before */ }

// Payroll.cs
public class Payroll
{
  [Service]
  public ILog Log { get; set; }
}
```

Pay attention to the names of files too. This is important; each type is in its own file. Now, as you run this program, suppose you want to change the implementation of Log without stopping the application. What you would do is

- Open up an editor with the Log.cs file and edit the file.

- Close the editor. Now Log.cs gets compiled into an in-memory assembly.

- Create the first type found in this new assembly. It will be a Log, for sure, but incompatible with the previous Log! However, it implements an ILog, which is good enough for us.

- Go over the objects already created by the container and update all [Service]-marked references to an ILog with the new object.

This last part could be tricky. First, you need a container that can go over its own injection points, though, to be honest, you could use good old-fashioned reflection for this purpose too. The reason I'm referring to a container is that it's more convenient to use. Also, notice this approach only works for property injection, and there's an implicit assumption that the service is *immutable* (has no state). If the service had state, you'd have to serialize it and then deserialize the data into the new object – not impossible, but a robust implementation needs to handle many corner cases.

So the moral of this story is that, in order to be able to substitute one runtime-constructed type for another, they both need to implement the same interface. And before you ask, *no*, you cannot dynamically change any base type (class or interface).

Summary

The principal goal of the Bridge design pattern, as we have seen, is to avoid excessive proliferation of data types where there are two or more "dimensions," that is, aspects of a system that can potentially multiply in number. The best approach to Bridge is still active avoidance (e.g., replace classes with enums, if possible), but if that's not possible, we simply abstract away both hierarchies and find a way of connecting them.

CHAPTER 9

Composite

It's a fact of life that objects are quite often composed of other objects (or, in other words, they aggregate other objects). Remember, we agreed to equate aggregation and composition at the start of this part of the book.

There are a few ways for an object to advertise that it's composed of something. The most obvious approach is for an object to either implement IEnumerable<T> (where T is whatever you're prepared to expose) or, alternatively, to expose public members that themselves implement IEnumerable<T>. This is not the only interface that communicates the idea of having multiple objects (there are many others, e.g., IAsyncEnumerable), but it's probably the most well-known.

Another option for advertising being a composite is to inherit from a known collection class such as Collection<T>, List<T>, or similar. This of course lets you not just implement IEnumerable<T> implicitly but also provides you with an internal storage mechanism, so issues such as adding new objects to the collection are automatically handled for you.

So what is the Composite pattern about? Essentially, we try to give single objects and groups of objects an identical interface and have those interface members work correctly regardless of which class is the underlying.

Grouping Graphic Objects

Think of an application such as PowerPoint where you can select several different objects and drag them as one. And yet, if you were to select a single object, you could grab that object too. Same goes for rendering: you can render an individual graphic object, or you can group several shapes together, and they get drawn as one group.

© Dmitri Nesteruk 2022
D. Nesteruk, *Design Patterns in .NET 6*, https://doi.org/10.1007/978-1-4842-8245-8_9

The implementation of this approach is rather easy because it relies on just a single base class such as the following:

```
public class GraphicObject
{
  public virtual string Name { get; set; } = "Group";
  public string Color;
  // todo members
}
public class Circle : GraphicObject
{
  public override string Name => "Circle";
}
public class Square : GraphicObject
{
  public override string Name => "Square";
}
```

This appears to be a fairly ordinary example with nothing standing out except for the fact that GraphicObject is abstract, as well as the virtual string Name property, which is, for some reason, set to "Group". So even though the inheritors of GraphicObject are, obviously, scalar entities, GraphicObject itself reserves the right to act as a *container* for further items.

The way this is done is by furnishing GraphicObject with a lazily constructed list of children:

```
public class GraphicObject
{
  ...
  private readonly Lazy<List<GraphicObject>> children = new();
  public List<GraphicObject> Children => children.Value;
}
```

So GraphicObject can act as both a singular, scalar element (e.g., you inherit it, and you get a Circle) and a container of elements. We can implement some methods that would print its contents:

```
public class GraphicObject
{
  private void Print(StringBuilder sb, int depth)
  {
    sb.Append(new string('*', depth))
      .Append(string.IsNullOrWhiteSpace(Color) ? string.Empty :
      $"{Color} ")
      .AppendLine($"{Name}");
    foreach (var child in Children)
      child.Print(sb, depth + 1);
  }

  public override string ToString()
  {
    var sb = new StringBuilder();
    Print(sb, 0);
    return sb.ToString();
  }
}
```

This code uses asterisks (*) for indicating the level of depth of each element. Armed with this, we can now construct a drawing that consists of both shapes and a group of shapes and print it out:

```
var drawing = new GraphicObject {Name = "My Drawing"};
drawing.Children.Add(new Square {Color = "Red"});
drawing.Children.Add(new Circle{Color="Yellow"});

var group = new GraphicObject();
group.Children.Add(new Circle{Color="Blue"});
group.Children.Add(new Square{Color="Blue"});
drawing.Children.Add(group);

WriteLine(drawing);
```

And here is the output we get:

```
My Drawing
*Red Square
*Yellow Circle
*Group
**Blue Circle
**Blue Square
```

So this is the simplest implementation of the Composite design pattern that is based on inheritance and optional containment of a list of sub-elements. The only issue, which the astute reader will point out, is that it makes absolutely no sense for scalar classes such as Circle or Square to have a Children member. What if someone were to use such an API? It would make very little sense.

In the next example, we're going to look at scalar objects that are truly scalar, with no extraneous members in their interface.

Neural Networks

Machine learning is the hot new thing, and I hope it stays this way, or I'll have to update this paragraph. Part of machine learning is the use of artificial neural networks: software constructs that attempt to mimic the way neurons work in our brains.

The central concept of neural networks is, of course, a *neuron*. A neuron can produce a (typically numeric) output as a function of its inputs, and we can feed that value on to other connections in the network. We're going to concern ourselves with connections only, so we'll model the neuron like so:

```
public class Neuron
{
  public List<Neuron> In, Out;
}
```

This is a simple neuron with outgoing and incoming connections to other neurons. What you probably want to do is to be able to connect one neuron to another, which can be done using

```
public void ConnectTo(Neuron other)
{
  Out.Add(other);
  other.In.Add(this);
}
```

This method does fairly predictable things: it sets up connections between the current (this) neuron and some other one. So far, so good.

Now, suppose we also want to create neuron *layers*. A layer is quite simply a specific number of neurons grouped together. This can easily be done just by inheriting from a Collection<T>, that is:

```
public class NeuronLayer : Collection<Neuron>
{
  public NeuronLayer(int count)
  {
    while (count --> 0)
      Add(new Neuron());
  }
}
```

Looks good, right? I've even thrown in the arrow --> operator for you to enjoy.[1] But now, we've got a bit of a problem.

The problem is this: we want to be able to have neurons connectable to neuron layers (in both directions), and we also want layers to be connectable to other layers. Broadly speaking, we want this to work:

```
var neuron1 = new Neuron();
var neuron2 = new Neuron();
var layer1 = new NeuronLayer(3);
```

---

[1] There is, of course, no --> operator; it's quite simply the postfix decrement -- followed by the greater than >. The effect, though, is exactly as the --> arrow suggests: in while (count --> 0) we iterate until count reaches zero.

```
var layer2 = new NeuronLayer(4);

neuron1.ConnectTo(neuron2); // works already :)
neuron1.ConnectTo(layer1);
layer2.ConnectTo(neuron1);
layer1.ConnectTo(layer2);
```

As you can see, we've got four distinct cases to take care of:

1. Neuron connecting to another neuron

2. Neuron connecting to layer

3. Layer connecting to neuron

4. Layer connecting to another layer

As you may have guessed, there's no way in Baator that we'll be making four overloads of the ConnectTo() method. What if there were three distinct classes? Would we realistically consider creating nine methods? I do not think so.

The way to have a single-method solution to this problem is to realize that both Neuron and NeuronLayer can be treated as enumerables. In the case of NeuronLayer, there's no problem – it is already enumerable. But in the case of Neuron, well...we need to do some work.

In order to get Neuron ready, we are going to

- Remove its own ConnectTo() method, since it's not general enough.

- Implement the IEnumerable<Neuron> interface, yielding...ourself (!) when someone wants to enumerate us.

Here's what the new Neuron class looks like:

```
public class Neuron : IEnumerable<Neuron>
{
  public readonly List<Neuron> In = new(), Out = new();

  public IEnumerator<Neuron> GetEnumerator()
  {
    yield return this;
  }

  IEnumerator IEnumerable.GetEnumerator()
```

```
  {
    return GetEnumerator();
  }
}
```

And now, the *piece de resistance*: since both Neuron and NeuronLayer now conform to IEnumerable<Neuron>, all that remains for us to do is to implement a single extension method that connects the two enumerables together:

```
public static class ExtensionMethods
{
  public static void ConnectTo(
    this IEnumerable<Neuron> self, IEnumerable<Neuron> other)
  {
    if (ReferenceEquals(self, other)) return;

    foreach (var from in self)
      foreach (var to in other)
      {
        from.Out.Add(to);
        to.In.Add(from);
      }
  }
}
```

And that's it! We now have a single method that can be called to glue together any entities consisting of Neuron classes. Now, if we decided to make some NeuronRing, provided it supports IEnumerable<Neuron>, we could easily connect it to either a Neuron, a NeuronLayer, or another NeuronRing!

Shrink Wrapping the Composite

No doubt many of you want some kind of prepackaged solution that would allow scalar objects to be treated as enumerables. Well, if your scalar class doesn't derive from another class, you can simply define a base class similar to the following:

```
public abstract class Scalar<T> : IEnumerable<T>
```

```
  where T : Scalar<T>
{
  public IEnumerator<T> GetEnumerator()
  {
    yield return (T) this;
  }

  IEnumerator IEnumerable.GetEnumerator()
  {
    return GetEnumerator();
  }
}
```

This class is generic, and the type parameter T refers to the object we're trying to "scalarize." Now, making any object expose itself as a collection of one element is as simple as...

```
public class Foo : Scalar<Foo> {}
```

...and the object is immediately available for use in, say, a foreach loop:

```
var foo = new Foo();
foreach (var x in foo)
{
  // will yield only one value of x
  // where x == foo referentially :)
}
```

This approach only works if your type doesn't have a parent because multiple inheritance is impossible. It would, of course, be nice to have some marker interface (inheriting from IEnumerable<T>, perhaps, though that's not strictly necessary) that would implement GetEnumerator() as extension methods. Sadly, the C# language designers did not leave this option available – GetEnumerator()s must be strictly *instance* methods to be picked up by foreach.

Lucky for us, we can abuse the C# default interface member mechanism in order to provide a default IEnumerable implementation in an interface instead of an abstract class:

```
public interface IScalar<out T> : IEnumerable<T>
{
  IEnumerator<T> IEnumerable<T>.GetEnumerator()
  {
    yield return (T) this;
  }

  IEnumerator IEnumerable.GetEnumerator()
  {
    return GetEnumerator();
  }
}
```

We can now greatly simplify our Neuron class:

```
public class Neuron : IScalar<Neuron>
{
  public readonly List<Neuron> In = new(), Out = new();
}
```

With this modification, our example continues to work without any problems. ConnectTo() correctly identifies that an IScalar is an IEnumerable and connects the different pieces of the application.

Of course, this example leverages a certain amount of trickery. Even though foreach works on an IScalar, a call to neuron.GetEnumerator() will not compile because accessing default interface members requires an explicit cast to the related interface. In our case, we can let it slide because foreach is all that we need to work.

Composite Specification

When I introduced the Open-Closed Principle, I gave a demo of the Specification pattern. The key aspects of the pattern were base types IFilter and ISpecification that allowed us to use inheritance to build an extensible filtering framework that conformed to the

OCP. Part of that implementation involved combinators – specifications that would combine several specifications together under an AND or OR operator mechanic.

Both AndSpecification and OrSpecification made use of two operands (which we called left and right), but that restriction was completely arbitrary: in fact, we could have combined more than two elements together, and furthermore, we could improve the OOP model with a reusable base class such as the following:

```
public abstract class CompositeSpecification<T> : ISpecification<T>
{
  protected readonly ISpecification<T>[] items;

  public CompositeSpecification(params ISpecification<T>[] items)
  {
    this.items = items;
  }
}
```

This should feel familiar because we've implemented the approach before. We made an ISpecification that is, in fact, a combination of different specifications passed as params in the constructor.

With this approach, the AndSpecification combinator can now be implemented with a bit of LINQ:

```
public class AndSpecification<T> : CompositeSpecification<T>
{
  public AndSpecification(params ISpecification<T>[] items) :
  base(items) {}

  public override bool IsSatisfied(T t)
  {
    return items.All(i => i.IsSatisfied(t));
  }
}
```

Similarly, if you wanted an OrSpecification, you would replace the call to All() with a call to Any(). You could even make specifications that would support other, more complicated criteria. For example, you could make a composite such that the item is required to satisfy at most/at least/specifically a number of specifications contained within.

You can now create composites of any size using the constructor with any number of arguments. If you want, you can make a utility factory method that would save you from typing generic arguments and make the syntax a bit neater:

```
public static class All
{
  [MethodImpl(MethodImplOptions.AggressiveInlining)]
  public static AndSpecification<T> Of<T>(params Specification<T>[] items)
  {
    return new(items);
  }
}
```

This would be usable as

```
var spec = All.Of(
  new ColorSpecification(Color.Green),
  new SizeSpecification(Size.Tiny)
);
```

Of course, when it comes to syntax helpers, in C# there are many different alternatives. For example, you could define an extension method on a ValueTuple composed of any number of different specifications, for example:

```
public static class CompositeSpecificationExtensions
{
  // extension method on typed value tuple
  public static AndSpecification<T> All<T>(
    this (Specification<T> first, Specification<T> second) specs)
  {
    return new(specs.first, specs.second);
  }
}
```

This could be used as

```
var spec = (
  new ColorSpecification(Color.Green),
  new SizeSpecification(Size.Tiny)
).All();
```

177

However, of course, to handle different numbers of arguments, you would have to generate a lot of these extension methods!

Summary

The Composite design pattern allows us to provide identical interfaces for individual objects and collections of objects. This can be accomplished in one of two ways:

- Make every scalar object you intend to work with a collection, or alternatively, get it to contain a collection and expose it somehow. You can use Lazy<T> so you don't allocate too many data structures if they are not actually needed. This is a very simple approach and is somewhat unidiomatic.

- Teach scalar objects to appear and act as collections. This is done by implementing IEnumerable<T> and then calling yield return this in GetEnumerator(). Strictly speaking, having a scalar value expose IEnumerable is also unidiomatic, but it is aesthetically better and has a smaller computational cost.

CHAPTER 10

Decorator

Suppose you're working with a class your colleague wrote and you want to extend that class' functionality. How would you do it, without modifying the original code? Well, one approach is inheritance: you make a derived class, add the functionality you need, and maybe even `override` something, and you're good to go.

Right, except this doesn't always work, and there are many reasons. The most common reason is that you cannot inherit the class – either because your target class needs to inherit something else (and multiple inheritance is impossible) or because the class you want to extend is `sealed`.

The Decorator pattern allows us to enhance existing types including, possibly, multiple enhancements applied on top of one another, without either modifying the original types (Open-Closed Principle) or causing an explosion of the number of derived types.

Here is what I mean by *multiple* enhancements: suppose we have a class called `Shape` that represents graphical shapes (circle, square, etc.) and we need to give shapes color or a transparency value. We can make two inheritors called `ColoredShape` and `TransparentShape`, but then we also need to take into account the fact that someone will want a `ColoredTransparentShape`. So we've generated three classes to support two enhancements; if we had three enhancements, we would need seven distinct classes. This can be illustrated as a Venn diagram (Figure 10-1) showing all the partitions generated by an intersection of three sets.

And let's not forget that we actually want different shapes (`Square`, `Circle`, etc.) – what base class would those inherit from? With three enhancements and two distinct shapes, the number of classes would jump up to 14. Clearly, this is an unmanageable situation – even if you are using a tool for code generation!

We'll consider this `Shape` scenario a bit later on, but for now, we'll take a look at different examples.

© Dmitri Nesteruk 2022
D. Nesteruk, *Design Patterns in .NET 6*, https://doi.org/10.1007/978-1-4842-8245-8_10

The Basics of Delegation

Before we talk about decorators, we need to discuss the concept of *delegation*. Delegation means, simply, that an object takes on the responsibilities of another object. There are two ways it can do this: it can inherit the original object, or it can aggregate it.

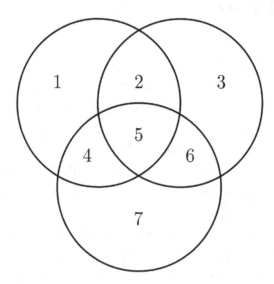

Figure 10-1. *Number of possible combinations of three different classes*

Aggregation naturally implies that we try to expose the original object's API as much as it is feasible. For example, given an object `Person` defined as...

```
public sealed class Person
{
  public void SayHello() { ... }
}
```

...any object that seeks to aggregate `Person` and needs to expose `SayHello()` has two choices:

- Expose the underlying `Person` object as `public`.

- Duplicate the `SayHello()` method, calling the underlying implementation.

In most cases, one would write something like the following:

```
public class Employee
{
  private Person person;
  public void SayHello() { person.SayHello(); }
}
```

This is *delegation*: the responsibility for saying hello is delegated to a different object. In our example, we can just write the implementation by hand. But imagine that, instead of Person, you had a class with dozens of methods that need to be delegated. In this case, doing it by hand is tedious, which is why developer tools such as Rider and ReSharper offer the **Generate | Delegated Members** functionality for automating the process.

Delegation is, in most cases, a simple affair. One challenge that comes up is to do with fluent interfaces. If you decide to aggregate a StringBuilder and delegate its AppendLine() call (which, I remind you, is fluent), developer tools will incorrectly generate the following:

```
public class SomeClass
{
  private StringBuilder builder;

  public StringBuilder AppendLine(string s) { return builder.
  AppendLine(s); }
}
```

What you're actually looking for is

```
public SomeClass AppendLine(string s)
{
  builder.AppendLine(s);
  return this;
}
```

I'm afraid you'll just have to fix this part yourself!

Apart from the hiccup with fluent interfaces, expect possibly incorrect code being generated around calls that are unsafe or unsafe language syntax such as pointers. And don't forget you don't *have to* replicate the underlying API exactly.

Points and Lines

To gain a fundamental appreciation for the Decorator design pattern, consider a graphics application that performs some mathematical modeling using points and lines and then needs to output points and lines to the screen. It may appear as though we ought to only have two classes (Point and Line), but in practice, graphical objects contain more information than mathematical ones.

For example, a 2D point only has x and y coordinates and in most circumstances can probably be passed by value without loss of performance. A graphical point, on the other hand, may need to specify the point size (since a point is typically rendered as a small circle), and a graphical line can also specify line thickness; whether it's solid, dotted, or dashed; and so on.

Our first instinct is to use inheritance. If we define a Point as…

```
class Point
{
  public double X, Y;
}
```

…then a graphical point, which I shall simply call GPoint, may be defined as

```
class GPoint : Point
{
  public string Color;
}
```

This may seem like a great idea from the outset, but it's really not, and I wouldn't recommend writing code like this. While the OOP approach is very appealing, we're losing out on the ability to turn Point into a struct. A Point is nothing more than a pair of values, and if you were to introduce any members, most of them would be ones it's not worth inheriting. For example, if you were to give Point a ToString() member, you would definitely override it in the inheritor, and calling base.ToString() is really the same as calling someReference.ToString(), so there's no advantage there.

Also, though we have polymorphism, we're unlikely to ever use it, since the mathematical and graphical representations are used in different areas of application.

Our typical scenarios are as follows:

- Turn a Point into a GPoint to show it on the screen.

- Get a Point from a GPoint in case we need some info about it.

- Have GPoint expose the same members as Point, but without inheritance.

```
public readonly struct Point
{
  public readonly double X, Y;
}

class GPoint
{
  public Point Point;
  public string Color;
  // add some useful constructors, then...
  public double X => Point.X;
  public double Y => Point.Y;
}
```

GPoint is a decorator. It decorates Point, giving it additional functionality, aggregating the original Point, and exposing its members. Notice that X and Y are *getters*. Our original Point is read-only; it cannot be modified, only replaced wholesale, the motivation being that mutable structs are generally dangerous (they introduce unexpected temporaries) and so are best avoided.

If, for some reason, you're concerned about lack of polymorphism, you can introduce an implicit conversion operator that simply takes the Point part out of GPoint:

```
public static implicit operator Point(GPoint gp)
{
  return gp.Point;
}
```

Whether or not the opposite implicit conversion makes sense is up for debate – I'd argue that it's better to simply introduce a well-made constructor.

Now, consider a Line class (note: class, not struct) implemented as

```
class Line
{
  public Point Start, End;
}
```

Once again, in addition to a mathematical line, we want a graphical line that defines, for example, the line thickness. This time round, the ideal solution is not so obvious. For example, we can simply implement GLine as

```
class GLine
{
  public Line Line = new();
  public double Thickness = 1.0;
}
```

This is a decorator similar to the one we've made for Point, but it assumes that the Points that make up the underlying Line do not need to be wrapped as GPoints. What if they do? In this case, we could go for a different definition:

```
class GLine
{
  public GPoint Start = new(), End = new();
  public double Thickness = 1.0;
}
```

Once again, an implicit conversion can be made though, this time round, this will make a copy of object state:

```
public static implicit operator Line(GLine gl)
{
  return new Line() { Start = gl.Start, End = gl.End };
}
```

Adapter-Decorator

You can also have a decorator that acts as an adapter. For example, suppose we want to use the CodeBuilder, but we want it to start acting as a string. Perhaps we want to take a CodeBuilder and stick it into an API that expects our object to implement the = operator for assigning from a string and a += operator for appending additional strings. Can we adapt CodeBuilder to these requirements? We sure can. All we have to do is add the appropriate functionality:

```
public static implicit operator CodeBuilder(string s)
{
  var cb = new CodeBuilder();
  cb.sb.Append(s);
  return cb;
}

public static CodeBuilder operator +(CodeBuilder cb, string s)
{
  cb.Append(s);
  return cb;
}
```

With this implementation, we can now start working with a CodeBuilder as if it were a string:

```
CodeBuilder cb = "hello";
cb += " world";
WriteLine(cb); // prints "hello world"
```

Curiously enough, the second line in the preceding code will work even if we didn't implement operator + explicitly. Why? You figure it out!

Simulating Multiple Inheritance

One of the simplest uses of the Decorator pattern is to use it in the context of multiple inheritance.

Multiple Inheritance with Interfaces

In addition to extending sealed classes, the Decorator pattern also shows up when you want to have multiple base classes...which of course you cannot have because C# does not support multiple inheritance. For example, suppose you have a Dragon that's both a Bird and a Lizard. It would make sense to write something like

```
public class Bird
{
  public void Fly() { ... }
}

public class Lizard
{
  public void Crawl() { ... }
}

public class Dragon : Bird, Lizard {} // cannot do this!
```

Sadly, this is impossible, so what do you do? Well, you extract interfaces from both Bird and Lizard:

```
public interface IBird
{
  void Fly();
}

public interface ILizard
{
  void Crawl();
}
```

Then, you make a Dragon class that implements these interfaces, aggregates instances of Bird and Lizard, and delegates the calls:

```
public class Dragon: IBird, ILizard
{
  private readonly IBird bird;
  private readonly ILizard lizard;
```

```
public Dragon(IBird bird, ILizard lizard)
{
  this.bird = bird;
  this.lizard = lizard;
}

public void Crawl() => lizard.Crawl();
public void Fly() => bird.Fly();
}
```

You'll notice that there are two options here: either you initialize the default instances of Bird and Lizard right inside the class or you offer the client more flexibility by taking both of those objects in the constructor. This would allow you to construct more sophisticated IBird/ILizard classes and make a dragon out of them. Also, this approach automatically supports constructor injection, should you go the IoC route.

One interesting problem with the decorator is the "diamond inheritance" problem of C++. Suppose a dragon crawls only until it's 10 years old and, from then on, it only flies. In this case, you'd have both the Bird and Lizard classes have an Age property with independent implementations:

```
public interface ICreature
{
  int Age { get; set; }
}

public interface IBird : ICreature
{
  void Fly();
}

public interface ILizard : ICreature
{
  void Crawl();
}

public class Bird : IBird
{
  public int Age { get; set; }
```

```csharp
  public void Fly()
  {
    if (Age >= 10)
      WriteLine("I am flying!");
  }
}

public class Lizard : ILizard
{
  public int Age { get; set; }
  public void Crawl()
  {
    if (Age < 10)
      WriteLine("I am crawling!");
  }
}
```

Notice that we've had to introduce a new interface ICreature just so we could expose the Age as part of both the IBird and ILizard interfaces. The real problem here is the implementation of the Dragon class, because if you use the code generation features of ReSharper or a similar tool, you will simply get

```csharp
public class Dragon : IBird, ILizard
{
  ...
  public int Age { get; set; }
}
```

This once again shows that generated code isn't always what you want. Remember, both Bird.Fly() and Lizard.Crawl() have *their own* implementations of Age, and those implementations need to be kept consistent in order for those methods to operate correctly. This means that the correct implementation of Dragon.Age is the following:

```csharp
public int Age
{
  get => bird.Age;
  set => bird.Age = lizard.Age = value;
}
```

Notice that our setter assigns both, whereas the getter simply uses the underlying bird – this choice is arbitrary, and we could have easily taken the lizard's age instead. The setter ensures consistency, so in theory, both values would always be equal...except during initialization, a place we haven't taken care of yet. A lazy man's solution to this problem would be to redefine the Dragon constructor thus:

```
public Dragon(IBird bird, ILizard lizard)
{
  this.bird = bird;
  this.lizard = lizard;
  bird.Age = lizard.Age;
}
```

As you can see, building a decorator is generally easy, except for two nuances: the difficulties in preserving a fluent interface and the challenge of diamond inheritance. I have demonstrated here how to solve both of these problems.

Multiple Inheritance with Default Interface Members

The collision between the Age properties of Bird and Lizard can be partially mitigated with C# 8's default interface members. While they do not give us "proper," C++-style multiple inheritance, they give us enough to go by.

First of all, we implement a base interface for a creature:

```
public interface ICreature
{
  int Age { get; set; }
}
```

This step is essential, because now we can define interfaces IBird and ILizard that have default method implementations that actually make use of the property:

```
public interface IBird : ICreature
{
  void Fly()
  {
```

```
    if (Age >= 10)
      WriteLine("I am flying");
  }
}

public interface ILizard : ICreature
{
  void Crawl()
  {
    if (Age < 10)
      WriteLine("I am crawling!");
  }
}
```

Finally, we can make a class that implements both of these interfaces. Of course, this class has to provide an implementation of the Age property, since no interface is able to do so:

```
public class Dragon : IBird, ILizard
{
  public int Age { get; set; }
}
```

And now we have a class that inherits the behavior of two interfaces. The only caveat is that explicit casts are required to actually make use of those behaviors:

```
var d = new Dragon {Age = 5};

if (d is IBird bird)
  bird.Fly();

if (d is ILizard lizard)
  lizard.Crawl();
```

It *is* possible to expose those methods directly on the object, but this requires that you introduce mirroring extension methods on Dragon that perform the cast to the right interface and call the underlying.

Dynamic Decorator Composition

Of course, as soon as we start building decorators over existing types, we come to the question of decorator *composition*, that is, whether or not it's possible to decorate a decorator with another decorator. I certainly hope it's possible – decorators should be flexible enough to do this!

For our scenario, let's imagine that we have an abstract base class called Shape with a single member called AsString() that returns a string describing this shape (Iap deliberately avoiding ToString() here):

```
public abstract class Shape
{
  public virtual string AsString() => string.Empty;
}
```

I chose to make Shape an abstract class with a default, no-op implementation. We could equally use an IShape interface for this example.

We can now define a concrete shape like, say, a circle or a square:

```
public sealed class Circle : Shape
{
  private float radius;

  public Circle() : this(0) {}

  public Circle(float radius)
  {
    this.radius = radius;
  }

  public void Resize(float factor)
  {
    radius *= factor;
  }

  public override string AsString() => $"A circle of radius {radius}";
}

// similar implementation of Square with 'side' member omitted
```

I deliberately made `Circle` and similar classes `sealed` so we cannot simply inherit from them. Instead, we are once again going to build decorators: this time, we'll build two of them – one for adding color to a shape...

```
public class ColoredShape : Shape
{
  private readonly Shape shape;
  private readonly string color;

  public ColoredShape(Shape shape, string color)
  {
    this.shape = shape;
    this.color = color;
  }

  public override string AsString()
    => $"{shape.AsString()} has the color {color}";
}
```

...and another to give a shape transparency:

```
public class TransparentShape : Shape
{
  private readonly Shape shape;
  private readonly float transparency;

  public TransparentShape(Shape shape, float transparency)
  {
    this.shape = shape;
    this.transparency = transparency;
  }

  public override string AsString() =>
    $"{shape.AsString()} has {transparency * 100.0f}% transparency";
}
```

As you can see, both of these decorators inherit from the abstract Shape class, so they are themselves Shapes and they decorate other Shapes by taking them in the constructor. This allows us to use them together, for example:

```
var circle = new Circle(2);
WriteLine(circle.AsString());
// A circle of radius 2

var redSquare = new ColoredShape(circle, "red");
WriteLine(redSquare.AsString());
// A circle of radius 2 has the color red

var redHalfTransparentSquare = new TransparentShape(redSquare, 0.5f);
WriteLine(redHalfTransparentSquare.AsString());
// A circle of radius 2 has the color red has 50% transparency
```

As you can see, the decorators can be applied to other Shapes in any order you wish, preserving consistent output of the AsString() method. One thing they do not guard against is cyclic repetition: you can construct a ColoredShape(ColoredShape(Square)), and the system will not complain; we could not detect this situation either, even if we wanted to.

So this is the *dynamic* decorator implementation: the reason we call it dynamic is because these decorators can be constructed at runtime, objects wrapping objects as layers of an onion. It is, on the one hand, very convenient, but on the other hand, you lose all type information as you decorate the object. For example, a decorated Circle no longer has access to its Resize() member:

```
var redSquare = new ColoredShape(circle, "red");
redCircle.Resize(2); // oops!
```

This problem is impossible to solve: since ColoredShape takes a Shape, the only way to allow resizing is to add Resize() to Shape itself, but this operation might not make sense for all shapes. This is a limitation of the dynamic decorator.

Decorator Cycle Policies

I want to show you a more sophisticated example of an interaction of two patterns –
Dynamic Decorator and Strategy. We are going to continue the Dynamic Decorator
approach to decorating classes with additional behaviors. Just as a reminder, the gist of
Dynamic Decorator is an ability to write code similar to the following:

```
var circle = new Circle(3);
WriteLine(circle); // A circle of radius 3

var redCircle = new ColoredCircle(circle, "red");
WriteLine(redCircle); // A circle of radius 3 has the color red
```

The implementation of these wrappers was shown already, so I will not repeat them
here. The problem I want to investigate now is related to the following scenario:

```
var weirdCircle = new ColoredCircle(redCircle, "blue");
WriteLine(weirdCircle);
// A circle of radius 3 has the color red has the color blue
```

As you can see, the output is a bit bizarre. Should we even be allowing to apply the
same decorator twice? Clearly, we have no way of detecting this at compile time, but
perhaps we can at least do something about it at runtime?

Well, we can certainly use a bit of reflection so that a decorator does not wrap *itself*.
That's easy. But what about a situation where the decorator wraps itself cyclically, for
example, ColoredShape(TransparentShape(ColoredShape(X)))? This cannot be
detected easily and requires the traversal of the entire chain of decorators that have been
applied thus far.

I can see three different strategies (we'll call them *policies*) of handling repetitions in
the decorator chain:

- CyclesAllowedPolicy: Allows cycles. It's exactly what we have
  right now.

- ThrowOnCyclePolicy: Throws an exception when cycles are detected.
  This needs to be done as early as possible, that is, in the constructor
  of the offending decorator.

- AbsorbCyclePolicy: The cycles are allowed, but effects from
  additional decorators beyond the first one are not applied.

We can try to define a general-purpose policy class such as the following:

```
public abstract class ShapeDecoratorCyclePolicy
{
  public abstract bool TypeAdditionAllowed(Type type, IList<Type>
  allTypes);
  public abstract bool ApplicationAllowed(Type type, IList<Type> allTypes);
}
```

This allows each policy to define two aspects: whether the decorator can be instantiated and whether the instantiated decorator can actually be applied. Each method takes two arguments: the type of the current decorator that we're attempting to construct and a list of allTypes, which is a list of all the types in the wrapper chain.

For example, suppose you're trying to make a ColoredShape(TransparentShape(Square)). Then, when applying the outermost decorator, we'll have

- type == ColoredShape and

- allTypes == [TransparentShape, Square]

We can now take all the three policies previously mentioned and define them in code. The implementation of CyclesAllowedPolicy is the simplest:

```
public class CyclesAllowedPolicy : ShapeDecoratorCyclePolicy
{
  public override bool TypeAdditionAllowed
    (Type type, IList<Type> allTypes) => true;
  }

  public override bool ApplicationAllowed
    (Type type, IList<Type> allTypes) => true;
}
```

The implementation of ThrowOnCyclePolicy attempts to throw an exception both on construction and on invocation as soon as the cycle is detected:

```
public class ThrowOnCyclePolicy : ShapeDecoratorCyclePolicy
{
  private bool handler(Type type, IList<Type> allTypes)
  {
```

```
  if (allTypes.Contains(type))
    throw new InvalidOperationException(
      $"Cycle detected! Type is already a {type.FullName}!");
  return true;
}

public override bool TypeAdditionAllowed(Type type, IList<Type> allTypes)
{
  return handler(type, allTypes);
}

public override bool ApplicationAllowed(Type type, IList<Type> allTypes)
{
  return handler(type, allTypes);
}
}
```

Finally, AbsorbCyclePolicy allows the chaining of decorators but lets you know that application is not allowed if a cycle is detected:

```
public class AbsorbCyclePolicy : ShapeDecoratorCyclePolicy
{
  public override bool TypeAdditionAllowed(Type type, IList<Type> allTypes)
  {
    return true;
  }

  public override bool ApplicationAllowed(Type type, IList<Type> allTypes)
  {
    return !allTypes.Contains(type);
  }
}
```

So far, it may not be clear how these policies are to be applied. In order to get them into the game, we'll introduce two ShapeDecorator base classes: one nongeneric and the other generic.

By the way, a generic-nongeneric pair of classes is a "pattern" that you will see quite often when programming. Why? Because of type checks. Given a generic type Foo<>, you cannot write x is Foo – all you can do is write x is Foo<Bar>. In other words, you have to explicitly specify the generic parameter.

This is a problem if you're doing any sort of cast where you don't care what that generic parameter actually is. And, yes, you can fiddle with reflection, but quite often the generic-nongeneric duality makes life a lot simpler.

So back to the problem at hand. We first define our ShapeDecorator as follows:

```
public abstract class ShapeDecorator : Shape
{
  protected internal readonly List<Type> types = new();
  protected internal Shape shape;

  public ShapeDecorator(Shape shape)
  {
    this.shape = shape;
    if (shape is ShapeDecorator sd)
        types.AddRange(sd.types);
  }
}
```

Despite having no abstract members, ShapeDecorator is an abstract class. It has two members. The first is the Shape that we intend to wrap. The second is more tricky: it is a list of all the additional decorator types that we're wrapping, assuming there are any. This is a recursive process: if we're wrapping a ShapeDecorator, we simply take its list of wrapped types.

You'll notice something interesting here – at no point do we actually add anything to the types collection. This is because the very process of addition is governed by appropriate policy, and in our implementation, policies only appear in the generic version of our ShapeDecorator. Here it is:

```
public abstract class ShapeDecorator<TSelf, TCyclePolicy> : ShapeDecorator
  where TCyclePolicy : ShapeDecoratorCyclePolicy, new()
{
  private readonly TCyclePolicy policy = new();
```

```
  public ShapeDecorator(Shape shape) : base(shape)
  {
    if (policy.TypeAdditionAllowed(typeof(TSelf), types))
      types.Add(typeof(TSelf));
  }
}
```

Okay, there's quite a lot to take in here.

First, ShapeDecorator<> takes two generic arguments. The first argument TSelf refers to the name of the class we're actually using to inherit this. We use this approach in many sections of the book. The second argument is the type of policy that we want to use when we detect cycles: this needs to be a type that inherits from ShapeDecoratorCyclePolicy and defines a default constructor.

The constructor of this type is a bit sophisticated too. First, it calls the base class, which we've already seen doing things with the types collection. But, assuming our chosen policy allows us to add the type to the list of types, we actually perform the addition.

What this means in practice is that, if you choose a policy that allows cycles in the construction of decorators and you create a ColoredShape(ColoredShape(Square)), your types list will contain [ColoredShape, ColoredShape].

With all that implemented, we can now finally create a ColoredShape:

```
public class ColoredShape
  : ShapeDecorator<ColoredShape, AbsorbCyclePolicy>
{

  private readonly string color;

  public ColoredShape(Shape shape, string color) : base(shape)
  {
    this.color = color;
  }

  public override string AsString()
  {
    var sb = new StringBuilder($"{shape.AsString()}");

    if (policy.ApplicationAllowed(types[0], types.Skip(1).ToList()))
      sb.Append($" has the color {color}");
```

```
    return sb.ToString();
  }
}
```

As you can see, functionally, it's the same wrapper as before. The only difference is that when constructing it, you can specify a cycle policy – in this particular case, we specify an `AbsorbCyclePolicy` because we want to allow cycles, but we don't want `AsString()` having any extraneous text in it.

Of course, the choice of where to place the policy is purely stylistic. If you want to define one policy per the entire hierarchy of decorators, for example, you can simply introduce another base class.

Now, an interesting thing happens in our implementation of `AsString()`. First, by default, `AsString()` always calls itself on the wrapped object. But then, it makes a decision on whether to apply the *current* decorator depending on the policy at hand. Remember that, at this stage, the `types` list has already been initialized with the types of the entire wrapper chain. `types[0]` is our current class, and `types.Skip(1)` contains the classes we're wrapping. Consequently, we can pass this information into the policy and determine whether the application of the current decorator is warranted. If it is, we apply it!

With all of this put together, we now get the following behavior:

```
var circle = new Circle(2);
var colored1 = new ColoredShape(circle, "red");
var colored2 = new ColoredShape(colored1, "blue");

WriteLine(circle.AsString());
// A circle of radius 2

WriteLine(colored1.AsString());
// A circle of radius 2 has the color red

WriteLine(colored2.AsString());
// A circle of radius 2 has the color red
```

The implementation here is completely *ad hoc* and makes a large number of design decisions. For example, policies are specified in a static way via generics. This is great if you plan to choose one policy and stick with it, but if you plan to alter policies at runtime (perhaps with the use of an IoC container?), then you can instead adopt a dynamic approach – see the "Dynamic Strategy" section of Chapter 24.

Static Decorator Composition

When you are given a dynamically decorated ColoredShape, there's no way to tell whether this shape is a circle, square, or something else without looking at the output of AsString(). So how would you "bake in" the underlying type of the decorated objects into the type of the object you have? Turns out you can do so with generics.

The idea is simple: our decorator, say ColoredShape, takes a generic argument that specifies what type of object it's decorating. Naturally, that object has to be a Shape, and since we're aggregating it, it's also going to need a constructor:

```
public class ColoredShape<T> : Shape
  where T : Shape, new()
{
  private readonly string color;
  private readonly T shape = new T();

  public ColoredShape() : this("black") {}
  public ColoredShape(string color) { this.color = color; }

  public override string AsString() =>
    return $"{shape.AsString()} has the color {color}";
}
```

Okay, so what's going on here? We have a new ColoredShape that's generic; it takes a T that's supposed to inherit a Shape. Internally, it stores an instance of T as well as color information. We've provided two constructors for flexibility: since C#, unlike C++, doesn't support constructor forwarding, the default constructor is going to be useful for composition (see, we have the new() requirement).

We can now provide a similar implementation of TransparentShape<T>, and armed with both, we can now build static decorators of the following form:

```
var blueCircle = new ColoredShape<Circle>("blue");
WriteLine(blueCircle.AsString());
// A circle of radius 0 has the color blue

var blackHalfSquare = new TransparentShape<ColoredShape<Square>>(0.4f);
WriteLine(blackHalfSquare.AsString());
// A square with side 0 has the color black has transparency 40
```

This static approach has certain advantages and disadvantages. The advantage is that we preserve the type information: given a Shape we can tell that the shape is a ColoredShape<Circle>, and perhaps we can act on this information somehow. Sadly, this approach has plenty of disadvantages:

- Notice how the radius/side values in the preceding example are both zero. This is because we cannot initialize those values in the constructor: C# does not have constructor forwarding.

- We still don't have access to the underlying members; for example, blueCircle.Resize() is still not legal.

- These sorts of decorators cannot be composed at runtime.

All in all, in the absence of CRTP and mixin inheritance,[1] the uses for static decorators in C# are very, very limited. Oh, and before you ask: cycle detection in this scenario is very difficult to do. It is certainly impossible to detect cycles at compile time, and trying to detect them at runtime will require very heavy use of reflection.

Functional Decorator

A functional decorator is a natural consequence of functional composition. If we can compose functions, we can equally wrap functions with other functions in order, for example, to provide before-and-after functionality such as logging.

Here's a very simple implementation. Imagine you have some work that needs to be done:

```
let doWork() =
  printfn "Doing some work"
```

We can now create a decorator function (a functional decorator!) that, given any function, measures how long it takes to execute:

```
let logger work name =
  let sw = Stopwatch.StartNew()
```

---

[1] Mixin inheritance is a C++ technique for adding functionality to classes by using inheritance. In the context of the decorator, it would allow us to compose a class of type T<U<V>> that would inherit from both U and V, giving us access to all the underlying members. Also, constructors would work correctly, thanks to constructor forwarding and C++'s variadic templates.

```
printfn "%s %s" "Entering method" name
work()
sw.Stop()
printfn "Exiting method %s; %fs elapsed" name sw.Elapsed.TotalSeconds
```

We can now use this wrapper around doWork, replacing a `unit -> unit` function with one with the same interface but that also performs some measurements:

```
let loggedWork() = logger doWork "doWork"
loggedWork()
// Entering method doWork
// Doing some work
// Exiting method doWork; 0.097824s elapsed
```

Pay attention to the round brackets in this example: it might be tempting to remove them, but that would drastically alter the types of data structures. Remember, any `let x = ...` construct will always evaluate to a variable (possibly of a `unit` type!) instead of a parameterless function unless you add an empty parameter list.

There are a couple of catches in this implementation. For one, doWork does not return a value; if it did, we would have to cache it in a type-independent manner, something that's possible to implement in C++ but extremely difficult to do in any .NET language. Another issue is that we have no way of determining the name of the wrapped function, so we end up passing it as a separate argument – not an ideal solution!

Summary

A decorator gives a class additional functionality while adhering to the OCP and mitigating issues related to `sealed` classes and multiple inheritance. Its crucial aspect is *composability*: several decorators can be applied to an object in any order. We've looked at the following types of decorators:

- *Dynamic decorators*, which can store references to the decorated objects and provide dynamic (runtime) composability.

- *Static decorators*, which preserve the information about the type of the objects involved in the decoration; these are of limited use since they do not expose underlying objects' members, nor do they allow us to efficiently compose constructor calls.

We also looked at detecting cycles in dynamic decorators and various policies (as per the Strategy pattern) that can be adopted when multiple decorators of the same type are applied in a sequence.

Finally, we discussed functional decorators. These are, essentially, just functions that wrap other functions.

CHAPTER 11

Façade

First of all, let's get the linguistic issue out of the way: that little curve under the letter Ç is called a *cedilla*, and the letter itself is pronounced as an S, so the word *façade* is pronounced as "fah-saad." The particularly pedantic among you are welcome to use the letter ç in your code, since compilers treat this just fine.[1]

Now, about the pattern itself... Essentially, the best analogy I can think of is a typical house. When you buy a house, you generally care about the exterior and the interior. You are less concerned about the internals: electrical systems, insulation, sanitation, that sort of thing. Those parts are all equally important, but we want them to "just work" without breaking. You're much more likely to be buying new furniture than changing the wiring of your boiler.

The same idea applies to software: sometimes you need to interact with a complicated system in a simple way. By "system" we could mean a set of components or just a single component with a rather complicated API. For example, think about the seemingly simple task of downloading a string of text from a URL. The fully fleshed-out solution to this problem using various `System.Net` data types looks something like this:

```
string url = "http://www.google.com/robots.txt";
var request = WebRequest.Create(url);
request.Credentials = CredentialCache.DefaultCredentials;
var response = request.GetResponse();
var dataStream = response.GetResponseStream();
var reader = new StreamReader(dataStream);
string responseFromServer = reader.ReadToEnd();
Console.WriteLine(responseFromServer);
reader.Close();
response.Close();
```

---

[1] Over the years I have seen many silly tricks involving the use of Unicode (typically UTF-8) encoding in C# source files. The most insidious case is one where a developer insisted on calling his extension methods' first argument `this` – it was, of course, a completely valid identifier because the letter i in `this` was a Ukrainian letter i, not a Latin one.

This is a lot of work! Furthermore, I almost guarantee that most of you wouldn't be able to write this code without looking it up online. That's because there are several underlying data types that make the operation possible. And if you wanted to do it all asynchronously, you would have to use a complementary API set comprised of XxxAsync() methods.

So whenever we encounter a situation where a complex interaction of different parts is required for something to get done, we might want to put it behind a façade, that is, a much simpler interface. In the case of downloading web pages, all of the preceding code reduces to a single line:

```
new WebClient().DownloadString(url);
```

In this example, the WebClient class is a *façade*, that is, a nice, user-friendly interface that does what you want quickly and without ceremony. Of course, the original APIs are also available to you so that, if you need something more complicated (e.g., to provide credentials), you can use the more technical parts to fine-tune the operation of your program.

With this one example, you've already grasped the gist of the Façade design pattern. However, just to illustrate the matter further (as well as tell the story of how OOP is used and abused in practice), I would like to present yet another example.

Magic Squares

While a proper Façade demo requires that we make super-complicated systems that actually warrant a façade to be put in front of them, let us consider a trivialized example: the process of making magic squares. A magic square is a matrix such as

$$\begin{bmatrix} 1 & 14 & 14 & 4 \\ 11 & 8 & 6 & 9 \\ 8 & 10 & 10 & 5 \\ 13 & 2 & 3 & 15 \end{bmatrix}$$

If you add up the values in any row, any column, or any diagonal, you'll get the same number – in this case, 33. If we want to generate our own magic squares, we can imagine it as an interplay of three different subsystems:

- Generator: A component that simply generates a sequence of random numbers of a particular size.

- Splitter: A component that takes a rectangular matrix and outputs a set of lists representing all rows, columns, and diagonals in the matrix.

- Verifier: A component that checks that the sums of all lists passed into it are the same.

We begin by implementing the Generator:

```
public class Generator
{
  private static readonly Random random = new Random();

  public List<int> Generate(int count)
  {
    return Enumerable.Range(0, count)
      .Select(_ => random.Next(1, 6))
      .ToList();
  }
}
```

Note that the generator yields one-dimensional lists, whereas the next component, Splitter, accepts a matrix:

```
public class Splitter
{
  public List<List<int>> Split(List<List<int>> array)
  {
    // implementation omitted
  }
}
```

The implementation of Splitter is rather long-winded, so I've omitted it here – take a look at the source code for its exact details. As you can see, the Splitter returns a list of lists. Our final component, Verifier, checks that those lists all add up to the same number:

```
public class Verifier
{
  public bool Verify(List<List<int>> array)
```

```
  {
    if (!array.Any()) return false;
    var expected = array.First().Sum();
    return array.All(t => t.Sum() == expected);
  }
}
```

So there you have it – we have three different subsystems that are expected to work in concert in order to generate random magic squares. But are they easy to use? If we gave these classes to a client, they would really struggle to operate them correctly. So how can we make their lives better?

The answer is simple: we build a façade, essentially a wrapper class that hides all these implementation details and provides a very simple interface. Of course, it uses all the three classes behind the scenes:

```
public class MagicSquareGenerator
{
  public List<List<int>> Generate(int size)
  {
    var g = new Generator();
    var s = new Splitter();
    var v = new Verifier();

    List<List<int>> square;

    do
    {
      square = new List<List<int>>();
      for (int i = 0; i < size; ++i)
        square.Add(g.Generate(size));
    }
    while (!v.Verify(s.Split(square)));

    return square;
  }
}
```

And there you have it! Now, if the client wants to generate a 3 × 3 magic square, all they have to do is call

```
var gen = new MagicSquareGenerator();
var square = gen.Generate(3);
```

And they'll get something like

$$\begin{bmatrix} 3 & 1 & 5 \\ 5 & 3 & 1 \\ 1 & 5 & 3 \end{bmatrix}$$

Okay, so this *is* a magic square, but maybe the user of this API has an additional requirement: they do not want numbers to repeat. How can we make it easy for them to implement this? First of all, we change Generate() to take each of the subsystems as generic parameters:

```
private List<List<int>> generate
  <TGenerator, TSplitter, TVerifier>(int size)
  where TGenerator : Generator, new()
  where TSplitter : Splitter, new()
  where TVerifier : Verifier, new()
{
  var g = new TGenerator();
  var s = new TSplitter();
  var v = new TVerifier();

  // rest of code as before
}
```

And now we simply make an overloaded Generate() that applies all three default generic parameters:

```
public List<List<int>> Generate(int size)
{
  return Generate<Generator, Splitter, Verifier>(size);
}
```

In the absence of default generic parameters, this is the only way we can provide sensible defaults and, at the same time, allow customization. Now, if the user wants to ensure all the values are unique, they can make a `UniqueGenerator`...

```csharp
public class UniqueGenerator : Generator
{
  public override List<int> Generate(int count)
  {
    List<int> result;
    do
    {
      result = base.Generate(count);
    } while (result.Distinct().Count() != result.Count);

    return result;
  }
}
```

...and then feed it into the façade, thereby getting a better magic square:

```csharp
var gen = new MagicSquareGenerator();
var square = gen
  .Generate<UniqueGenerator, Splitter, Verifier>(3);
```

This gives us

$$\begin{bmatrix} 8 & 1 & 6 \\ 3 & 5 & 7 \\ 4 & 9 & 2 \end{bmatrix}$$

Of course, it's really impractical to generate magic squares this way, but what this example demonstrates is that you can hide complicated interactions between different systems behind a façade and that you can also incorporate a certain amount of configurability so that users can customize the internal operations of the mechanism should the need arise.

One thing to note: If you never intended to use virtual members inside your classes (say, by defining only interfaces), you could use `structs` instead of `classes` without loss of generality.

Building a Trading Terminal

I've spent a lot of time working in areas of quant finance and algorithmic trading. As you can probably guess, what's required of a good trading terminal is quick delivery of information into a trader's brain: you want things to be rendered as fast as possible, without any lag.

Most of financial data (except for the charts) is actually rendered in plain text: white characters on a black screen. This is, in a way, similar to the way the terminal/console/command-line interface works in your own operating system, but there is a subtle difference.

The first part of a terminal window is the *buffer*. This is where the rendered characters are stored. A buffer is a rectangular area of memory, typically a 1D or 2D char array.[2] A buffer can be much larger than the visible area of the terminal window, so it can store some historical output that you can scroll back to.

Typically, a buffer has a pointer (e.g., an integer) specifying the current input line. That way, a full buffer doesn't reallocate all lines; it just overwrites the oldest one.

Then there's the idea of a *viewport*. A viewport renders a part of the particular buffer. A buffer can be huge, so a viewport just takes a rectangular area out of that buffer and renders that. Naturally, the size of the viewport has to be less than or equal to the size of the buffer.

Finally, there's the console (terminal window) itself. The console shows the viewport, allows scrolling up and down, and even accepts user input. The console is, in fact, a façade: a simplified representation of what is a rather complicated setup behind the scenes.

Typically, most users interact with a single buffer and viewport. It *is*, however, possible to have a console window where you have, say, the area split vertically between two viewports, each having their corresponding buffers. This can be done using utilities such as the screen Linux command.

---

[2] Most buffers are typically one-dimensional. The reason for this is that it's easier to pass a single pointer somewhere than a double pointer, and using an array or vector doesn't make much sense when the size of the structure is deterministic and immutable. Another advantage to the 1D approach is that, when it comes to GPU processing, a system such as CUDA uses up to six dimensions for addressing *anyway*, so after a while, computing a 1D index from an N-dimensional block/grid position becomes second nature.

An Advanced Terminal

One problem with a typical operating system terminal is that it is *extremely slow* if you pipe a lot of data into it. For example, a Windows terminal window (cmd.exe) uses GDI to render the characters, which is completely unnecessary. In a fast-paced trading environment, you want the rendering to be hardware-accelerated: characters should be presented as pre-rendered textures placed on a surface using an API such as OpenGL.[3]

A trading terminal consists of *multiple* buffers and viewports. In a typical setup, different buffers might be getting updated concurrently with data from various exchanges or trading bots, and all of this information needs to be presented on a single screen.

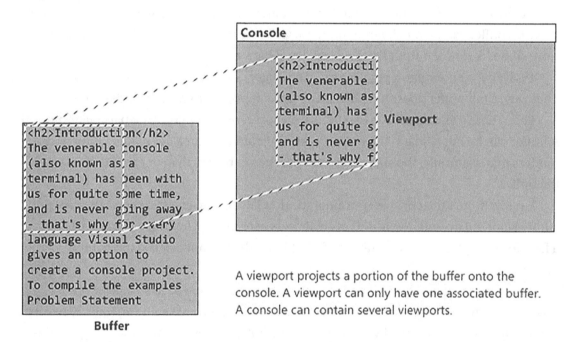

A viewport projects a portion of the buffer onto the console. A viewport can only have one associated buffer. A console can contain several viewports.

Figure 11-1. *One way a text console can be logically organized*

Buffers also provide functionality that is a lot more exciting than just a 1D or 2D linear storage. For example, a TableBuffer might be defined as

---

[3] We also use ASCII, since Unicode is rarely, if ever, required. Having 1 char = 1 byte is a good practice if you don't need to support extra character sets. While not relevant to the discussion at hand, it also greatly simplifies the implementation of string processing algorithms on both GPUs and FPGAs.

```
public class TableBuffer : IBuffer
{
  private readonly TableColumnSpec[] spec;

  private readonly int totalHeight;
  private readonly List<string[]> buffer;
  private static readonly Point invalidPoint = new Point(-1,-1);
  private readonly short[,] formatBuffer;

  public TableBuffer(TableColumnSpec [] spec, int totalHeight)
  {
    this.spec = spec;
    this.totalHeight = totalHeight;

    buffer = new List<string[]>();
    for (int i = 0; i < (totalHeight - 1); ++i)
    {
      buffer.Add(new string[spec.Length]);
    }

    formatBuffer = new short[spec.Max(s => s.Width),totalHeight];
  }

  public struct TableColumnSpec
  {
    public string Header;
    public int Width;
    public TableColumnAlignment Alignment;
  }
}
```

In other words, a buffer can take some specification and build a table (yes, a good old-fashioned ASCII-formatted table!) and present it on-screen.[4]

---

[4] Many trading terminals have abandoned pure ASCII representation in favor of more mixed-mode approaches, such as simply using monospace fonts in ordinary UI controls or rendering many little text-based consoles in separate windowing API rather than sticking to a single canvas.

A viewport is in charge of getting data from the buffer. Some of its characteristics include the following:

- A reference to the buffer it's showing.

- Its size.

- If the viewport is smaller than the buffer, it needs to specify which part of the buffer it is going to show. This is expressed in absolute x-y coordinates.

- The location of the viewport on the overall console window.

- The location of the cursor, assuming this viewport is currently taking user input.

Where's the Façade?

The console itself *is* the façade in this particular system. Internally, the console has to manage a lot of different internal settings:

```
public class Console : Form
{
  private readonly Device device;
  private readonly PresentParameters pp;
  private IList<Viewport> viewports;
  private Size charSize;
  private Size gridSize;
  // many more fields here
}
```

Initialization of the console is also, typically, a very nasty affair. At the very least, you need to specify the size of individual characters and the width and height of the console (in terms of the number of characters). In some situations, you do actually want to specify console parameters in excruciating detail, but when in a hurry, you just want a sensible set of defaults.

However, since it's a façade, it actually tries to give a really accessible API. This might either take a number of sensible parameters to initialize all the guts from:

```
private Console(bool fullScreen, int charWidth, int charHeight,
  int width, int height, Size? clientSize)
{
  int windowWidth =
    clientSize == null ? charWidth*width : clientSize.Value.Width;
  int windowHeight =
    clientSize == null ? charHeight*height : clientSize.Value.Height;

  // and a lot more code

  // single buffer and viewport created here
  // linked together and added to appropriate collections
  // image textures generated
  // grid size calculated depending on whether we want fullscreen mode
}
```

Alternatively, one might pack all those arguments into a single object, which, again, has some sensible defaults:

```
public static Console Create(ConsoleCreationParameters ccp) { ... }

public class ConsoleCreationParameters
{
  public Size? ClientSize;
  public int CharacterWidth = 10;
  public int CharacterHeight = 14;
  public int Width = 20;
  public int Height = 30;
  public bool FullScreen;
  public bool CreateDefaultViewAndBuffer = true;
}
```

As you can see, with the façade we've built, there are no less than three ways of setting up the console:

- Use the low-level API to configure the console explicitly, viewports and buffers included.

- Use the `Console` constructor that requires you to provide fewer values and makes a couple of useful assumptions (e.g., that you want just one viewport with an underlying buffer).

- Use the constructor that takes a `ConsoleCreationParameters` object. This requires you to provide even fewer pieces of information, as every field of that structure has a suitable default.

IoC Modules

Let's look back at the Abstract Factory example we discussed in Chapter 4. There, we had different shapes (circle, square) and different ways of rendering shapes: whether with 90° or rounded corners. This time round, we'll consider the situation that there is *no* abstract factory to help us because we decided to use an IoC container instead.

Now, if you were to configure an IoC container such as Autofac directly, you would probably write something like

```
var cb = new ContainerBuilder();
cb.RegisterType<Rectangle>().As<IRectangle>();
cb.RegisterType<Square>().As<ISquare>();
// more similar lines
// ...
// and then build the container
var c = cb.Build();
```

Now, at some point in time, you decide to switch to rounded shapes. How would you do it? One approach would be to simply rewrite the code to

```
cb.RegisterType<RoundedRectangle>().As<IRectangle>()
// and so on
```

But rewriting code is not a robust approach. Instead, what we can do is define an IoC module: a separate class that serves as a de facto façade, grouping configurations together.

In Autofac, you could define a module like this:

```
class BasicModule : Module
{
  protected override void Load(ContainerBuilder builder)
  {
    builder.RegisterType<Square>().As<ISquare>();
    builder.RegisterType<Rectangle>().As<IRectangle>();
  }
}
```

Similarly, you could define a RoundedModule so that rounded shapes are returned instead. Now, all you have to do is RegisterModule() when the container is being built and then use the registrations therein!

```
var b = new ContainerBuilder();
//b.RegisterModule<BasicModule>();
b.RegisterModule<RoundedModule>();
var c = b.Build();
var square = c.Resolve<ISquare>();
square.Draw(); // Rounded square
```

As the code shows, if you want to switch between ordinary and rounded shapes, you would simply swap one module for another. This way, the modules act as *de facto* façades for types that will be resolved by the application.

In addition to basic registrations, modules can themselves be configurable: you'd just have to use the nongeneric RegisterModule() call if you want to give them parameters.

Summary

The Façade design pattern is a way of putting a simple interface in front of one or more complicated subsystems. As we have seen in the magic square example, in addition to providing a convenient interface, it's possible to expose the internal mechanics and allow for further customization by advanced users. Similarly, in our final example, a complicated setup involving many buffers and viewports can be used directly, or if you just want a simple console with a single buffer and associated viewport, you can get it through a very accessible and intuitive API.

CHAPTER 12

Flyweight

A flyweight (also sometimes called a *token* or a *cookie*) is a temporary component that acts as a "smart reference" to something. Typically, flyweights are used in situations where you have a very large number of very similar objects and you want to minimize the amount of memory that is dedicated to storing all those values.

Let's take a look at some scenarios where this pattern becomes relevant.

User Names

Imagine a massively multiplayer online game. I bet you 1 bitcoin there's more than one user called John Smith – quite simply because it is a very common name. So, if we were to store that name over and over (in UTF-16), we would be spending ten characters per name (plus a few more bytes for every `string`). Instead, we could store the name once and then store a reference to every user with that name. That's quite a saving.

Furthermore, the last name Smith is very popular on its own. Thus, instead of storing full names, splitting the name into first and last would allow further optimizations, as you could simply store `"Smith"` in an indexed store and then simply store the index instead of the actual string.

Let's see how we can implement such a space-saving system. We're going to measure the results by forcing garbage collection and measuring the amount of memory taken using dotMemory.

So here's the first, naive implementation of a `User` class. Notice that the full name is kept as a single string:

```
public class User
{
  public string FullName { get; }
```

© Dmitri Nesteruk 2022

D. Nesteruk, *Design Patterns in .NET 6*, https://doi.org/10.1007/978-1-4842-8245-8_12

```
  public User(string fullName)
  {
    FullName = fullName;
  }
}
```

The implication of this code is that "John Smith" and "Jane Smith" are distinct strings, each occupying their own memory. Now, we can construct an alternative type, User2, that is a little bit smarter in terms of its storage while exposing the same API (I've avoided extracting an IUser interface here for brevity):

```
public class User2
{
  private static List<string> strings = new();
  private int[] names;

  public User2(string fullName)
  {
    int getOrAdd(string s)
    {
      int idx = strings.IndexOf(s);
      if (idx != -1) return idx;
      else
      {
        strings.Add(s);
        return strings.Count - 1;
      }
    }

    names = fullName.Split(' ').Select(getOrAdd).ToArray();
  }

  public string FullName => string.Join(" ", names.Select(i =>
  strings[i]));
}
```

As you can see, the actual strings are stored in a single List. The full name, as it is fed into the constructor, is split into the constituent parts. Each part gets inserted (unless it's already there) into the list of strings, and the names array simply stores the indices of the names in the list, however many there are. This means that, strings notwithstanding, the amount of non-static memory User2 takes up is 64 bits (two Int32s).

Now is a good time to pause and explain where exactly the flyweight is. Essentially, the flyweight is the index that we are storing. A flyweight is a tiny object with a very small memory footprint that points to something larger that is stored elsewhere.

The only question remaining is whether or not this approach actually makes sense. While it's very difficult to simulate this on actual users (this would require a live data set), we are going to do the following:

- Generate 100 first and 100 last names as random strings. The algorithm for making a random string is as follows:

```
public static string RandomString()
{
  Random rand = new();
  return new string(
    Enumerable.Range(0, 10)
              .Select(i => (char) ('a' + rand.Next(26))).ToArray());
}
```

- Make a concatenation (cross product) of every first and last name and initialize 100 × 100 users:

```
var users = new List<User>(); // or User2
foreach (var firstName in firstNames)
foreach (var lastName in lastNames)
  users.Add(new User($"{firstName} {lastName}"));
```

- Just to be safe, we force GC at this point.

- Finally, we use the dotMemory unit testing API to output the total amount of memory taken up by the program.

Running this entirely unscientific (but indicative) test on my machine tells me that the User2 implementation saves us 329,305 bytes. Is this significant? Well, let's try to calculate: a single ten-character string takes up 34 bytes (14 bytes[1] + 2 × 10 bytes for

---

[1] The size of a string actually depends on the bitness of the operating system as well as the version of .NET that you are using.

the letters), so 340,000 bytes for all the strings. This means we reduced the amount of memory taken by 97%! If this isn't cause for celebration, I don't know what is.

It's important to note that the result may vary drastically between different .NET platform incarnations.

Text Formatting

Say you're working with a text editor and you want to add formatting to text – for example, make text bold or italic or capitalize it. How would you do this? One option is to treat each character individually: if your text is composed of X characters, you make a bool array of size X and simply flip each of the flags if you want to alter text. This would lead to the following implementation:

```
public class FormattedText
{
  private string plainText;

  public FormattedText(string plainText)
  {
    this.plainText = plainText;
    capitalize = new bool[plainText.Length];
  }

  public void Capitalize(int start, int end)
  {
    for (int i = start; i <= end; ++i)
      capitalize[i] = true;
  }

  private bool[] capitalize;
}
```

I'm using capitalization here (because that's what a text console can render), but you can think of other forms of formatting being here too. For every type of formatting, you'd be making another Boolean array, initializing it to the right size in the constructor (and imagine the nightmare if the text changes!) and then, of course, you would need to take into account those Boolean flags whenever you actually want to show the text somewhere:

```csharp
public override string ToString()
{
  var sb = new StringBuilder();
  for (var i = 0; i < plainText.Length; i++)
  {
    var c = plainText[i];
    sb.Append(capitalize[i] ? char.ToUpper(c) : c);
  }
  return sb.ToString();
}
```

This approach does in fact work:

```csharp
var ft = new FormattedText("This is a brave new world");
ft.Capitalize(10, 15);
WriteLine(ft); // This is a BRAVE new world
```

But of course we are wasting memory. Even if the text has *no* formatting whatsoever, we still allocate the array. True, we could have made it lazy so that it's only created whenever someone uses the `Capitalize()` method, but then we would still lose a lot of memory on first use, particularly with large texts.

This is precisely the situation the Flyweight design pattern is made for! In this particular case, we're going to define a flyweight as a `Range` class that stores information about the start and end positions of a substring within a string, as well as all the formatting information we desire:

```csharp
public class TextRange
{
  public int Start, End;
  public bool Capitalize; // also Bold, Italic, etc.

  public bool Covers(int position)
  {
    return position >= Start && position <= End;
  }
}
```

Now, we can define a `BetterFormattedText` class that simply stores a list of all the formatting that was applied:

```
public class BetterFormattedText
{
  private readonly string plainText;
  private readonly List<TextRange> formatting
    = new List<TextRange>();

  public BetterFormattedText(string plainText)
  {
    this.plainText = plainText;
  }

  public TextRange GetRange(int start, int end)
  {
    var range = new TextRange {Start = start, End = end};
    formatting.Add(range);
    return range;
  }

  public class TextRange { ... }
}
```

Notice that `TextRange` is an inner class – this is a design decision, and you could easily keep it external. Now, instead of a dedicated `Capitalize()` method, we simply have a method called `GetRange()` that does three things: it creates a new range, adds it to the formatting list, but also returns it to the client to be operated upon.

All that remains now is to make a new implementation of `ToString()` that incorporates this flyweight-based approach. Here it is:

```
public override string ToString()
{
  var sb = new StringBuilder();

  for (var i = 0; i < plainText.Length; i++)
  {
    var c = plainText[i];
    foreach (var range in formatting)
```

```
    if (range.Covers(i) && range.Capitalize)
        c = char.ToUpperInvariant(c);
    sb.Append(c);
  }

  return sb.ToString();
}
```

As you can see, we simply iterate each of the characters. For each character, we check all the ranges with the Covers() method, and if that range covers this point and has special formatting, we show that formatting to the end user. Here is how you would use the new API:

```
var bft = new BetterFormattedText("This is a brave new world");
bft.GetRange(10, 15).Capitalize = true;
WriteLine(bft); // This is a BRAVE new world
```

Admittedly, ours is a fairly inefficient implementation of Flyweight (traversal of every character is just too tedious), but hopefully it's obvious that the general approach saves a lot of memory in the long run.

Using Flyweights for Interop

Sometimes, managed code is not enough. For example, you need to run some calculations on the GPU, and those are (typically) programmed using CUDA C and the like. You end up having to use a C or C++ library from your C# code, so you make calls from the managed (.NET) side to the unmanaged (native code) side.

This isn't really a problem if you want to pass simple bits of data, such as numbers or arrays, back and forth. .NET has functionality for pinning an array and sending it to the "unmanaged" side for processing. It works fine, most of the time.

The problems arise when you allocate some object-oriented construct (i.e., a class) inside unmanaged code and want to return it to the managed caller. Nowadays, this is typically handled by serializing (encoding) all the data on one side and then unpacking it on the other side. This can be done in many formats, including simple ones such as returning XML or JSON or complicated, industry-grade solutions such as Google's Protocol Buffers.

In some cases, though, you don't really need to return the full object itself. Instead, you simply want to return a handle so that this handle can be subsequently used on the unmanaged side again. You don't even need the extra memory traffic passing objects back and forth. There are many reasons you'd want to do this, but the main reason is that you want only one side to manage the object's lifetime, since managing it on both sides is a nightmare that nobody really needs.

What you do in this case is you return a flyweight. This can be anything – a string identifier, an integer, a GUID – anything that lets you refer to the object later on. The managed side then holds on to the token and uses that token to pass back to the unmanaged side when some operations on the underlying object are required.

This approach introduces an issue with lifetime management. Suppose we want the underlying object to live for as long as we have the token. How can we implement this? Well, this would mean that, on the unmanaged side, the token lives forever, whereas on the managed side, we wrap it in an IDisposable with the Dispose() method sending a message back to the unmanaged side that the token has been disposed. But what if we copy the token and have two or more instances of it? Then we end up having to build a reference-counted system for tokens: something that is quite possible, but introduces extra complexity in our system.

There is also a symmetric problem: what if the managed side has destroyed the object that the token represents? If we try to use the token, additional checks need to be made to ensure the token is actually valid, and some sort of meaningful return value needs to be given to the unmanaged call in order to tell the managed side that the token has gone stale. Again, this is extra work.

Summary

The Flyweight pattern is fundamentally a space-saving technique. Its exact incarnations are diverse: sometimes you have the flyweight being returned as an API token that allows you to perform modifications of whoever has spawned it, whereas at other times the flyweight is implicit, hiding behind the scenes – as in the case of our User, where the client isn't meant to know about the flyweight actually being used.

In the .NET Framework, the principal flyweight-like object is, of course, Span<T>. Just like the TextRange we implemented when working with strings, Span<T> is a type that has information about a part of an array: the starting position and length. Operations on the Span get applied to the object the Span refers to, and .NET provides a rich API for creating spans on different types of objects. Span also makes heavy use of C# 7's ref-related APIs (such as ref returns).

CHAPTER 13

Proxy

When we looked at the Decorator design pattern, we saw different ways of enhancing the functionality of an object. The Proxy design pattern is similar, but its goal is generally to preserve exactly (or as closely as possible) the object's original API while offering certain internal enhancements.

Proxy is an unusual design pattern in that it isn't really homogeneous. The different kinds of proxies people build are quite numerous and serve entirely different purposes. In this chapter we'll take a look at a selection of different proxy types, and you can find more online.

Protection Proxy

The idea of a protection proxy, as the name suggests, is to provide access control to an existing object. For example, you might be starting out with an object called Car that has a single Drive() method that lets you drive the car unconditionally (here we go, another synthetic example):

```
public class Car // : ICar
{
  public void Drive()
  {
    WriteLine("Car being driven");
  }
}
```

© Dmitri Nesteruk 2022
D. Nesteruk, *Design Patterns in .NET 6*, https://doi.org/10.1007/978-1-4842-8245-8_13

But, later on, you decide that you want to only let people drive the car if they are old enough. What if you don't want to change Car itself and you want the extra checks to be done somewhere else (SRP)? Let's see... First, you extract the ICar interface (note this operation doesn't affect Car in any significant way):

```
public interface ICar
{
  void Drive();
}
```

The protection proxy we're going to build is going to depend on a Driver that's defined like this:

```
public class Driver
{
  public int Age { get; set; }

  public Driver(int age)
  {
    Age = age;
  }
}
```

The proxy itself is going to take a Driver in the constructor and is going to expose the same ICar interface as the original car, the only difference being that some internal checks occur making sure the driver is old enough:

```
public class CarProxy : ICar
{
  private Car car = new Car();
  private Driver driver;

  public CarProxy(Driver driver)
  {
    this.driver = driver;
  }

  public void Drive()
  {
```

```
  if (driver.Age >= 16)
    car.Drive();
  else
    WriteLine("Driver too young");
  }
}
```

Here is how one would use this proxy:

```
ICar car = new CarProxy(new Driver(12));
car.Drive(); // Driver too young
```

There's one piece of the puzzle that we haven't really addressed. Even though both Car and CarProxy implement ICar, their constructors are not identical! This means that the interfaces of the two objects are the same. Is this a problem? This depends:

- If your code was dependent on Car rather than ICar (violating the DIP), then you would need to search and replace every use of this type in your code. Not impossible with tools like ReSharper/Rider, just really annoying.

- If your code was dependent on ICar but you were explicitly invoking Car constructors, you would have to find all those constructor invocations and feed each of them a Driver.

- If you were using dependency injection, you are good to go provided you register a Driver in the container.

So, among other things, the protection proxy we've built is an illustration of the benefits of using an IoC container with constructor injection support.

Property Proxy

C# makes the use of properties easy: you can use either "full" or automatic properties, and now there's expression-based notation for getters and setters, so you can keep properties really concise. However, that's not always what you want: sometimes, you want a getter or setter of each property in your code to do something in addition to just the default actions. For example, you might want setters that prevent self-assignment and also (for illustrative purposes) output some info about what value is being assigned and to what property.

So instead of using ordinary properties, you might want to introduce a *property proxy* – a class that, for all intents and purposes, behaves like a property but is actually a separate class with domain-specific behaviors (and associated performance costs). You would start building this class by wrapping a simple value and adding whatever extra information you want the property to have (e.g., the property name):

```csharp
public class Property<T> where T : new()
{
  private T value;
  private readonly string name;

  public T Value
  {
    get => value;

    set
    {
      if (Equals(this.value, value)) return;
      Console.WriteLine($"Assigning {value} to {name}");
      this.value = value;
    }
  }

  public Property() : this(default(T)) {}
  public Property(T value, string name = "")
  {
    this.value = value;
    this.name = name;
  }
}
```

For now, all we have is a simple wrapper, but where's the *proxy* part of it all? After all, we want a Property<int> to behave as close to an int as possible. To that end, we can define a couple of implicit conversion operators:

```csharp
public static implicit operator T(Property<T> property)
{
  return property.Value; // int n = p_int;
}
```

```
public static implicit operator Property<T>(T value)
{
  return new Property<T>(value); // Property<int> p = 123;
}
```

The first operator lets us implicitly convert the property type to its underlying value; the second operator lets us initialize a property from a value (without a name, of course). Sadly, C# does not allow us to override the assignment = operator.

How would you use this property proxy? Well, there are two ways I can think of. One, and the most obvious, is to expose the property as a public field:

```
public class Creature
{
  public Property<int> Agility = new(10, nameof(Agility))
}
```

Unfortunately, this approach is not a "proper" proxy because, while it replicates the interface of an ordinary property, it doesn't give us the behavior we want:

```
var c = new Creature();
c.Agility = 12; // <nothing happens!>
```

When you assign a value, as you would with an ordinary property, absolutely nothing happens. Why? Well, the reason is that we invoked the implicit conversion operator, which, instead of changing an existing property, just gave us a new property instead! It's definitely not what we wanted, and furthermore, we've lost the name value as it was never propagated by the operator.

So the solution here, if we really want the property to both look like a duck and quack like a duck, is to create a wrapper (delegating) property and keep the proxy as a private backing field:

```
public class Creature
{
  private readonly Property<int> agility = new(10, nameof(agility));

  public int Agility
  {
```

```
    get => agility.Value;
    set => agility.Value = value;
  }
}
```

With this approach, we finally get the desired behavior:

```
var c = new Creature();
c.Agility = 12; // Assigning 12 to Agility
```

Purists might argue that this isn't an ideal proxy (since we've had to both generate a new class and rewrite an existing property), but this is purely a limitation of the C# programming language.

Composite Proxy: SoA/AoS

Many applications, such as game engines, are very sensitive to data locality. For example, consider the following class:

```
class Creature
{
  public byte Age;
  public int X, Y;
}
```

If you had several creatures in your game, kept in an array, the memory layout of your data would appear as

```
Age X Y Age X Y Age X Y ... and so on
```

This means that, if you wanted to update the X coordinate of all objects in an array, your iteration code would have to jump over the other fields to get each of the Xs.

Turns out that CPUs generally like data locality, that is, data being kept together. This is often called the AoS/SoA (Array of Structures/Structure of Arrays) problem. For us, it would be much better if the memory layout was in SoA form, as follows:

```
Age Age Age ... X X X ... Y Y Y
```

How can we achieve this? Well, we can build a data structure that keeps exactly such a layout and then expose Creature objects as proxies.

Here's what I mean. First of all, we create a Creatures collection (arrays are used for simplicity) that enforces data locality for each of the "fields":

```
class Creatures
{
  private readonly int size;
  private byte [] age;
  private int[] x, y;

  public Creatures(int size)
  {
    this.size = size;
    age = new byte[size];
    x = new int[size];
    y = new int[size];
  }
}
```

Now, a Creature type can be constructed as a proxy that points to an element within the Creatures container:

```
public struct Creature
{
  private readonly Creatures creatures;
  private readonly int index;

  public Creature(Creatures creatures, int index)
  {
    this.creatures = creatures;
    this.index = index;
  }

  public ref byte Age => ref creatures.age[index];
  public ref int X => ref creatures.x[index];
  public ref int Y => ref creatures.y[index];
}
```

This data structure is what's called a *hollow proxy*. It is a data structure that doesn't store any useful (actionable) information, nor does it provide any special behaviors. All it does is provide a level of indirection. It is essentially a bunch of pointers into an existing data structure. Its existence is only motivated by syntactic convenience.

Note that the preceding class is *nested* within Creatures. The reason for this is that its property getters need to access private members of Creatures, which would be impossible if the class was on the same scope as the container.

So now that we have this proxy, we can give the Creatures container additional features, such as an indexer or a GetEnumerator() implementation:

```
public class Creatures
{
  // members here
  public Creature this[int index]
    => new Creature(this, index);

  public IEnumerator<Creature> GetEnumerator()
  {
    for (int pos = 0; pos < size; ++pos)
      yield return new Creature(this, pos);
  }
}
```

And that's it! We can now look at a side-by-side comparison of the AoS approach and the new SoA approach:

```
// AoS
var creatures = new Creature[100];
foreach (var c in creatures)
{
  c.X++; // not memory-efficient
}

// SoA
var creatures2 = new Creatures(100);
foreach (var c in creatures2)
{
  c.X++; // better!
}
```

Naturally, what I've shown here is a simplistic model. It would be more useful with arrays replaced by more flexible data structures like List<T>, and a lot more features could be added in order to make Creatures even more user-friendly.

Composite Proxy with Array-Backed Properties

Suppose you're working on an application that generates bricklaying designs. You need to decide what surfaces you want to cover with bricks, so you make a list of checkboxes as follows:

- ☐ Pillars
- ☐ Walls
- ☐ Floors
- ☐ All

Most of these are easy and can be bound one-to-one to Boolean variables, but the last option, All, cannot. How would you implement it in code? Well, you could try something like the following:

```
public class MasonrySettings
{
  public bool Pillars, Walls, Floors;

  public bool All
  {
    get { return Pillars && Walls && Floors; }
    set {
      Pillars = value;
      Walls = value;
      Floors = value;
    }
  }
}
```

This implementation might work, but it's not 100% correct. The last checkbox called All is actually not even boolean because it can be in three states:

- Checked if all items are checked

- Unchecked if all items are unchecked

- Grayed if some items are checked and others are not

This makes it a bit of a challenge: how do we make a variable for the state of this element that can be reliably bound to UI?

First of all, those combinations using && are ugly. We already have a tool called array-backed properties that can help us take care of that, transforming the class to

```
public class MasonrySettings
{
  private bool[] flags = new bool[3];

  public bool Pillars
  {
    get => flags[0];
    set => flags[0] = value;
  }

  // similar for Floors and Walls
}
```

Now, care to guess that type the All variable should have? Personally I'd go for a bool? (aka Nullable<bool>) where the null can indicate an indeterminate state. This means that we check the homogeneity of each element in the array and return its first element if it's homogeneous (i.e., all elements are the same) and null otherwise:

```
public bool? All
{
  get
  {
    if (flags.Skip(1).All(f => f == flags[0]))
      return flags[0];
    return null;
  }
```

```
set
{
  if (!value.HasValue) return;
  for (int i = 0; i < flags.Length; ++i)
    flags[i] = value.Value;
}
}
```

The getter here is fairly self-explanatory. When it comes to the setter, its value gets assigned to every element in the array. If the argument is null, we don't do anything. An alternative implementation could, for example, flip every Boolean member inside the array – your choice!

Virtual Proxy

There are situations where you only want the object constructed when it's accessed and you don't want to allocate it prematurely. If this was your starting strategy, you would typically use a Lazy<T> or similar mechanism, feeding the initialization code into its constructor lambda. However, there are situations where you are adding lazy instantiation at a later point in time and you cannot change the existing API.

In this situation, what you end up building is a *virtual proxy*: an object that has the same API as the original, giving the appearance of an instantiated object, but behind the scenes the proxy only instantiates the object when it's actually necessary.

Imagine a typical image interface:

```
interface IImage
{
  void Draw();
}
```

An eager (opposite of lazy) implementation of a Bitmap (nothing to do with System.Drawing.Bitmap!) would load the image from a file on construction, even if that image isn't actually required for anything. And, yes, the following code is an emulation:

```
class Bitmap : IImage
{
  private readonly string filename;
```

```
public Bitmap(string filename)
{
  this.filename = filename;
  WriteLine($"Loading image from {filename}");
}

public void Draw()
{
  WriteLine($"Drawing image {filename}");
}
}
```

The very act of construction of this `Bitmap` will trigger the loading of the image:

```
var img = new Bitmap("pokemon.png");
// Loading image from pokemon.png
```

That's not quite what we want. What we want is the kind of bitmap that only loads itself when the `Draw()` method is used. Now, I suppose we could jump back into `Bitmap` and make it lazy, but we're going to assume the original implementation is set in stone and is not modifiable.

So what we can then build is a virtual proxy that will use the original `Bitmap`, provide an identical interface, and also reuse the original `Bitmap`'s functionality:

```
class LazyBitmap : IImage
{
  private readonly string filename;
  private Bitmap bitmap;

  public LazyBitmap(string filename)
  {
    this.filename = filename;
  }

  public void Draw()
  {
```

```
  if (bitmap == null) // lazy loading
    bitmap = new Bitmap(filename);

  bitmap.Draw();
 }
}
```

Here we are. As you can see, the constructor of this LazyBitmap is a lot less "heavy": all it does is store the name of the file to load the image from, and that's it – the image doesn't actually get loaded.[1]

All of the magic happens in Draw(): this is where we check the bitmap reference to see whether the underlying (eager!) bitmap has been constructed. If it hasn't, we construct it and then call its Draw() function to actually draw the image.

Now imagine you have some API that uses an IImage type:

```
public static void DrawImage(IImage img)
{
  WriteLine("About to draw the image");
  img.Draw();
  WriteLine("Done drawing the image");
}
```

We can use this API with an instance of LazyBitmap instead of Bitmap (hooray, polymorphism!) to render the image, loading it in a lazy fashion:

```
var img = new LazyBitmap("pokemon.png");
DrawImage(img); // image loaded here

// About to draw the image
// Loading image from pokemon.png
// Drawing image pokemon.png
// Done drawing the image
```

---

[1] Not that it matters for this particular example, but this implementation is not thread-safe. Imagine two threads that both do a null check, pass it, and then both assign bitmap one after another – the constructor will be called twice. This is why we use System.Lazy, which is thread-safe by design.

Communication Proxy

Suppose you call a method Foo() on an object of type Bar. Your typical assumption is that Bar has been allocated on the same machine as the one running your code, and you similarly expect Bar.Foo() to execute in the same process.

Now imagine that you make a design decision to move Bar and all its members off to a different machine on the network. But you still want the old code to work! If you want to keep going as before, you'll need a *communication proxy* – a component that proxies the calls "over the wire" and of course collects results, if necessary.

Let's implement a simple ping-pong service to illustrate this. First, we define an interface:

```
interface IPingable
{
  string Ping(string message);
}
```

If we are building ping-pong in-process, we can implement Pong as follows:

```
class Pong : IPingable
{
  public string Ping(string message)
  {
    return message + " pong";
  }
}
```

Basically, you ping a Pong, and it appends the word " pong" to the end of the message and returns that message. Notice that I'm not using a StringBuilder here, but instead making a new string on each turn: this lack of mutation helps replicate this API as a web service.

We can now try out this setup and see how it works in-process:

```
void UseIt(IPingable pp)
{
  WriteLine(pp.ping("ping"));
}
```

```
var pp = new Pong();
for (int i = 0; i < 3; ++i)
{
  UseIt(pp);
}
```

And the end result is that we print "ping pong" three times, just as we wanted.

So now, suppose you decide to relocate the Pingable service to a web server, far, far away. Perhaps you even decide to expose it through a special framework such as ASP.NET:

```
[Route("api/[controller]")]
public class PingPongController : Controller
{
  [HttpGet("{msg}")]
  public string Get(string msg)
  {
    return msg + " pong";
  }
}
```

With this setup, we'll build a communication proxy called RemotePong that will be used in place of Pong:

```
class RemotePong : IPingable
{
  string Ping(string message)
  {
    string uri = "http://localhost:9149/api/pingpong/" + message;
    return new WebClient().DownloadString(uri);
  }
}
```

With this implemented, we can now make a single change:

```
var pp = new RemotePong(); // was Pong
for (int i = 0; i < 3; ++i)
{
  UseIt(pp);
}
```

And that's it. You get the same output, but the actual implementation can be running on Kestrel in a Docker container somewhere halfway around the world.

Dynamic Proxy for Logging

Say you're testing a piece of code and you want to record the number of times particular methods are called and what arguments they are called with. You have a couple of options, including the following:

- Using AOP approaches such as PostSharp or Fody to create assemblies where the required functionality is weaved into the code

- Using profiling/tracing software instead

- Creating dynamic proxies for your objects in tests

A *dynamic proxy* is a proxy created at runtime. It allows us to take an existing object and, provided a few rules are followed, to override or wrap some of its behaviors to perform additional operations.

So imagine that you are writing tests that cover the operation of a BankAccount, a class that implements the following interface:

```
public interface IBankAccount
{
    void Deposit(int amount);
    bool Withdraw(int amount);
}
```

Suppose that your starting point is a test such as the following:

```
var ba = new BankAccount();
ba.Deposit(100);
ba.Withdraw(50);
WriteLine(ba);
```

When performing those operations, you also want a *count* of the number of methods that have been called. So, effectively, you want to wrap a BankAccount with some sort of dynamically constructed proxy that implements the IBankAccount interface and keeps a log of all the methods called.

We shall construct a new class that we'll call Log<T> that is going to be a dynamic proxy for any type T:

```
public class Log<T> : DynamicObject
  where T : class, new()
{
  private readonly T subject;
  private Dictionary<string, int> methodCallCount = new ();
  //            ↑ not thread-safe, obviously

  protected Log(T subject)
  {
    this.subject = subject;
  }
}
```

Our class takes a subject, which is the class it is wrapping, and has a simple dictionary of method call counts.

Now this class inherits from DynamicObject, which is great because we want to make a log of the calls made to its various methods, and only then does it actually invoke those methods. Here's how we can implement this:

```
public override bool TryInvokeMember(
  InvokeMemberBinder binder, object[] args, out object result)
{
  try
  {
    if (methodCallCount.ContainsKey(binder.Name))
      methodCallCount[binder.Name]++;
    else
      methodCallCount.Add(binder.Name, 1);

    result = subject
      ?.GetType()
      ?.GetMethod(binder.Name)
      ?.Invoke(subject, args);
    return true;
  }
```

```
  catch
  {
    result = null;
    return false;
  }
}
```

As you can see, all we're doing is logging the number of calls made to a particular method and then invoking the method itself using reflection.

Now, there's only one tiny problem for us to handle: how do we get our Log<T> to pretend as if it were implementing some interface I? This is where dynamic proxy frameworks come in. The one we're going to be using is called ImpromptuInterface.[2] This framework provides an extension method called ActLike() that allows a dynamic object to pretend that it implements a particular interface.

Armed with this, we can give our Log<T> a static factory method that would construct a new instance of T, wrap it in a Log<T>, and then expose it as some interface I:

```
public static I As<I>() where I : class
{
  if (!typeof(I).IsInterface)
    throw new ArgumentException("I must be an interface type");

  // duck typing here!
  return new Log<T>(new T()).ActLike<I>();
}
```

The end result of it all is that we can now perform a simple replacement and get a record of all the calls made to the bank account class:

```
//var ba = new BankAccount();
var ba = Log<BankAccount>.As<IBankAccount>();

ba.Deposit(100);
ba.Withdraw(50);

WriteLine(ba);
```

---

[2] You can get it from NuGet; the source code is at https://github.com/ekonbenefits/impromptu-interface

244

```
// Deposit called 1 time(s)
// Withdraw called 1 time(s)
```

Naturally, in order for this to work, we've had to override `Log<T>.ToString()` to output call counts. Sadly, the wrapper we've made will not automatically proxy over calls to `ToString()`/`Equals()`/`GetHashCode()` because every `object` has them intrinsically built in. If you do want to connect these to the underlying, you'd have to add overrides in `Log<T>` and then use the `subject` field to make the appropriate calls.

Composite Proxy

Having met the Composite design pattern earlier in the book, you might be wondering just how Composite is able to interact with Proxy, considering how different the two patterns and their uses are. Well, let me show you an example.

Quite often, when using a `StringBuilder`, I find it necessary to put specific lines of text into specific locations in the builder. Sometimes, I need to insert lines at the beginning and end up having to use `Insert()` in doing so. If I have to compose a large file with many parts, what I do is typically construct a separate `StringBuilder` for each part and then merge them into a final builder toward the end.

Having to declare lots of different `StringBuilder` entities is tiring. You may end up writing to the wrong one and not even notice. It is far better to simply have some sort of *prioritized* `StringBuilder` where, when adding entries, you can optionally refer to the order of the entries. For example, we can assume that smaller integer values mean the builder is earlier in the file and larger integer values mean the data is kept at a later position.

What does this have to do with the Composite pattern, though? The answer is this: behind the scenes we, of course, keep *several* `StringBuiler` entities. These are created on demand as you use the API.

To get this to work, we're going to have to trick the system a little. First of all, we'll define a class as follows:

```
public class PriorityStringBuilder
{
  private StringBuilder sb = new StringBuilder();
}
```

Now, we use Rider/R#/your favorite IDE to **generate Delegating Members** for sb. Having done so, we now need to do some cleanup: for example, the IDEs may forget to mark StringBuilder methods that take pointers as unsafe, or it may mess up nullability annotations. For this particular example, we do *not* need to try and recover a fluent interface – you'll see why in a moment.

Having created the sb field, we now replace it with the following:

```
public class PriorityStringBuilder
{
  private readonly int defaultPriority;
  private readonly SortedDictionary<int, StringBuilder> data = new ();
  private StringBuilder sb => data[defaultPriority];

  public PriorityStringBuilder(int defaultPriority = 100)
  {
    this.defaultPriority = defaultPriority;
    data[defaultPriority] = new StringBuilder();
  }

  // generated members here
}
```

There's quite a lot going on here, so let me explain what we did:

- The class was given a constructor where you get to specify the default priority for adding text. By default, this has a value of 100, meaning that, to add text at an earlier stage, you'd use some priority <100 and, to add it later, you can use a higher value. We'll see in a moment how to use those.

- We removed the StringBuilder field and replaced it with a SortedDictionary, which stores not one but any number of StringBuilder objects with different priorities.

- The sb field is no longer a field: it's a property that returns the builder associated with default priority. This should remind you of the Array-Backed Properties approach we met earlier.

In order to support priority, we're going to break the interface somewhat by removing the current indexer. By default, StringBuilder's indexer works just like that of a string: it returns a character at a specified position. We don't want that. Instead, we'll use the index value to specify the priority we need, resulting in the following implementation:

```
public StringBuilder this[int priority]
{
  get
  {
    if (!data.ContainsKey(priority))
      data.Add(priority, new StringBuilder());
    return data[priority];
  }
}
```

And, finally, the icing on the cake: we implement ToString(), which simply takes the data from all the StringBuilders and puts it into one string:

```
public override string ToString()
{
  return string.Join(string.Empty,
    data.Values.Select(s => s.ToString()));
}
```

To demonstrate the use of this, consider a simple HTML document where you first construct the body of the page, but then need to wrap it with appropriate tags:

```
var b = new PriorityStringBuilder();
b.AppendLine("<p>Hello, World!</p>");
b[50].AppendLine("<html>")
  .AppendLine("<body>");
b[150].AppendLine("</body")
  .AppendLine("</html>");
Console.WriteLine(b);
```

This gives the predictable output:

```
<html>
<body>
<p>Hello, World!</p>
</body
</html>
```

Naturally, the approach presented here can do with some improvements. For example, our use of the term *priority* is imprecise since one might argue that text with higher priority should come *earlier* in the output, not later. But the solution presented here works well, and we leave it up to you to figure out how to best avoid magic numbers.

Summary

This chapter has presented a number of proxies. Unlike the Decorator pattern, Proxy doesn't try to expand the public API surface of an object by adding new members (unless it can't be helped). All it tries to do is enhance or modify the underlying behavior of existing members.

Plenty of different proxies exist:

- Protection proxies provide access control wrappers to control access to resources.

- Property proxies are stand-in objects that can replace fields and perform additional operations during assignment and/or access.

- Composite proxies are stand-in objects that help you access composite objects.

- Virtual proxies provide virtual access to the underlying object and can implement behaviors such as lazy object loading. You may feel like you're working with a real object, but the underlying implementation may not have been created yet and can, for example, be loaded on demand.

- Communication proxies allow us to change the physical location of the object (e.g., move it to the cloud) but allow us to use pretty much the same API. Of course, in this case the API is just a shim for a remote service such as some available REST API.

- Logging proxies allow you to perform logging in addition to calling the underlying functions.

- Dynamic proxies are proxies constructed at runtime, for whatever purpose. Plenty of different implementations exist, including explicit dynamic proxy support in popular IoC containers.

There are lots of other proxy types out there, and chances are that the ones you build yourself will not fall into a preexisting category, but will instead perform some action specific to your domain.

CHAPTER 14

Value Object

The decision as to whether to make an object a `class` or a `struct` is very important, and not just from the performance perspective. Quite often what we really want is a "value plus" – to be able to provide a wrapper around a single value (such as an `int`) that would do one of the following:

- Carry additional information (data or metadata).

- Provide additional behaviors.

- Provide additional levels of indirection.

Some fairly obvious examples of value object types include

- *Money*: Carries information about monetary value (likely as integer rather than FP) and currency

- `DateTime`, `TimeSpan`, and similar classes

- `System.Guid` (essentially a 128-bit value)

The vehicle for this is, of course, a `struct`, which enjoys the well-known trappings such as pass-by-value, value (rather than referential) equality, and others.

There are, in fact, several different `struct` incarnations, which are all very similar:

- An ordinary `struct`

- A `record struct`, which is a `struct` with many useful synthesized members

- A `ref struct`, which is a special, stack-only structure

In addition, each of these also has its `readonly` variation (`readonly struct`, `readonly record struct`, and `readonly ref struct`, respectively) that helps enforce immutability. It is best practice to keep structs immutable, since modifications of mutable struct members can often lead to no-op effects, where the developer thinks they've modified a variable, whereas they've inadvertently made a copy instead.

© Dmitri Nesteruk 2022
D. Nesteruk, *Design Patterns in .NET 6*, https://doi.org/10.1007/978-1-4842-8245-8_14

Whichever type of struct we choose, we can use it to construct an object that is intended to be passed by value and to convey additional information and functions. From a certain perspective, a value object can be considered as a proxy or decorator.

Two-Dimensional Point

Let us take a look at how to implement a value object that represents a simple two-dimensional point in Cartesian space. We'll start with a simple (non-record) definition:

```
public readonly struct Point
{
  public readonly double X, Y;
  public Point(double x, double y) => (X, Y) = (x, y);
  public static Point Origin = new Point(0, 0);
}
```

With such a definition, we must provide this structure with a bare minimum of operations, including

- *Equality operations*: An implementation of IEquatable<T>, the Equals(), and the == and != operators

- Support for GetHashCode()

You may also optionally choose to provide

- A sensible ToString() implementation

- A deconstruction method

- *Relational members*: The IComparable<T> interface, the CompareTo() method, and various relational operators

Most of these constructs can be automatically generated by either opting for a record struct or, alternatively, by using Rider or ReSharper. In any case, there is no need to type all this boilerplate code manually.

At this point, you could also furnish your type with whatever operators may be applicable. For example, in the case of a 2D point, you could add support for adding two points together or for multiplying a point by a number:

```
public static Point operator +(in Point p1, in Point p2)
{
  return new Point(p1.X + p2.X, p1.Y + p2.Y);
}

public static Point operator *(in Point p, double value)
{
  return new Point(p.X * value, p.Y * value);
}
```

The type can now be used as follows:

```
Point p = new Point(1, 2);
var p2 = p + p * 3.5;
Console.WriteLine(p2); // (4.5,9)
```

Percentage Value

Primitive values can have special meanings. Consider percentages: multiplying by 50 is different from multiplying by 50% because the latter is really multiplication by 0.5. But you still want to refer to 50% as 50% in your code, right? Let's see if we can build a Percentage type.

First of all, we need to agree on construction. Let's assume that we do, in fact, store a decimal behind the scenes that is actually a multiplier. In that case, we can begin our Percentage class as follows:

```
[DebuggerDisplay("{value*100.0f}%")]
public readonly record struct Percentage(decimal value)
{
  private readonly decimal value = value;
  // more members here
}
```

We have different choices for how to actually construct percentage values. One approach would be to adopt extension methods:

```csharp
public static class PercentageExtensions
{
  public static Percentage Percent(this int value)
  {
    return new Percentage(value/100.0m);
  }

  public static Percentage Percent(this decimal value)
  {
    return new Percentage(value/100.0m);
  }
}
```

We want this percentage to act the same as percentage values in, for example, Microsoft Excel. Multiplying by 50% should effectively multiply by 0.5; other operations should work in a similar fashion. Thus, we need to define many operators such as

```csharp
public static decimal operator *(decimal f, Percentage p)
{
  return f * p.value;
}
```

Let's not forget that the percentage can also operate on other percentages: for example, you can add 5% and 10% together, and similarly, you can take 50% of 50% (getting 25%). So you need more operators such as

```csharp
public static Percentage operator +(Percentage a, Percentage b)
{
  return new Percentage(a.value + b.value);
}
```

In addition, we need a meaningful `ToString()` implementation, since `Equals()`, `GetHashCode()`, and other members are generated automatically:

```csharp
public override string ToString()
{
  return $"{value*100}%";
}
```

And that's your percentage value object. Now, if you need to operate on percentages in your application and store them explicitly as percentages, you can do so:

```
Console.WriteLine(10m * 5.Percent());            // 0.50
Console.WriteLine(2.Percent() + 3m.Percent());   // 5.00%
```

With this approach, you can write methods that specifically take percentage values rather than general-purpose floating- point values:

```
public void GiveSalaryBonus(Percentage pc) { ... }
```

You can enhance this model further. For example, a Discount type can inherit from the Percentage type and allow only a limited range of values between 0% and 100%, since neither negative discounts nor discounts above 100% make any sense.

Units of Measure

You might have heard about major disasters, such as the loss of a $125 million Mars Climate Orbiter spacecraft, being due to mismatches in measurement units. Measurement units show up all over the place in software engineering projects and are a prime candidate for the Value Object pattern.

What we want to do, put simply, is to somehow attach information about the measurement units and their dimensions directly to the actual value. Exactly *how* it gets attached to a unit is up for debate. Broadly speaking, programming languages could implement this by

- Using unit information only at compile time and completely throwing it away at runtime

- Performing the checks at compile time, but leaving the unit information intact so it can be reused (e.g., as a library)

While the latter option is arguably more usable, F# goes for the former option, that is, being able to attach unit information to numeric values but almost completely wiping out all the unit data during compilation.

In F#, you can decorate a type with a [<Measure>] attribute to denote that it is some measurement unit:

```
[<Measure>] type kg // kilograms
[<Measure>] type m  // meters
[<Measure>] type s  // seconds
```

Notice that measurement units do not specify their underlying numeric type: a weight measurement can use a `float`, `decimal`, `uint16`, or any other numeric type. Naturally, such calculations are constrained such that a uniform type has to be used everywhere in the calculation, since F# does not allow implicit conversions, even if those conversions are widening (e.g., `int` to `float`):

```
let more_weight = 3<kg> + 4.0<kg>
// The type 'float<kg>' does not match the type 'int<kg>'
```

Having defined a set of units, these can be applied to numeric values:

```
let length = 3.0<m>
let time = 5.0<s>
let weight = 2.0<kg>
```

Measurements involving several units can be expressed as such. For instance, force is measured in Newtons $\left(\dfrac{kg \cdot m}{s^2} \right)$:

```
[<Measure>] type N = kg m / s^2 // Newtons
```

This allows us to perform calculations with compile-time dimensional analysis. Dimensional analysis ensures that the data you're assigning has the right units, so that, for example, dividing distance by time gives you speed, but assigning this value to a force variable is simply not possible and will not pass compile-time checks.

For example, this will work just fine:

```
let force: float<N> = (weight * length) / (time*time)
printf $"%f{force}" // 0.24
```

On the other hand, this will not compile:

```
let force: float<N> = (weight * length) / (time)
// The unit of measure 'N' does not match the unit of measure 'kg m/s'
```

It's important to understand that units of measure in F# are used for static (compile-time) checking. When the code is compiled, all measurement information attached to values is eliminated completely so you cannot, for example, implement a `ToString()` that incorporates unit information.

If we did want to incorporate unit information at compile time, it would require us to create an endless number of `struct` definitions that would all specify explicitly their measurement units, then use those types instead of the plain numeric data types.

Summary

Value Object is a pattern that promotes a primitive value into an OOP-like construct with the express purpose of providing additional information. At the very least, you're including type information, but in addition you can adorn it with attributes and behaviors (including extension methods) that make it more usable than a plain value.

Value objects also often arise out of efficiency concerns. If you have a piece of code that generates a large number of small objects, you end up increasing pressure on the Garbage Collector to take care of these constructs once you're done with them. Value objects instead allow you to allocate everything on the stack, provided, of course, that you do not exceed stack space.

PART IV

Behavioral Patterns

When most people hear about behavioral patterns, it's often related to pet training or general behavioral psychology, which often boils down to biological entities doing what you want them to do. Well, in a way, all of coding is about programs doing what you want, so behavioral software design patterns cover a very wide range of behaviors that are, nonetheless, quite common in programming.

As an example, consider the domain of software engineering. We have languages that are compiled, which involves lexing, parsing, and a million other things (the Interpreter pattern), and having constructed an abstract syntax tree (AST) for a program, you might want to analyze the program for possible bugs (the Visitor pattern). All of these are behaviors that are common enough to be expressed as patterns, and this is why we are here today.

Unlike creational patterns (which are concerned exclusively with the creation of objects) or structural patterns (which are concerned with composition/aggregation/ inheritance of objects), behavioral design patterns do not follow a central theme. While there are certain similarities between different patterns (e.g., Strategy and Template Method do the same thing in different ways), most patterns present unique approaches to solving a particular problem.

CHAPTER 15

Chain of Responsibility

Consider the typical example of corporate malpractice: insider trading. Say a particular trader has been caught red-handed trading on inside information. Who is to blame for this? If management didn't know, it's the trader. But maybe the trader's peers were in on it, in which case the group manager might be the one responsible. Or perhaps the practice is institutional, in which case it's the CEO who would take the blame.[1]

This is an example of a responsibility chain: you have several different elements of a system who can all process a piece of information one after another. As a concept, it's rather easy to implement, since all that's implied is the use of an ordinary list.

Scenario

Imagine a computer game where each creature has a name and two characteristic values – Attack and Defense:

```
public class Creature
{
  public string Name;
  public int Attack, Defense;

  public Creature(string name, int attack, int defense) { ... }
}
```

Now, as the creature progresses through the game, it might pick up an item (e.g., a magic sword), or it might end up getting enchanted. In either case, its attack and defense values will be modified by something we'll call a CreatureModifier.

---

[1] In all likelihood, if we're talking about banking, *nobody* gets punished. Nobody was punished for the subprime mortgage crisis. In the LIBOR fixing scandal, only one trader got convicted (six bankers were accused in the UK but later cleared). What does this have to do with design patterns? Absolutely nothing! Just wanted to share.

© Dmitri Nesteruk 2022
D. Nesteruk, *Design Patterns in .NET 6*, https://doi.org/10.1007/978-1-4842-8245-8_15

Furthermore, situations where *several* modifiers are applied are not uncommon, so we need to be able to stack modifiers on top of a creature, allowing them to be applied in the order they were attached.

Let's see how we can implement this.

Method Chain

In the classic Chain of Responsibility (CoR) implementation, we shall define CreatureModifier as follows:

```csharp
public class CreatureModifier
{
  protected Creature creature;
  protected CreatureModifier next;

  public CreatureModifier(Creature creature)
  {
    this.creature = creature;
  }

  public void Add(CreatureModifier cm)
  {
    if (next != null) next.Add(cm);
    else next = cm;
  }

  public virtual void Handle() => next?.Handle();
}
```

There are a lot of things happening here, so let's discuss them in turn:

- The class takes and stores a reference to the Creature it plans to modify.

- The class doesn't really do much, but it's not abstract: all its members have implementations.

- The next member points to an optional CreatureModifier following this one. The implication is, of course, that the modifier can also be some inheritor of CreatureModifier.

- The Add() method adds another creature modifier to the modifier chain. This is done iteratively: if the current modifier is null, we set it to that; otherwise, we traverse the entire chain and put it on the end. Naturally, this traversal has $O(n)$ complexity.

- The Handle() method simply handles the next item in the chain, if it exists; it has no behavior of its own. The fact that it's virtual implies that it's meant to be overridden.

So far, all we have is an implementation of a poor man's append-only singly linked list. But when we start inheriting from it, things will hopefully become clearer. For example, here is how you would make a modifier that would double the creature's attack value:

```
public class DoubleAttackModifier : CreatureModifier
{
  public DoubleAttackModifier(Creature creature)
    : base(creature) {}

  public override void Handle()
  {
    WriteLine($"Doubling {creature.Name}'s attack");
    creature.Attack *= 2;
    base.Handle();
  }
}
```

All right, finally we're getting somewhere. So this modifier inherits from CreatureModifier and in its Handle() method does two things: doubles the attack value and calls Handle() from the base class. That second part is critical: the only way in which a *chain* of modifiers can be applied is if every inheritor remembers to call the base at the end of its own Handle() implementation.

Here is another, more complicated modifier. This modifier increases the defense of creatures with attack of 2 or less by 1:

```
public class IncreaseDefenseModifier : CreatureModifier
{
  public IncreaseDefenseModifier(Creature creature)
    : base(creature) {}
```

```
public override void Handle()
{
  if (creature.Attack <= 2)
  {
    WriteLine($"Increasing {creature.Name}'s defense");
    creature.Defense++;
  }

  base.Handle();
}
}
```

Again we call the base class at the end. Putting it all together, we can now make a creature and apply a combination of modifiers to it:

```
var goblin = new Creature("Goblin", 1, 1);
WriteLine(goblin); // Name: Goblin, Attack: 1, Defense: 1

var root = new CreatureModifier(goblin);
root.Add(new DoubleAttackModifier(goblin));
root.Add(new DoubleAttackModifier(goblin));
root.Add(new IncreaseDefenseModifier(goblin));

// eventually...
root.Handle();
WriteLine(goblin); // Name: Goblin, Attack: 4, Defense: 1
```

As you can see, the preceding goblin is a 4/1 because its attack got doubled and the defense modifier, while added, did not affect its defense score.

Here's another curious point. Suppose you decide to cast a spell on a creature such that no bonus can be applied to it. Is it easy to do? Quite easy, actually, because all you have to do is avoid calling the base handle() – this avoids executing the entire chain:

```
public class NoBonusesModifier : CreatureModifier
{
  public NoBonusesModifier(Creature creature)
    : base(creature) {}
```

```
  public override void Handle()
  {
    WriteLine("No bonuses for you!");
    // no call to base.Handle() here
  }
}
```

That's it! Now, if you slot the NoBonusesModifier at the *beginning* of the chain, no further elements will be applied.

Broker Chain

The example with the pointer chain is very artificial. In the real world, you'd want creatures to be able to take on and lose bonuses arbitrarily, something that an append-only linked list doesn't support. Furthermore, you don't want to modify the underlying creature stats permanently (as we did) – instead, you want to keep modifications temporary.

One way to implement Chain of Responsibility is through a centralized component. This component can keep a list of *all* modifiers available in the game and can facilitate queries for a particular creature's attack or defense by ensuring that all relevant bonuses are applied.

The component that we are going to build is called an *event broker*. Since it's connected to every participating component, it represents the Mediator design pattern. And, further, since it responds to queries through events, it leverages the Observer design pattern.

Let's build one. First of all, we'll define a structure called Game that will represent, well, a game that's being played:

```
public class Game // mediator pattern
{
  public event EventHandler<Query> Queries; // effectively a chain

  public void PerformQuery(object sender, Query q)
  {
    Queries?.Invoke(sender, q);
  }
}
```

The class Game is what we generally call an *event broker*: a central component that brokers (passes) events between different parts of the system. Here it is implemented using ordinary .NET events, but you can equally imagine an implementation using some sort of message queue.

In the game, we are using an event called Queries. Essentially, this lets us raise this event and have it handled by every subscriber (listening component). But what do events have to do with querying a creature's attack or defense?

Well, imagine that you want to query a creature's statistic. You could certainly try to read a field, but remember, we need to apply all the modifiers before the final value is known. So instead we'll encapsulate a query in a separate object (this is the Command pattern[2]) defined as follows:

```
public class Query
{
  public string CreatureName;
  public enum Argument
  {
    Attack, Defense
  }
  public Argument WhatToQuery;
  public int Value; // bidirectional!
}
```

All we've done in the preceding class is encapsulated the concept of querying a particular value from a creature. All we need to provide is the name of the creature and which statistic we're interested in. It is precisely this value (well, a reference to it) that will be constructed and used by Game.Queries to apply the modifiers and return the final Value.

Now, let's move on to the definition of Creature. It's very similar to what we had before. The only difference in terms of fields is a reference to a Game:

---

[2] Actually, there's a bit of confusion here. The concept of Command-Query Separation (CQS) suggests the separation of operations into commands (which mutate state and yield no value) and queries (which do not mutate anything but yield a value). The GoF does not have a concept of a query, so we let *any* encapsulated instruction to a component be called a command.

```
public class Creature
{
  private Game game;
  public string Name;
  private int attack, defense;

  public Creature(Game game, string name, int attack, int defense)
  {
    // obvious stuff here
  }
  // other members here
}
```

Notice how attack and defense are private fields now. This means that, to get at the *final* (post-modifier) attack value, you would need to call a separate read-only property, for example:

```
public int Attack
{
  get
  {
    var q = new Query(Name, Query.Argument.Attack, attack);
    game.PerformQuery(this, q);
    return q.Value;
  }
}
```

This is where the magic happens! Instead of just returning a value or statically applying some reference-based chain, what we do is create a Query with the right arguments and then send the query off to be handled by whoever is subscribed to Game.Queries. Every single listening component gets a chance to modify the baseline attack value.

So let's now implement the modifiers. Once again, we'll make a base class, but this time round it won't have a body for the Handle() method:

```
public abstract class CreatureModifier : IDisposable
{
  protected Game game;
  protected Creature creature;
```

```csharp
  protected CreatureModifier(Game game, Creature creature)
  {
    this.game = game;
    this.creature = creature;
    game.Queries += Handle; // subscribe
  }

  protected abstract void Handle(object sender, Query q);

  public void Dispose()
  {
    game.Queries -= Handle; // unsubscribe
  }
}
```

Right, so this time round the `CreatureModifier` class is even more sophisticated. It obviously keeps a reference to the creature it's meant to modify, but also to the Game that's being played. Why? Well, as you can see, what's happening is that, in the constructor, it subscribes to the `Queries` event so that its inheritors can inject themselves as a set of modifiers is applied one after another. We also implement `IDisposable` so as to unsubscribe from the query events and prevent memory leaks.[3]

The `CreatureModifier.Handle()` method is deliberately made abstract so that inheritors can implement it and handle the modification process depending on the `Query` that's being sent. Let's take a look at how this is used by reimplementing `DoubleCreatureModifier` in this new paradigm:

```csharp
public class DoubleAttackModifier : CreatureModifier
{
  public DoubleAttackModifier(Game game, Creature creature)
    : base(game, creature) {}

  protected override void Handle(object sender, Query q)
  {
    if (q.CreatureName == creature.Name &&
      q.WhatToQuery == Query.Argument.Attack)
```

---

[3] This is precisely what is done in Reactive Extensions. See Chapter 20 for more information.

```
        q.Value *= 2;
    }
}
```

Right, so now we have a concrete implementation of Handle(). Extra care needs to be taken here to identify that the query is, in fact, a query that we want to process. Since a DoubleAttackModifier only cares about queries for an attack value, we verify this particular argument (WhatToQuery) and also make sure that the query is related to the creature we're meant to investigate.

If we now add an IncreaseDefenseModifier (increases defense by 2, implementation omitted), we can now run the following scenario:

```
var game = new Game();
var goblin = new Creature(game, "Strong Goblin", 2, 2);
WriteLine(goblin); // Name: Strong Goblin, attack: 2, defense: 2

using (new DoubleAttackModifier(game, goblin))
{
  WriteLine(goblin); // Name: Strong Goblin, attack: 4, defense: 2
  using (new IncreaseDefenseModifier(game, goblin))
  {
    WriteLine(goblin); // Name: Strong Goblin, attack: 4, defense: 4
  }
}

WriteLine(goblin); // Name: Strong Goblin, attack: 2, defense: 2
```

What's happening here? Well, prior to being modified, the goblin is a 2/2. Then, we manufacture a scope, within which the goblin is affected by a DoubleAttackModifier, so inside the scope, it is a 4/2 creature. As soon as we exit the scope, the modifier's destructor triggers, and it disconnects itself from the broker and thus no longer affects the values when they are queried. Consequently, the goblin itself reverts to being a 2/2 creature once again.

Functional Chain of Responsibility

Functional composition in F# allows us to use the >> operator to define a chain of functions that can be invoked in sequential fashion, thus representing a chain of responsibilities in processing some data.

For example, this can be used in validation. Consider a Person record type defined as

```
type Person = {
  Age : int
  IsCitizen : bool
}
```

A person can only vote if they are 16 or older and are a citizen; furthermore, we want to ensure their age is a reasonable number so as to avoid the fraudulent case of the dead voting.

Each of the validation requirements can be formalized by a function:

```
let oldEnough person = person.Age >= 16
let ageReasonable person = person.Age < 130
let isCitizen person = person.IsCitizen
```

A higher-order function can then be used to chain-apply each of these validators and propagate a true value if everything is OK and false if one of the validations has been tripped:

```
let check(f : Person -> bool) (person, result) =
  if not result then (person, false)
  else (person, f(person))
```

All the validation functions can now be wrapped with check() and composed together using the >> operator:

```
let validationChain = check(oldEnough) >> check(ageReasonable) >> check(isCitizen)
```

And now the entire validation chain can be invoked with a single function call. We pass in the object to validate and then check the second tuple value, which tells us whether the entire chain succeeded or not:

```
let sam = { Age = 40; IsCitizen = true };
printf "Can Sam vote? %b" ((validationChain(sam, true)) |> snd)
// Can Sam vote? true
```

It's important to note that this form of functional composition is pretty much immutable, meaning that it's impossible to modify at runtime. If you want to make it modifiable, you'd have to give up on the idea of compile-time composition and use a mutable data structure, thus negating the benefits that F# brings to the table.

Summary

Chain of Responsibility is a very simple design pattern that lets components process a command (or a query) in turn. The simplest implementation of CoR is one where you simply make a reference chain and, in theory, you could replace it with just an ordinary List or, perhaps, a LinkedList if you wanted fast removal as well.

A more sophisticated Broker Chain implementation that also leverages Mediator and Observer patterns allows us to process queries on an event, letting each subscriber perform modifications of the originally passed object (it's a single reference that goes through the entire chain) before the final values are returned to the client.

CHAPTER 16

Command

Think about a trivial variable assignment, such as `meaningOfLife = 42`. The variable got assigned, but there's no record anywhere that the assignment took place. Nobody can give us the previous value. We cannot take the *fact* of assignment and serialize it somewhere. This is problematic, because without a record of the change, we are unable to roll back to previous values, perform audits, or do history-based debugging.[1]

The Command design pattern proposes that, instead of working with objects directly by manipulating them through their APIs, we send them *commands*: instructions on how to do something. A command is nothing more than a data class with its members describing what to do and how to do it. Let's take a look at a typical scenario.

Scenario

Let's try to model a typical bank account that has a balance and an overdraft limit. We'll implement `Deposit()` and `Withdraw()` methods on it:

```
public class BankAccount
{
  private int balance;
  private int overdraftLimit = -500;

  public void Deposit(int amount)
  {
    balance += amount;
    WriteLine($"Deposited ${amount}, balance is now {balance}");
  }
```

---

[1] We *do* have dedicated historical debugging tools such as Visual Studio's IntelliTrace or UndoDB.

© Dmitri Nesteruk 2022
D. Nesteruk, *Design Patterns in .NET 6*, https://doi.org/10.1007/978-1-4842-8245-8_16

```
public void Withdraw(int amount)
{
  if (balance - amount >= overdraftLimit)
  {
    balance -= amount;
    WriteLine($"Withdrew ${amount}, balance is now {balance}");
  }
}
public override string ToString()
{
  return $"{nameof(balance)}: {balance}";
}
}
```

Now we can call the methods directly, of course, but let us suppose that, for audit purposes, we need to make a record of every deposit and withdrawal made and we cannot do it right inside BankAccount because – guess what – we've already designed, implemented, and tested that class.[2]

Implementing the Command Pattern

We'll begin by defining an interface for a command:

```
public interface ICommand
{
  void Call();
}
```

Having made the interface, we can now use it to define a BankAccountCommand that will encapsulate information about what to do with a bank account:

```
public class BankAccountCommand : ICommand
{
  private BankAccount account;
```

---

[2] You *can* design your code in a command-first fashion, that is, ensure that commands are the only publicly accessible API that your objects provide.

```
public enum Action
{
  Deposit, Withdraw
}
private Action action;
private int amount;

public BankAccountCommand
  (BankAccount account, Action action, int amount) { ... }
}
```

The information contained in the command includes the following:

- The account to operate upon.

- The action to take; both the set of options and the variable to store
  the action are defined in the class.

- The amount to deposit or withdraw.

Once the client provides this information, we can take it and use it to perform the deposit or withdrawal:

```
public void Call()
{
  switch (action)
  {
    case Action.Deposit:
      account.Deposit(amount);
      succeeded = true;
      break;
    case Action.Withdraw:
      succeeded = account.Withdraw(amount);
      break;
    default:
      throw new ArgumentOutOfRangeException();
  }
}
```

With this approach, we can create the command and then perform modifications of the account right on the command:

```
var ba = new BankAccount();
var cmd = new BankAccountCommand(ba,
  BankAccountCommand.Action.Deposit,  100);
cmd.Call(); // Deposited $100, balance is now 100
WriteLine(ba); // balance: 100
```

This will deposit 100 dollars into our account. Easy! And if you're worried that we're still exposing the original Deposit() and Withdraw() member functions to the client, well, the only way to hide them is to make commands inner classes of the BankAccount itself.

Undo Operations

Since a command encapsulates all information about some modification to a BankAccount, it can equally roll back this modification and return its target object to its prior state.

To begin with, we need to decide whether to stick undo-related operations into our Command interface. I will do it here for purposes of brevity, but in general, this is a design decision that needs to respect the Interface Segregation Principle that we discussed at the beginning of the book. For example, if you envisage some commands being final and not subject to undo mechanics, it might make sense to split ICommand into, say, ICallable and IUndoable.

Anyways, here's the updated ICommand:

```
public interface ICommand
{
  void Call();
  void Undo();
}
```

And here is a naive (but working) implementation of BankAccountCommand.Undo(), motivated by the assumption that Deposit() and Withdraw() are symmetric operations:

```
public void Undo()
{
  switch (action)
  {
    case Action.Deposit:
      account.Withdraw(amount);
      break;
    case Action.Withdraw:
      account.Deposit(amount);
      break;
    default:
      throw new ArgumentOutOfRangeException();
  }
}
```

Why is this implementation broken? Because if you tried to withdraw an amount equal to the GDP of a developed nation, you would not be successful, but when rolling back the transaction, we don't have a way of telling that it failed!

To get this information, we modify Withdraw() to return a success flag:

```
public bool Withdraw(int amount)
{
  if (balance - amount >= overdraftLimit)
  {
    balance -= amount;
    Console.WriteLine($"Withdrew ${amount}, balance is now {balance}");
    return true; // succeeded
  }
  return false; // failed
}
```

That's much better! We can now modify the entire BankAccountCommand to do two things:

- Store internally a succeeded flag when a withdrawal is made. We assume that Deposit() cannot fail.

- Use this flag when Undo() is called.

Here we go:

```
public class BankAccountCommand : ICommand
{
  ...
  private bool succeeded;
}
```

Okay, so now that we have the flag, we can improve our implementation of Undo():

```
public void Undo()
{
  if (!succeeded) return;
  switch (action)
  {
    case Action.Deposit:
      account.Deposit(amount); // assumed to always succeed
      succeeded = true;
      break;
    case Action.Withdraw:
      succeeded = account.Withdraw(amount);
      break;
    default:
      throw new ArgumentOutOfRangeException();
  }
}
```

Tada! We can finally undo withdrawal commands in a consistent fashion:

```
var ba = new BankAccount();
var cmdDeposit = new BankAccountCommand(ba,
  BankAccountCommand.Action.Deposit,  100);
var cmdWithdraw = new BankAccountCommand(ba,
  BankAccountCommand.Action.Withdraw,  1000);
cmdDeposit.Call();
cmdWithdraw.Call();
WriteLine(ba); // balance: 100
cmdWithdraw.Undo();
```

```
cmdDeposit.Undo();
WriteLine(ba); // balance: 0
```

The goal of this exercise was, of course, to illustrate that in addition to storing information about the action to perform, a command can also store some intermediate information that is, once again, useful for things like audits. If you detect a series of 100 failed withdrawal attempts, you can investigate a potential hack.

Composite Commands (aka Macros)

A transfer of money from account A to account B can be simulated with two commands:

1. Withdraw $X from A.

2. Deposit $X to B.

It would be nice if, instead of creating and calling these two commands, we could just create and call a single command that encapsulates both of the preceding commands. This is the essence of the Composite design pattern that we'll discuss later.

Let's define a skeleton composite command. I'm going to inherit from List<BankAccountCommand> and, of course, implement the ICommand interface:

```
abstract class CompositeBankAccountCommand
  : List<BankAccountCommand>, ICommand
{
  public virtual void Call()
  {
    ForEach(cmd => cmd.Call());
  }

  public virtual void Undo()
  {
    foreach (var cmd in
      ((IEnumerable<BankAccountCommand>)this).Reverse())
    {
      cmd.Undo();
    }
  }
}
```

As you can see, the `CompositeBankAccountCommand` is both a list and a `Command`, which fits the definition of the Composite design pattern. I've implemented both `Undo()` and `Redo()` operations. Note that the `Undo()` process goes through commands in reverse order; hopefully, I don't have to explain *why* you'd want this as default behavior. The cast is there because a `List<T>` has its own, `void`-returning, mutating `Reverse()` that we definitely do not want. If you don't like what you see here, you can use a `for` loop or some other base type that doesn't do in-place reversal.

So now, how about a composite command specifically for transferring money? I would define it as follows:

```
class MoneyTransferCommand : CompositeBankAccountCommand
{
  public MoneyTransferCommand(BankAccount from,
    BankAccount to, int amount)
  {
    AddRange(new []
    {
      new BankAccountCommand(from,
        BankAccountCommand.Action.Withdraw,  amount),
      new BankAccountCommand(to,
        BankAccountCommand.Action.Deposit,  amount)
    });
  }
}
```

All we're doing here is providing a constructor to initialize the object with. We keep reusing the base class `Undo()` and `Redo()` implementations. The entire arrangement is illustrated in Figure 16-1.

But wait. That's not right, is it? The base class implementations don't quite cut it because they don't incorporate the idea of failure. If I fail to withdraw money from A, I shouldn't deposit that money to B: the entire chain should cancel itself.

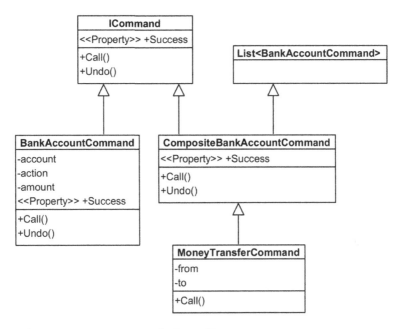

Figure 16-1. *Composite command class diagram*

To support this idea, more drastic changes are required. We need to

- Add a Success flag to Command. This of course implies that we can no longer use an interface – we need an abstract class.

- Record the success or failure of *every* operation.

- Ensure that the command can only be undone if it originally succeeded.

- Introduce a new in-between class called DependentCompositeCommand that is very careful about actually rolling back the commands.

Let's assume that we've performed the refactoring such that Command is now an abstract class with a Boolean Success member; the BankAccountCommand now overrides both Undo() and Redo().

When calling each command, we only do so if the previous one succeeded; otherwise, we simply set the success flag to false:

```
public override void Call()
{
  bool ok = true;
  foreach (var cmd in this)
  {
    if (ok)
    {
      cmd.Call();
      ok = cmd.Success;
    }
    else
    {
      cmd.Success = false;
    }
  }
}
```

There is no need to override the Undo() because each of our commands checks its own Success flag and undoes the operation only if it's set to true. Here's a scenario that demonstrates the correct operation of the new scheme when the source account doesn't have enough funds for the transfer to succeed:

```
var from = new BankAccount();
from.Deposit(100);
var to = new BankAccount();

var mtc = new MoneyTransferCommand(from, to, 1000);
mtc.Call();
WriteLine(from); // balance: 100
WriteLine(to);   // balance: 0
```

One can imagine an even stronger form of this paradigm where a composite command only succeeds if *all* of its parts succeed (think about a transfer where the withdrawal succeeds but the deposit fails because the account is locked – would you want it to go through?) – this is a bit harder to implement, and I leave it as an exercise for you.

The entire purpose of this section was to illustrate how a simple command-based approach can get quite complicated when real-world business requirements are taken into account. Whether or not you actually *need* this complexity...well, that is up to you.

Functional Command

The Command design pattern is typically implemented using classes. It is, however, possible to also implement this pattern in a functional way.

First of all, one might argue that an ICommand interface with a single Call() method is simply unnecessary: we already have delegates such as Func and Action that can serve as *de facto* interfaces for our purposes. Similarly, when it comes to invoking the commands, we can invoke said delegates directly instead of calling a member of some interface.

Here's a trivial illustration of the approach. We begin by defining a BankAccount simply as

```
public class BankAccount
{
  public int Balance;
}
```

We can then define different commands to operate on the bank account as independent methods. These could, alternatively, be packaged into ready-made function objects – there's no real difference between the two:

```
public void Deposit(BankAccount account, int amount)
{
  account.Balance += amount;
}

public void Withdraw(BankAccount account, int amount)
{
  if (account.Balance >= amount)
    account.Balance -= amount;
}
```

Every single method represents a command. We can therefore bundle up the commands in a simple list and process them one after another:

```
var ba = new BankAccount();
var commands = new List<Action>();

commands.Add(() => Deposit(ba, 100));
commands.Add(() => Withdraw(ba, 100));

commands.ForEach(c => c());
```

You may feel that this model is a great simplification of the one we had previously when talking about ICommand. After all, any invocation can be reduced to a parameterless Action that simply captures the needed elements in the lambda. However, this approach has significant downsides, namely:

- *Direct references*: A lambda that captures a specific object by necessity extends its lifetime. While this is great in terms of correctness (you'll never invoke a command with a nonexistent object), there are situations where you want commands to persist longer than the objects they need to affect.

- *Logging*: If you wanted to record every single action being performed on an account, you would *still* need some sort of command processor. But how can you determine which command is being invoked? All you're looking at is an Action or similarly nondescript delegate. How do you determine whether it's a deposit or a withdrawal or something entirely different, like a composite command?

- *Marshaling*: Quite simply, you cannot marshal a lambda. You could maybe marshal an expression tree (as in an Expression<Func<>>), but even then, parsing expression trees is not the easiest of things. A conventional OOP-based approach is easier because a class can be deterministically (de)serialized.

- *Secondary operations*: Unlike functional objects, an OOP command (or its interface) can define operations other than invocation. We've looked at examples such as Undo(), but other operations could include things like Log(), Print(), or something else. A functional approach doesn't give you this sort of flexibility.

To sum up, while the functional pattern does represent some action that needs to be done, it only encapsulates its principal behavior. A function is difficult to inspect/traverse, it is difficult to serialize, and if it captures context, this has obvious lifetime implications. Use with caution!

Queries and Command-Query Separation

The notion of Command-Query Separation (CQS) is the idea that operations in a system fall broadly into the following two categories:

- Commands, which are instructions for the system to perform some operation that involves mutation of state, but yields no value

- Queries, which are requests for information that yield values but do not mutate state

The GoF book does not define a query as a separate pattern, so in order to settle this issue once and for all, I propose the following, very simple, definition:

> A *query* is a special type of command that does not mutate state. Instead, a query instructs components to provide some information, such as a value calculated on the basis of interaction with one or more components.

There. We can now argue that both parts of CQS fall under the Command design pattern, the only difference being that queries have a return value – not in the `return` sense, of course, but rather in having a mutable field/property that any command processor can initialize or modify.

Summary

The Command design pattern is simple: what it basically suggests is that components can communicate with one another using special objects that encapsulate instructions, rather than specifying those same instructions as arguments to a method.

Sometimes, you don't want such an object to mutate the target or cause it to do something specific; instead, you want to use such an object to get some info from the target, in which case we typically call such an object a query. While, in most cases, a query is an immutable object that relies on the return type of the method, there *are* situations (see, e.g., the Chain of Responsibility "Broker Chain" example) where you want the result that's being returned to be modified by other components. But the components themselves are still not modified; only the result is.

Commands are used a lot in UI systems to encapsulate typical actions (e.g., copy or paste), and then a single command to be invoked by several different means is allowed. For example, you can copy by using the top-level application menu, a button on the toolbar, the context menu, or pressing a keyboard shortcut.

Finally, these actions can be combined into composite commands (macros) – sequences of actions that can be recorded and then replayed at will. Notice that a composite command can itself be composed of other composite commands (as per the Composite design pattern).

CHAPTER 17

Interpreter

> Any good software engineer will tell you that a compiler and an interpreter
> are interchangeable.
>
> —*Tim Berners-Lee*

The goal of the Interpreter design pattern is, you guessed it, to interpret input,
particularly *textual* input, although to be fair it really doesn't matter. The notion of
an interpreter is greatly linked to Compiler Theory and similar courses taught at
universities. Since we don't have nearly enough space here to delve into the complexities
of different types of parsers and whatnot, the purpose of this chapter is to simply show
some examples of the kinds of things you might want to interpret.

Here are a few fairly obvious ones:

- Numeric literals such as `42` or `1.234e12` need to be interpreted to be
  stored efficiently in binary. In C#, these operations are covered via
  methods such as `Int.Parse()`.

- Regular expressions help us find patterns in text, but what you
  need to realize is that regular expressions are essentially a separate,
  embedded domain-specific language (DSL). And naturally, before
  using them, they must be interpreted correctly.

- Any structured data, be it CSV, XML, JSON, or something more
  complicated, requires interpretation before it can be used.

- At the pinnacle of the application of Interpreter, we have fully fledged
  programming languages. After all, a compiler or interpreter for a
  language like C or Python must actually understand the language
  before compiling something executable.

© Dmitri Nesteruk 2022
D. Nesteruk, *Design Patterns in .NET 6*, https://doi.org/10.1007/978-1-4842-8245-8_17

Given the proliferation and diversity of challenges related to interpretation, we shall simply look at some examples. These serve to illustrate how one can build an interpreter: making one from scratch or using a specialized library or parser framework.

Integer Parsing

The parsing of numbers is the number one operation that gets redefined (optimized) by developers of algorithmic trading systems. The default implementations are very powerful and can handle many different number formats, but in real life the stock market typically feeds you data with a single uniform format (e.g., just positive integers), allowing the construction of much faster (orders of magnitude) parsers.

Consider a method such as uint.Parse(). This method is very powerful – not only can it parse the string "12345" but it can do the following:

- Perform validation, throwing an exception if the number doesn't parse.

- Parse numbers prefixed by zero (e.g., 007) or with a plus (e.g., +3).

- Parse numbers that have a decimal point (provided AllowDecimalPoint is set).

- Detect numbers greater than maximum or less than minimum, resulting in OverflowException.

A further complication is that uint.Parse() is a wrapper for an entire call chain that provides number styles or default NumberFormatInfo arguments, implements a try/catch for throwing overflow exceptions, and so on.

This is great, but if you know that the market price is coming in as a well-formatted positive integer within some specific range, you can write your own parsing method that will be several times faster. Here is a completely naïve implementation:

```
public uint ParseNaive(string s)
{
  uint result = 0;
  foreach (char c in s)
  {
    result *= 10;
```

```
    result += (uint)(c - '0');
  }
  return result;
}
```

On my machine, a comparison between uint.Parse() and the preceding ParseNaive() using BenchmarkDotNet gives the following result:

Method	Mean	Error	StdDev
UintParse	25.539 ns	0.3983 ns	0.8743 ns
ParseNaive	8.589 ns	0.2082 ns	0.2557 ns

This zero-effort method offers a threefold increase in performance, and a real-world integer parsing method used "in anger" in an algorithmic trading system gives subnanosecond performance, which implies a 25× performance improvement when compared with the BCL uint.Parse() call. Unfortunately, even with the SIMD support currently available in .NET, such operations are typically written in C++ using SIMD intrinsics (or directly in Assembler).[1]

Numeric Expression Evaluator

Let's imagine that we decide to parse *very* simple mathematical expressions such as 3+(5-4), that is, we'll restrict ourselves to addition, subtraction, and brackets. We want a program that can read such an expression and, of course, calculate the expression's final value.

We are going to build the calculator *by hand*, without resorting to any parsing framework. This should hopefully highlight *some* of the complexity involved in parsing textual input.

---

[1] It's also worth noting that when markets transmit textual information, they do not use Unicode, but prefer 1-byte-per-char encodings. In most cases that would be ASCII, whereas regional exchanges such as the Moscow Exchange (MOEX) are likely to use their respective 1-byte encodings (e.g., Windows-1251). This is an issue because .NET uses UTF-16, which is why quite often we define our own 1-byte str ASCII string type, a kind of bidirectional proxy to an ordinary string.

Lexing

The first step to interpreting an expression is called *lexing*, and it involves turning a sequence of characters into a sequence of *tokens*. A token is typically a primitive syntactic element, and we should end up with a flat sequence of these. In our case, a token can be

- An integer

- An operator (plus or minus)

- An opening or closing parenthesis

Thus, we can define the following structure:

```
public record Token(Token.Type MyType, string Text)
{
  public enum Type
  {
    Integer, Plus, Minus, Lparen, Rparen
  }

  public readonly Type MyType = MyType;
  public readonly string Text = Text;

  public override string ToString() => $"`{Text}`";
}
```

You'll note that Token is not an enum because, apart from the type, we also want to store the text that this token relates to, since it is not always predefined. (We could, alternatively, store some Range that would refer to the original string.)

So now, given a string containing an expression, we can define a lexing process that will turn a text into a List<Token>:

```
static List<Token> Lex(string input)
{
  var result = new List<Token>();

  for (int i = 0; i < input.Length; i++)
  {
```

```
switch (input[i])
{
  case '+':
    result.Add(new Token(Token.Type.Plus, "+"));
    break;
  case '-':
    result.Add(new Token(Token.Type.Minus, "-"));
    break;
  case '(':
    result.Add(new Token(Token.Type.Lparen, "("));
    break;
  case ')':
    result.Add(new Token(Token.Type.Rparen, ")"));
    break;
  default:
    // todo
  }
}

  return result;
}
```

Parsing predefined tokens is easy. In fact, we could have added them as a...

```
Dictionary<BinaryOperation.Type,  char>
```

...to simplify things. But parsing a number is not so easy. If we hit a 1, we should wait and see what the next character is. For this we define a separate routine:

```
var sb = new StringBuilder(input[i].ToString());
for (int j = i + 1; j < input.Length; ++j)
{
  if (char.IsDigit(input[j]))
  {
    sb.Append(input[j]);
    ++i;
  }
```

```
else
{
  result.Add(new Token(Token.Type.Integer, sb.ToString()));
  break;
}
}
```

Essentially, while we keep reading (pumping) digits, we add them to the buffer. When we're done, we make a Token out of the entire buffer and add it to the resulting list.

Parsing

The process of *parsing* turns a sequence of tokens into meaningful, typically object-oriented, structures. At the top, it's often useful to have an abstract class or interface that all elements of the tree implement:

```
public interface IElement
{
  int Value { get; }
}
```

The type's Value evaluates this element's numeric value. Next, we can create an element for storing integral values (such as 1, 5, or 42):

```
public class Integer : IElement
{
  public Integer(int value)
  {
    Value = value;
  }

  public int Value { get; }
}
```

If we don't have an Integer, we must have an operation such as addition or subtraction. In our case, all operations are *binary*, meaning they have two parts. For example, 2+3 in our model can be represented in pseudocode as BinaryOperation{Literal{2}, Literal{3}, addition}:

```
public class BinaryOperation : IElement
{
  public enum Type
  {
    Addition,
    Subtraction
  }

  public Type MyType;
  public IElement Left, Right;

  public int Value
  {
    get
    {
      switch (MyType)
      {
        case Type.Addition:
          return Left.Value + Right.Value;
        case Type.Subtraction:
          return Left.Value - Right.Value;
        default:
          throw new ArgumentOutOfRangeException();
      }
    }
  }
}
```

But anyways, on to the parsing process. All we need to do is turn a sequence of Tokens into a binary tree of IExpressions. From the outset, it can look as follows:

```
static IElement Parse(IReadOnlyList<Token> tokens)
{
  var result = new BinaryOperation();
  bool haveLHS = false;
  for (int i = 0; i < tokens.Count; i++)
  {
    var token = tokens[i];
```

```
  // look at the type of token
  switch (token.MyType)
  {
    // process each token in turn
  }
}
return result;
}
```

The only thing we need to discuss from the preceding code is the haveLHS variable. Remember, what we are trying to get is a tree, and at the *root* of that tree we expect a BinaryExpression, which, by definition, has left and right sides. But when we are on a number, how do we know if it's the left or right side of an expression? That's right. We don't, which is why we track this using haveLHS.

Now let's go through these case by case. First, integers – these map directly to our Integer construct, so all we have to do is turn text into a number. (Incidentally, we could have also done this at the lexing stage if we wanted to.)

```
case Token.Type.Integer:
  var integer = new Integer(int.Parse(token.Text));
  if (!haveLHS)
  {
    result.Left = integer;
    haveLHS = true;
  } else
  {
    result.Right = integer;
  }
  break;
```

The plus and minus tokens simply determine the type of the operation we're currently processing, so they're easy:

```
case Token.Type.Plus:
  result.MyType = BinaryOperation.Type.Addition;
  break;
```

```
case Token.Type.Minus:
  result.MyType = BinaryOperation.Type.Subtraction;
  break;
```

And then there's the left parenthesis. Yep, just the left. We don't detect the right one explicitly. Basically, the idea here is simple: find the closing right parenthesis (I'm ignoring nested brackets for now), rip out the entire subexpression, `Parse()` it recursively, and set as the left- or right-hand side of the expression we're currently working with:

```
case Token.Type.Lparen:
  int j = i;
  for (; j < tokens.Count; ++j)
    if (tokens[j].MyType == Token.Type.Rparen)
      break; // found it!
  // process subexpression w/o opening
  var subexpression = tokens.Skip(i+1).Take(j - i - 1).ToList();
  var element = Parse(subexpression);
  if (!haveLHS)
  {
    result.Left = element;
    haveLHS = true;
  } else result.Right = element;
  i = j; // advance
  break;
```

In a real-world scenario, you'd want a lot more safety features in here: not just handling nested parentheses (which I think is a must), but handling incorrect expressions where the closing parenthesis is missing. If it is indeed missing, how would you handle it? Throw an exception? Try to parse whatever's left and assume the closing is at the very end?

Something else? All of these issues are left as the exercise to you.

Using Lexer and Parser

With both Lex() and Parse() implemented, we can finally parse the expression and calculate its value:

```
var input = "(13+4)-(12+1)";
var tokens = Lex(input);
WriteLine(string.Join("\t", tokens));
// `(`    `13`    `+`    `4`    `)`    `-`    `(`    `12`    `+`    `1`    `)`

var parsed = Parse(tokens);
WriteLine($"{input} = {parsed.Value}");
// (13-4)-(12+1) = -4
```

Interpretation in the Functional Paradigm

If you look at a set of elements that are produced by either the lexing or the parsing process, you will quickly see that they are trivial structures that would map very neatly onto F#'s discriminated unions. This, in turn, allows us to subsequently use pattern matching when there comes a time to traverse a (recursive) discriminated union in order to transform it into something else.

Here's an example: suppose you are given a definition of a mathematical expression and you want to print or evaluate it.[2] Let's define the structure in XML so we don't have to go through a difficult parsing process:

```
<math>
  <plus>
    <value>2</value>
    <value>3</value>
  </plus>
</math>
```

---

[2] This is a small illustration of something that's a real-life commercial product called MathSharp – a tool that converts MathML notation to ready-to-compile code. See http://activemesa.net/mathsharp for more information.

We can create a recursive discriminated union to represent this structure:

```fsharp
type Expression =
  Math of Expression list
  | Plus of lhs:Expression * rhs:Expression
  | Value of value:string
```

There is a one-to-one correspondence between the XML elements and the corresponding Expression cases (e.g., <math> → Math). In order to instantiate cases, we would need to use reflection. One trick I adopt here is to precompute the case constructors using APIs from the Microsoft.FSharp.Reflection namespace:

```fsharp
let cases = FSharpType.GetUnionCases (typeof<Expression>)
            |> Array.map(fun f ->
              (f.Name,  FSharpValue.PreComputeUnionConstructor(f)))
            |> Map.ofArray
```

We can then write a function that constructs a union case given a name and a set of parameters:

```fsharp
let makeCase parameters =
  try
    let caseInfo = cases.Item name
    (caseInfo parameters) :?> Expression
  with
  | exp -> raise <| new Exception(String.Format(
    "Failed to create {0} : {1}", name, exp.Message))
```

In this listing, the name variable is captured implicitly, since the makeCase function is an inner function. But let's not jump ahead. What we're interested in is, of course, parsing and transforming some piece of XML. Here's how that process would begin:

```fsharp
use stringReader = new StringReader(text)
use xmlReader = XmlReader.Create(stringReader)
let doc = XDocument.Load(xmlReader)
let parsed = recursiveBuild doc.Root
```

So what is this `recursiveBuild` function? As the name suggests, it's a function that recursively turns an XML element into a case of our discriminated union. Here is the full listing:

```
let rec recursiveBuild (root:XElement) =
  let name = root.Name.LocalName |> makeCamelCase

  let makeCase parameters =
    // as before

  let elems = root.Elements() |> Seq.toArray
  let values = elems |> Array.map(fun f -> recursiveBuild f)
  if elems.Length = 0 then
    let rootValue = root.Value.Trim()
    makeCase [| box rootValue |]
  else
    try
      values |> Array.map box |> makeCase
    with
      | _ -> makeCase [| values |> Array.toList |]
```

Let's try to go slowly through what's going on here:

- Since our union cases are camel-cased and the XML file is lowercase, I convert the name of the XML element (which we call `root`) to camel case.

- We materialize the sequence of child elements of the current elements into an array.

- For each inner element, we call `recursiveBuild` recursively (surprise!).

- Now we check how many child elements the current element has. If it's zero, it could be just a `<value>` with text in it. If it's not, there are two possibilities:

  - The item takes a bunch of primitives that can all be boxed into parameters.

  - The item takes a bunch of expressions.

This constructs the expression tree. If we want to evaluate the numeric value of the expression, this is now simple, thanks to pattern matching:

```
let rec eval expr =
  match expr with
  | Math m -> eval m.Head
  | Plus (lhs, rhs) -> eval lhs + eval rhs
  | Value v -> v |> int
```

Similarly, you could define a function for printing an expression:

```
let rec print expr =
  match expr with
  | Math m -> print m.Head
  | Plus (lhs, rhs) -> String.Format("({0}+{1})", print lhs, print rhs)
  | Value v -> v
```

Putting it all together, we can now print the expression in human-readable form and evaluate its result:

```
let parsed = recursiveBuild doc.Root
printf "%s = %d" (print parsed) (eval parsed)
// (2+3) = 5
```

Both functions are, of course, crude implementations of the Visitor design pattern without any traditional OOP trappings (though they are, of course, present behind the scenes). Some things to note are

- Our Value case is of string. If we wanted it to store an integer or a floating-point number, our parsing code would have to pry this information away using trial and error.

- Instead of making top-level functions, we can give Expression its own methods and even properties. For example, we can give it a property called Val that evaluates its numeric value:

  ```
  type Expression =
    // union members here
    member self.Val =
      let rec eval expr =
  ```

```
match expr with
  | Math m -> eval(m.Head)
  | Plus (lhs, rhs) -> eval lhs + eval rhs
  | Value v -> v |> int
eval self
```

- Strictly speaking, discriminated unions violate the Open-Closed Principle since there is no way to augment them through inheritance. As a result, if you decide to support new cases, you'd have to modify the original union type.

To sum up, discriminated unions, pattern matching, and also list comprehensions (which we haven't used in our demo, but you'd typically use them in a scenario like this) all make the Interpreter and Visitor patterns easy to implement under the functional paradigm.

Transpiler

Transpilation is the process of translation of one programming language into another. This can be done in different ways, including proper compilation (transpilation = trans-compilation) or just the textual conversion from one language to another.

The reasons for doing this are numerous:

- Having a single language that can be represented on every platform (e.g., Haxe).

- Converting one language into another where the supported paradigms are different. For example, C# has a ready-made parser (Roslyn) but is unable to operate on GPUs. Thus, a transpiler from C# to CUDA C makes sense.

- Converting languages as part of legacy code migration/rewrite.

In the context of .NET, it is perhaps best to reduce our discussion to the C# programming language, since we have Roslyn as a ready-made toolkit for parsing and emitting C#. While emitting C# is probably outside the bounds of this discussion (unless we're talking code generation), converting C# to some other language is something we can discuss in the context of Roslyn.

The first thing we do if we want to parse C# is to turn it into an abstract syntax tree (AST). With Roslyn, this is rather simple:

```
var tree = CSharpSyntaxTree.ParseText(sourceCode);
```

The trouble with an AST is that, by itself, it's often useless. It tells us the structure of the code, but doesn't tell us how that code behaves. For example, if I encounter a function call to Foo(), I cannot say *where* Foo() is or what its signature is.

What you're after is a *semantic model*. To get a semantic model, you need to compile a project that includes both the syntax tree you've just parsed and any required references. The following listing compiles an in-memory DLL:

```
var compilation = CSharpCompilation.Create("whatever")
  .WithOptions(new CSharpCompilationOptions(OutputKind.
  DynamicallyLinkedLibrary))
  .WithReferences(MetadataReference.CreateFromFile(typeof (Int32).Assembly.
  Location))
  .AddSyntaxTrees(tree);
```

Once compilation is done, we get the model:

```
var model = compilation.GetSemanticModel(tree, true);
```

We can now walk the model we've built using a visitor (see the Visitor pattern later in the book). In the case of C# syntax, the type we're after is CSharpSyntaxWalker. This type is very neatly designed: it has dozens of overridable methods for visiting every type of node that the C# syntax has. For example, if we want to process a using directive, we choose an override in our derived class:

```
public override void VisitUsingDirective(UsingDirectiveSyntax node)
{
  ...
}
```

Inside each VisitXxx() method, you can examine the node and perform various actions, such as building your own translation in a StringBuilder-like member. Now, it's important to understand that once you override something, this replaces the default behavior of the walker. By default, the walker traverses source code in a "natural" way: inside a class declaration, it will traverse members; inside method declarations, it will traverse statements. Notice that the default traversal is a no-op, because it relies entirely on your overrides to do actual work. Therefore, you will be calling a lot of `base.VisitXxx()` methods to ensure all the elements are covered appropriately.

The typical use of a syntax walker is as follows: we inherit from `CSharpSyntaxWalker` and pass in the constructor anything that the walker needs to do its work. At the very least, you want to pass in the `Compilation` and the `SemanticModel`, as well as any service data you might need. And then, once you've made your walker, you simply call `walker.Visit(tree.GetRoot())` to process your entire AST.

For a complete example of how to use Roslyn to convert C# into another language, take a look at Blackmire,[3] which is a demo project for converting C# to C++.

Summary

First, it needs to be said that, comparatively speaking, the Interpreter design pattern is somewhat uncommon – the challenges of building parsers are today considered inessential, which is why we see the topic being removed from Computer Science courses in many universities. So, unless you plan to work in language design or, say, making tools for static code analysis, you are unlikely to find the skills in building parsers in high demand.

One particular domain where interpreters do come in handy is in the so-called ETL (Extract, Transform, and Load) tasks. An ETL operation typically extracts data from one source, transforms that data, and then loads it into a different container. For example, a program might download an XML from a predefined location, parse it, extract the necessary bits, change them, and put them into a database.

ETL tasks are not always done by hand. These tasks can be handled by

- Mapping libraries such as AutoMapper that map objects onto one another

- Dedicated software such as Altova MapForce for visual editing of data mapping rules

- Heavyweight data integration suites such as Microsoft BizTalk that handle a multitude of different formats and rules

---

[3] `http://github.com/activemesa/blackmire`

That said, the challenge of interpretation is a whole separate field of Computer Science that a single chapter of a design patterns book cannot reasonably do justice to. If you are interested in the subject, I recommend you check out frameworks such as Lex/Yacc, ANTLR, and many others that are specifically geared for lexer/parser construction. I can also recommend writing static analysis plugins for popular IDEs – this is a great way to get a feel for how real ASTs look, how they are traversed and modified.

CHAPTER 18

Iterator

An iterator, put simply, is an object that is used to traverse some structure or another. Typically, the iterator references the currently accessed element and has a method to move forward. A bidirectional iterator also lets you walk backward, and a random-access iterator allows you to access an element at an arbitrary position.

In .NET, that thing that enables an iterator typically implements the `IEnumerator<T>` interface. It has the following members:

- `Current` refers to the element at the current position.

- `MoveNext()` lets you move on to the next element of the collection and returns `true` if we succeeded and `false` otherwise.

- `Reset()` sets the enumerator to the initial position.

The enumerator is also disposable, but we don't care about that too much. The point is any time you write...

```
foreach (x in y)
  Console.WriteLine(x);
```

...what you're really doing is the equivalent of

```
var enumerator = ((IEnumerable<Foo>)y).GetEnumerator();
while (enumerator.MoveNext())
{
  temp = enumerator.Current;
  Console.WriteLine(temp);
}
```

In other words, a class that implements `IEnumerable<T>` is required to have a method called `GetEnumerator()` that returns an `IEnumerator<T>`. And you use that enumerator to traverse the object.

© Dmitri Nesteruk 2022
D. Nesteruk, *Design Patterns in .NET 6*, https://doi.org/10.1007/978-1-4842-8245-8_18

Needless to say, it is very rare for you to have to make your own IEnumerator. Typically, you can write code such as...

```
IEnumerable<int> GetSomeNumbers()
{
  yield return 1;
  yield return 2;
  yield return 3;
}
```

...and the rest of the operations will be taken care of by the compiler. Alternatively, you can just use an existing collection class (array, List<T>, etc.), which already has all the plumbing you need.

In addition to IEnumerable, .NET also comes with an IAsyncEnumerable, which is a way of letting the client iterate over an IEnumerable but in an asynchronous way. We won't focus on it in this book.

Array-Backed Properties

Not all things are easy to iterate. For example, you cannot iterate all fields in a class unless you're using reflection. But sometimes you need to. Here, let me show you a scenario.

Suppose you're making a game with creatures in it. These creatures have various attributes, such as strength, agility, and intelligence. You could implement them as

```
public class Creature
{
  public int Strength { get; set; }
  public int Agility { get; set; }
  public int Intelligence { get; set; }
}
```

But now you also want to output some aggregate statistics about the creature. For example, you decide to calculate the sum of all its abilities:

```
public double SumOfStats => Strength + Agility + Intelligence;
```

This code is impossible to automatically refactor if you add an additional `Wisdom` property (ooh, is that too much D&D nerdiness for you?), but let me show you something that's even worse. If you want the average of all the abilities, you would write

```
public double AverageStat => SumOfStats / 3.0;
```

Whoa there! That 3.0 is a bona fide *magic number*, completely unsafe if the structure of the code changes. Let me show you yet another example of ugliness. Suppose you decide to calculate the maximum ability value of a creature. You'd need to write something like

```
public double MaxStat => Math.Max(
  Math.Max(Strength, Agility), Intelligence);
```

Well, you get the idea. This code is not robust and will break on any small change, so we're going to fix it, and the implementation is going to make use of *array-backed properties*.

The idea of array-backed properties is simple – all the backing fields of related properties exist in one array:

```
private int [] stats = new int[3];
```

Each of the properties then projects its getter and setter into the array. To avoid using integral indices, you can introduce private constants:

```
private const int strength = 0;
public ref int Strength => ref stats[strength];
// same for other properties
```

And now, of course, calculating the sum/average/maximum statistics is really easy because the underlying field is an array, and arrays are supported in LINQ:

```
public double AverageStat => stats.Average();
public double SumOfStats => stats.Sum();
public double MaxStat => stats.Max();
```

If you want to add an extra property, all you need to do is

- Extend the array by one element.
- Create a property with a getter and setter.

And that's it! The stats will still be calculated correctly. Furthermore, if you want, you can eschew all of those methods we made in favor of...

```
public IEnumerable<int> Stats => stats;
```

...and just let the client perform their own LINQ queries directly, for example, creature.Stats.Average().

Finally, if you want stats to be the enumerable collection, that is, letting people write foreach (var stat in creature), you can simply implement IEnumerable (and perhaps an indexer too):

```
public class Creature : IEnumerable<int>
{
  // as before

  public IEnumerator<int> GetEnumerator()
    => stats.AsEnumerable().GetEnumerator();

  IEnumerator IEnumerable.GetEnumerator()
    => GetEnumerator();

  public ref int this[int index] => ref stats[index];
}
```

This approach is functional, but there are plenty of downsides. One of those downsides has to do with change notifications. For example, suppose that your UI application binds a UI element to the SumOfStats property. You change Strength, but how would SumOfStats let you know that it did, in fact, change too? If SumOfStats was defined as a basic sum of different properties, we could have treated that summation as an expression tree, parsed it, and extracted the dependencies. But because we're using LINQ, this is now impossible or, at the very least, very difficult. We could attempt to supply some special metadata to indicate that some properties are array-backed and then read this metadata when determining dependencies, but as you can guess, this has both computational and cognitive costs.

The biggest issue with this approach is the amount of typing that's required in order to get this to work. All I can suggest here is, rather than attempting to fiddle with attribute-based decorations and either source generators or IL weaving, consider simply defining your entities externally – in XML, T4, or something similar. This allows for ultimate flexibility in defining whatever adornments you want for your entities, whether it's change notification, validation, implementation of array-backed properties, or any other aspect of a myriad of things entities might need to incorporate.

Let's Make an Iterator

In order to appreciate just how ugly iterators can get if you do decide to make them directly, we are going to implement a classic Comp Sci example – tree traversal. Let's begin by defining a single node of a binary tree:

```
public class Node<T>
{
  public T Value;
  public Node<T> Left, Right, Parent;

  public Node(T value)
  {
    Value = value;
  }

  public Node(T value, Node<T> left, Node<T> right)
  {
    Value = value;
    Left = left;
    Right = right;

    left.Parent = right.Parent = this;
  }
}
```

I've thrown in an additional constructor that initializes its node with both left and right child nodes. This allows us to define a tree using chained constructors such as

```
//     1
//    / \
//   2   3
var root = new Node<int>(1,
  new Node<int>(2), new Node<int>(3));
```

Okay, so now we want to traverse the tree. If you remember your Data Structures and Algorithms courses, you'll know that there are (at least) three ways: in-order, preorder, and postorder. Suppose we decide to define an InOrderIterator. Here's what it would look like:

```
public class InOrderIterator<T>
{
  public Node<T> Current { get; set; }
  private readonly Node<T> root;
  private bool yieldedStart;

  public InOrderIterator(Node<T> root)
  {
    this.root = Current = root;
    while (Current.Left != null)
      Current = Current.Left;
  }

  public bool MoveNext()
  {
    // todo
  }
}
```

Not bad so far: just as if we were implementing IEnumerator<T>, we have a property called Current and a MoveNext() method. But here's the thing: since the iterator is stateful, every invocation of MoveNext() has to take us to the next element in our current traversal scheme. This isn't as easy as it sounds:

```
public bool MoveNext()
{
  if (!yieldedStart)
  {
    yieldedStart = true;
    return true;
  }
```

```
  if (Current.Right != null)
  {
    Current = Current.Right;
    while (Current.Left != null)
      Current = Current.Left;
    return true;
  }
  else
  {
    var p = Current.Parent;
    while (p != null && Current == p.Right)
    {
      Current = p;
      p = p.Parent;
    }
    Current = p;
    return Current != null;
  }
}
```

Whoa there! Bet you didn't expect this! Well, this is exactly what you get if you implement your own iterators directly: an unreadable mess. But it works! We can use the iterator directly, C++ style:

```
var it = new InOrderIterator<int>(root);
while (it.MoveNext())
{
  Write(it.Current.Value);
  Write(',');
}
WriteLine();
// prints 213
```

Or, if we want, we can construct a dedicated `BinaryTree` class that exposes this in-order iterator as a default one:

```
public class BinaryTree<T>
{
  private Node<T> root;

  public BinaryTree(Node<T> root)
  {
    this.root = root;
  }

  public InOrderIterator<T> GetEnumerator()
  {
    return new InOrderIterator<T>(root);
  }
}
```

Notice we don't even have to implement IEnumerable (thanks to duck typing[1]). We can now write

```
var root = new Node<int>(1,
  new Node<int>(2), new Node<int>(3));
var tree = new BinaryTree<int>(root);
foreach (var node in tree)
  WriteLine(node.Value); // 2 1 3
```

Improved Iteration

Our implementation of in-order iteration is virtually unreadable and is nothing like what you read in textbooks. Why? Lack of recursion. After all, MoveNext() cannot preserve its state, so every time it gets invoked, it starts from scratch without remembering its

---

[1] *Duck typing* is the idea that "if it walks like a duck and it quacks like a duck, it is a duck." In programming parlance, duck typing implies that the right code will be used even when it doesn't implement any particular interface to identify it. In our case, the foreach keyword doesn't care in the least whether your type implements IEnumerable or not – all it's looking for is the implementation of GetEnumerator() in the iterated class. If it finds it, everything works.

context: it only remembers the previous element, which needs to be found before we find the next one in the iteration scheme we're using.

And this is why yield return exists: you can construct a state machine behind the scenes. This means that if I wanted to create a more natural in-order implementation, I could simply write it as

```csharp
public IEnumerable<Node<T>> NaturalInOrder
{
  get
  {
    IEnumerable<Node<T>> TraverseInOrder(Node<T> current)
    {
      if (current.Left != null)
      {
        foreach (var left in TraverseInOrder(current.Left))
          yield return left;
      }
      yield return current;
      if (current.Right != null)
      {
        foreach (var right in TraverseInOrder(current.Right))
          yield return right;
      }
    }
    foreach (var node in TraverseInOrder(root))
      yield return node;
  }
}
```

Notice that all the calls here are recursive. Now what we can do is use this directly, for example:

```csharp
var root = new Node<int>(1,
  new Node<int>(2), new Node<int>(3));
var tree = new BinaryTree<int>(root);
WriteLine(string.Join(",", tree.NaturalInOrder.Select(x => x.Value)));
// 2,1,3
```

Woo-hoo! This is way better. The algorithm itself is readable, and once again, we can take the property and just do LINQ on it, no problem.

Iterator Specifics

The state machine generated behind the scenes by foreach results in a strictly forward-only iterator, which may not necessarily be what you want. Close by, in C++ land, there is a hierarchy of sorts, which consists, among other things, of the following:

- *Forward iterator*, which only moves from the start of the collection to the end. A typical example of a collection that would only support a forward-only iterator is a singly linked list, which cannot be traversed easily in any other way.

- *Bidirectional iterator*, which allows iteration both forward and backward. A typical structure that supports this is a doubly linked list (e.g., C#'s LinkedList<T>).

- *Random-access iterator*, an iterator that allows lookup of an arbitrary position in the collection. This would also allow backward and forward iteration, but also lets you jump into an arbitrary (possibly nonexistent) location within, for example, a List<T>.

These more advanced forms of iteration are supported by frameworks such as LINQ. For example, LINQ defines both a Reverse() method for reverse iteration and an ElementAt() for random access. Curiously enough, an attempt is made to provide these operations in a universal manner, meaning that ElementAt() is available on all underlying collections, even collections such as a linked list for which random-access iteration, while possible, is not computationally cheap.

The implementation of LINQ has also run afoul of some natural interface restrictions, which in turn has driven the creation of default interface methods. For example, a LINQ method for ElementAt() may have a default implementation that simply does MoveNext N times from the start of a collection. LINQ does, however, provide optimizations, so that calling ElementAt() on an array or an IList<T> results in much faster code. This implementation only works faster because, at some point, the LINQ method tries to cast the underlying IEnumerable<T> to an IList<T> and return myList[N] if the cast succeeds.

But imagine a situation where a new interface – say, IReadOnlyList<T> – has been created. This is a different interface that we do not check for. We could go directly into the BCL sources (specifically, Enumerable.cs) and fix ElementAt(), adding yet another type check, but it obviously breaks the OCP and also doesn't scale very well: imagine if we have more and more special interfaces in the future that need to be optimized.

This is where default interface members come in: we can give the ElementAt() random-access behavior to IReadOnlyList<T>. This way, the original LINQ implementation is untouched, yet if we statically know that we are working with this exact interface, we can ensure that it gets processed in a faster way, by adding the code right to the interface. It is, naturally, a half-measure: since this method and the original one are unrelated (they are both just extension methods), as soon as you cast the reference to an IEnumerable<T>, all the magic disappears.

Iterator Adapter

Quite often you want an object to be iterable in some special way. For example, suppose you want to calculate the sum of all elements in a matrix – LINQ doesn't provide a Sum() method over a rectangular array, so what you can do is build an adapter such as

```csharp
public class OneDAdapter<T> : IEnumerable<T>
{
  private readonly T[,] arr;
  private int w, h;

  public OneDAdapter(T[,] arr)
  {
    this.arr = arr;
    w = arr.GetLength(0);
    h = arr.GetLength(1);
  }

  public IEnumerator<T> GetEnumerator()
  {
    for (int y = 0; y < h; ++y)
    for (int x = 0; x < w; ++x)
      yield return arr[x, y];
  }
```

```
IEnumerator  IEnumerable.GetEnumerator()
{
  return GetEnumerator();
}
}
```

This adapter could then be used whenever you want to iterate a 2D array in 1D manner. It could be improved further by having the function `yield return ref` the values, but sadly this is not possible.

Having implemented the adapter, calculation of the sum of all elements in a 2D rectangular array is now as simple as

```
var data = new [,] { { 1, 2 }, { 3, 4 } };
var sum = new OneDAdapter<int>(data).Sum(); // 10
```

Of course, we're still stuck with C#'s inability to derive type arguments in constructors, so perhaps a factory method could be useful here.

Here's another example – this one supports reverse iteration of a 1D array:

```
public class ReverseIterable<T> : IEnumerable<T>
{
  private readonly T[] arr;

  public ReverseIterable(T[] arr) => this.arr = arr;
  public IEnumerator<T> GetEnumerator()
  {
    for (int i = arr.Length - 1; i >= 0; --i)
      yield return arr[i];
  }

  IEnumerator  IEnumerable.GetEnumerator()
  {
    return GetEnumerator();
  }
}
```

Again, if you don't want to specify the type parameter explicitly, you'd have to create another, nongeneric `ReverseIterable` class and provide a factory method:

```
public static class ReverseIterable
{
  public static ReverseIterable<T> From<T>(T[] arr)
  {
    return new ReverseIterable<T>(arr);
  }
}
```

Of course, as we've discussed countless times before, this implies that the constructor is made public, and the only way to make it private is to make the factory a nested class of the iterator adapter.

Composite Iteration

We are now going to solve a real-world programming problem that has to do with access and iteration of nested objects.

Picture a simple scenario in the Building Information Modeling (BIM) space: a building that has floors and a floor that has rooms. Assuming the existence of classes (in pseudocode) Building{Floors}, Floor{Rooms}, and Room, what exactly can we determine, given a particular object?

- Given a Building, we can get its Floors. To get every single room, we would probably use LINQ's SelectMany().

- Given a Floor, we can iterate its Rooms, but we cannot reliably (by default) determine the building this floor is in.

- Given a Room, we cannot determine what floor it's on, nor the building it's in, without making special accommodations for this.

These missing requirements that we cannot yet do are very common. If you look at an API of an application such as Microsoft Excel, you often see that "everything refers to everything else." In other words, a worksheet cell in an Excel spreadsheet may have a reference not just to the containing worksheet but also the containing document.

It is entirely possible to implement all of this functionality by hand. However, a lot of it would take quite a bit of time to do, which is unnecessary, considering that a lot of the code is trivial. So let's instead consider how we would go about automating this process using source generators.

The `Building` is an obvious starting point:

```
public partial class Building
{
  public string Name;
  public List<Floor> Floors = new();
}
```

A `Floor`, on the other hand, needs to refer to the containing `Building`, so we can initially define it as

```
public partial class Floor
{
  public int Index;
  public List<Room> Rooms = new();
  public Building Building;
}
```

Now, onto source generators. The first thing a source generator can determine (by using Roslyn to analyze the class) is that a `Building` is made up of several `Floors`. It can therefore synthesize a partial `Building` class containing

```
public Building AddFloor(Floor floor)
{
  floor.Building = this;
  floors.Add(floor);
  return this;
}
```

This ensures that, when adding a floor, the `Building` reference is set correctly. A similarly synthesized `AddRoom()` method can be given to `Floor`, and additional methods (e.g., `Remove()`) can be synthesized in a similar fashion to avoid potential dangling references.

But that's not all! There are two more things we want to do. One of them is related to iteration (we're discussing the Iterator pattern, after all), and another has to do with finding parent references. Both of these features rely on the source analyzer knowing that a `Building` contains `Floors`, which contain `Rooms` – this is not difficult to implement with Roslyn, since we have all the building blocks already.

Thus, with this knowledge, `Building` would get an additional member that lets you iterate all the rooms (this is effectively a composite iterator):

```
public IEnumerable<Room> Rooms => Floors.SelectMany(f => f.Rooms);
```

With this member synthesized, we can now write `foreach (var room in building.Rooms)` and go through every single room. Naturally, this relies on a public member called `Rooms`, which is in contrast with our member `rooms`. How you choose to synthesize the public member is up to you. The most natural choice would be an `IReadOnlyList<>`.

The only thing that remains is backward references, that is, how a room can tell what building it's in. Sure, you can write `room.Floor.Building`, but if you want to avoid the extra work, you can give `Room` a synthesized member such as...

```
public Building Building => Floor.Building;
```

...and then write `room.Building` instead.

The examples presented here can be automatically synthesized to arbitrary depth. They can also be enhanced so that, for example, we also get all sorts of useful constructor overloads, unpacked methods (e.g., an `AddFloor()` that takes `Floor` constructor arguments rather than a preconstructed object), and so on.

Summary

The Iterator design pattern has been deliberately hidden in C# in favor of the simple `IEnumerator`/`IEnumerable` duopoly upon which everything is built. Notice that these interfaces only support forward iteration – there is no `MoveBack()` in `IEnumerator`. The existence of `yield` allows you to very quickly return elements as a collection that can be consumed by someone else while being blissfully unaware of the state machine that gets built behind the scenes.

CHAPTER 19

Mediator

A large proportion of the code we write has different components (classes) communicating with one another through direct references. However, there are situations where you don't want objects to be aware of each other's presence. Or perhaps you *do* want them to be aware of one another, but you still don't want them to communicate through references, because as soon as you keep and hold a reference to an object, you extend that object's lifetime beyond what might originally be desired (unless you use a WeakReference, of course).

So the mediator is a mechanism for facilitating communication between the components. Naturally, the mediator itself needs to be accessible to every component taking part, which means it should either be a publicly available static variable or, alternatively, just a reference that gets injected into every component.

Chat Room

Your typical Internet chat room is the classic example of the Mediator design pattern, so let's implement this before we move on to the more complicated stuff.

The most trivial implementation of a participant in a chat room can be as simple as

```
public class Person
{
  public string Name;
  public ChatRoom Room;
  private List<string> chatLog = new List<string>();

  public Person(string name) => Name = name;
```

© Dmitri Nesteruk 2022
D. Nesteruk, *Design Patterns in .NET 6*, https://doi.org/10.1007/978-1-4842-8245-8_19

```csharp
public void Receive(string sender, string message)
{
  string s = $"{sender}: '{message}'";
  WriteLine($"[{Name}'s chat session] {s}");
  chatLog.Add(s);
}

public void Say(string message) => Room.Broadcast(Name, message);

public void PrivateMessage(string who, string message)
{
  Room.Message(Name, who, message);
}
}
```

So we've got a person with a Name (user id), a chat log, and a reference to the actual ChatRoom. We have a constructor and then three methods:

- Receive() allows us to receive a message. Typically what this function would do is show the message on the user's screen and also add it to the chat log.

- Say() allows the person to broadcast a message to everyone in the room.

- PrivateMessage() is private messaging functionality. You need to specify the name of the person the message is intended for.

Both Say() and PrivateMessage()[1] just relay operations to the chat room. Speaking of which, let's actually implement ChatRoom – it's not particularly complicated:

```csharp
public class ChatRoom
{
  private List<Person> people = new();

  public void Broadcast(string source, string message) { ... }
  public void Join(Person p) { ... }
```

---

[1] In the real world, I would probably call the method PM(), considering how commonplace that acronym has become.

```
  public void Message(string source, string destination,
    string message) { ... }
}
```

So I have decided to go with pointers here. The ChatRoom API is very simple:

- Join() gets a person to join the room. We are not going to implement Leave(), instead deferring the idea to a subsequent example in this chapter.

- Broadcast() sends the message to everyone…well, not quite everyone: we don't need to send the message back to the person who sent it.

- Message() sends a private message.

The implementation of Join() is as follows:

```
public void Join(Person p)
{
  string joinMsg = $"{p.Name} joins the chat";
  Broadcast("room", joinMsg);

  p.Room = this;
  people.Add(p);
}
```

Just like a classic IRC chat room, we broadcast the message that someone has joined to everyone in the room. The first argument of Broadcast(), the origin parameter, in this case, is specified as "room" rather than the person who's joined. We then set the person's room reference and add them to the list of people in the room.

Now, let's look at Broadcast(): this is where a message is sent to every room participant. Remember, each participant has its own Person.Receive() method for processing the message, so the implementation is somewhat trivial:

```
public void Broadcast(string source, string message)
{
  foreach (var p in people)
    if (p.Name != source)
      p.Receive(source, message);
}
```

Whether or not we want to prevent a broadcast message to be relayed to ourselves is a point of debate, but I'm actively avoiding it here. Everyone else gets the message, though.

Finally, here's private messaging implemented with `Message()`:

```csharp
public void Message(string source, string destination, string message)
{
  people.FirstOrDefault(p => p.Name == destination)
    ?.Receive(source, message);
}
```

This searches for the recipient in the list of `people` and, if the recipient is found (because who knows, they could have left the room), dispatches the message to that person.

Coming back to `Person`'s implementations of `Say()` and `PrivateMessage()`, here they are:

```csharp
public void Say(string message) => Room.Broadcast(Name, message);

public void PrivateMessage(string who, string message)
{
  Room.Message(Name, who, message);
}
```

As for `Receive()`, well, this is a good place to actually display the message on-screen as well as add it to the chat log:

```csharp
public void Receive(string sender, string message)
{
  string s = $"{sender}: '{message}'";
  WriteLine($"[{Name}'s chat session] {s}");
  chatLog.Add(s);
}
```

We go the extra mile here by displaying not just whom the message came from but whose chat session we're currently in – this will be useful for diagnosing who said what and when.

Here's the scenario that we'll run through:

```
var room = new ChatRoom();

var john = new Person("John");
var jane = new Person("Jane");

room.Join(john);
room.Join(jane);

john.Say("hi room");
jane.Say("oh, hey john");

var simon = new Person("Simon");
room.Join(simon);
simon.Say("hi everyone!");

jane.PrivateMessage("Simon", "glad you could join us!");
```

Here is the output:

```
[john's chat session] room: "jane joins the chat"
[jane's chat session] john: "hi room"
[john's chat session] jane: "oh, hey john"
[john's chat session] room: "simon joins the chat"
[jane's chat session] room: "simon joins the chat"
[john's chat session] simon: "hi everyone!"
[jane's chat session] simon: "hi everyone!"
[simon's chat session] jane: "glad you could join us, simon"
```

Figure 19-1 an illustration of the chat room operations.

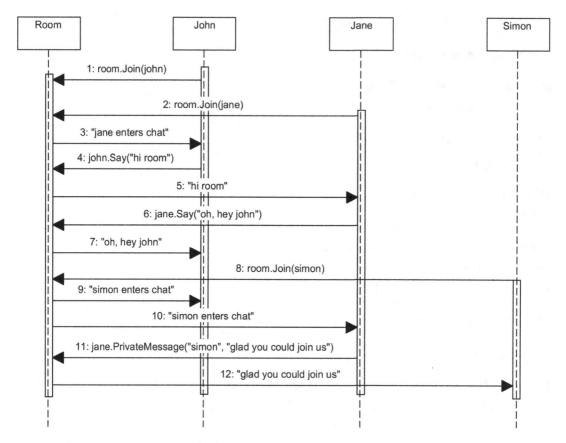

Figure 19-1. *Chat room operations*

Mediator with Events

In the chat room example, we've encountered a consistent theme: the participants need notification whenever someone posts a message. This seems like a perfect scenario for the Observer pattern, which is discussed later in the book: the idea of the mediator having an event that is shared by all participants – participants can then subscribe to the event to receive notifications, and they can also cause the event to fire, thus triggering said notifications.

Instead of redoing the chat room once again, let's go for a simpler example: imagine a game of football (soccer for my readers in the USA) with players and a football coach. When the coach sees their team scoring, they naturally want to congratulate the player. Of course, they need some information about the event, like *who* scored the goal and how many goals they have scored so far.

We can introduce a base class for any sort of event data:

```
abstract class GameEventArgs : EventArgs
{
  public abstract void Print();
}
```

I've added the Print() method deliberately to print the event's contents to the command line. Now, we can derive from this class in order to store some goal-related data:

```
class PlayerScoredEventArgs : GameEventArgs
{
  public string PlayerName;
  public int GoalsScoredSoFar;

  public PlayerScoredEventArgs
    (string playerName, int goalsScoredSoFar)
  {
    PlayerName = playerName;
    GoalsScoredSoFar = goalsScoredSoFar;
  }

  public override void Print()
  {
    WriteLine($"{PlayerName} has scored! " +
              $"(their {GoalsScoredSoFar} goal)");
  }
}
```

We are once again going to build a mediator, but it will have *no* behaviors! Seriously, with an event-driven infrastructure, they are no longer needed:

```
class Game
{
  public event EventHandler<GameEventArgs> Events;

  public void Fire(GameEventArgs args)
  {
```

```
    Events?.Invoke(this, args);
  }
}
```

As you can see, we've just made a central place where all game events are being generated. The generation itself is polymorphic: the event uses a GameEventArgs type, and you can test the argument against the various types available in your application. The Fire() utility method just helps us safely raise the event.

We can now construct the Player class. A player has a name, the number of goals they scored during the match, and a reference to the mediator Game, of course:

```
class Player
{
  private string name;
  private int goalsScored = 0;
  private Game game;

  public Player(Game game, string name)
  {
    this.name = name;
    this.game = game;
  }

  public void Score()
  {
    goalsScored++;
    var args = new PlayerScoredEventArgs(name, goalsScored);
    game.Fire(args);
  }
}
```

The Player.Score() method is where we make PlayerScoredEventArgs and post them for all subscribers to see. Who gets this event? Why, a Coach, of course:

```
class Coach
{
  private Game game;
```

```
  public Coach(Game game)
  {
    this.game = game;

    // celebrate if player has scored <3 goals
    game.Events += (sender, args) =>
    {
      if (args is PlayerScoredEventArgs scored
        && scored.GoalsScoredSoFar < 3)
      {
        WriteLine($"coach says: well done, {scored.PlayerName}");
      }
    };
  }
}
```

The implementation of the Coach class is trivial; our coach doesn't even get a name. But we do give them a constructor where a subscription is created to the game's Events such that, whenever something happens, the coach gets to process the event data in the provided lambda.

Notice that the argument type of the lambda is GameEventArgs – we don't know if a player has scored or has been sent off, so we need a cast to determine we've got the right type.

The interesting thing is that all the magic happens at the setup stage: there's no need to explicitly subscribe to particular events. The client is free to create objects using their constructors, and then when the player scores, the notifications are sent:

```
var game = new Game();
var player = new Player(game, "Sam");
var coach = new Coach(game);

player.Score(); // coach says: well done, Sam
player.Score(); // coach says: well done, Sam
player.Score();
```

The output is only two lines long because, on the third goal, the coach isn't impressed anymore.

Introduction to MediatR

MediatR is one of a number of libraries written to provide a shrink-wrapped Mediator implementation in .NET.[2] It provides the client a central `Mediator` component, as well as interfaces for requests and request handlers. It supports both synchronous and async/await paradigms and provides support for both directed messages and broadcasting.

MediatR is designed to work with an IoC container. It comes with examples for how to get it running with most popular containers out there; I'll be using Autofac for my examples.

The first steps are general: we simply set up MediatR under our IoC container and also register our own types through the interfaces they implement:

```
var builder = new ContainerBuilder();
builder.RegisterType<Mediator>()
  .As<IMediator>()
  .InstancePerLifetimeScope(); // singleton

builder.Register<ServiceFactory>(context =>
{
  var c = context.Resolve<IComponentContext>();
  return t => c.Resolve(t);
});

builder.RegisterAssemblyTypes(typeof(Demo).Assembly)
  .AsImplementedInterfaces();
```

The central `Mediator`, which we registered as a singleton, is in charge of routing requests to request handlers and getting responses from them. Each request is expected to implement the `IRequest<T>` interface, where `T` is the type of the response that is expected for this request. If there is no data to return, you can use a nongeneric `IRequest` instead.

Here's a simple example:

```
public class PingCommand : IRequest<PongResponse> {}
```

---

[2] MediatR is available on NuGet; source code can be found at `https://github.com/jbogard/MediatR`

So in our trivial demo, we intend to send a `PingCommand` and receive a `PongResponse`. The response doesn't have to implement any interface; we'll define it like this:

```
public record struct PongResponse(DateTime Timestamp);
```

The glue that connects requests and responses together is MediatR's `IRequestHandler` interface. It has a single member called `Handle` that takes a request and a cancellation token and returns the result of the call:

```
[UsedImplicitly]
public class PingCommandHandler
  : IRequestHandler<PingCommand, PongResponse>
{
  public async Task<PongResponse> Handle(PingCommand request,
    CancellationToken  cancellationToken)
 {
    return await Task
      .FromResult(new  PongResponse(DateTime.UtcNow))
      .ConfigureAwait(false);
  }
}
```

Note the use of the async/await paradigm, with the `Handle` method returning a `Task<T>`. If you don't need your request to produce a response, then, instead of using an `IRequestHandler`, you can use the `AsyncRequestHandler` base class, whose `Handle()` method returns a humble nongeneric `Task`. Oh, and in case your request is synchronous, you can inherit from the `RequestHandler<TRequest, TResponse>` class instead.

This is all that you need to do to actually set up two components and get them talking through a central mediator. Note that the mediator itself does not feature in any of the classes we've created: it works behind the scenes.

Putting everything together, we can use our setup as follows:

```
var container = builder.Build();
var mediator = container.Resolve<IMediator>();
var response = await mediator.Send(new PingCommand());
Console.WriteLine($"We got a pong at {response.Timestamp}");
```

You'll notice that request/response messages are targeted: they are dispatched to a single handler. MediatR also supports notification messages, which can be dispatched to multiple handlers. In this case, your request needs to implement the INotification interface:

```
public class Ping : INotification {}
```

And now you can create any number of INotification<Ping> classes that get to process these notifications:

```
public class Pong : INotificationHandler<Ping>
{
  public Task Handle(Ping notification,
                   CancellationToken  cancellationToken)
  {
    Console.WriteLine("Got a ping");
    return Task.CompletedTask;
  }
}
public class AlsoPong : INotificationHandler<Ping> { ... }
```

For notifications, instead of using the Send() method, we use the Publish() method:

```
await mediator.Publish(new Ping());
```

There is more information about MediatR available on its official Wiki page.

Service Bus as Mediator

All of our discussions of Mediator have centered on in-process implementations: as one component generates some sort of event, another component in the same process gets to process it. This isn't quite how it works in the real world. For example, in a chat room, the chat room participants reside on different corners of the world, whereas the chat room itself is hosted on some central server. The participants send messages and receive replies over the wire.

In practice, what you have is a form of bidirectional communication that leverages much more functionality than the programming language alone provides. In the case of general-purpose textual communication on the Internet, for example, you could use SignalR, which would, in turn, leverage one of the underlying web-based mechanisms (WebSockets, server-sent events, long polling) for performing remote procedure calls from a server to its clients.

In the case of a corporate message exchange system, a mediator would leverage whatever underlying technology is used to send messages: something like Microsoft Message Queuing (MSMQ), Azure Service Bus, or something similar.

As soon as these forms of communication become asynchronous, we end up encountering yet another problem: how do we know that a message has been delivered? In our synchronous call example, we could have certainty, but in a setup where you fire off a message, you need a mechanism that ensures *durability*: in other words, you need to ensure that, even in the case of a power outage that takes out some participant, the message still persists somewhere and gets to stick around until whoever is meant to process it comes back online. This is ensured by separate mechanisms such as Transactional Message Queuing.

Of course, sometimes you simply do not care. You fire off messages into the abyss. And, if they're lost, well, that's just tough luck.

Summary

The Mediator design pattern is all about having an in-between component that everyone in a system has access to and can use to communicate with one another. Instead of direct references, communication can happen through identifiers (usernames, unique ids, GUIDs, etc.).

The simplest implementation of a mediator is a member list and a function that goes through the list and does what it's intended to do – whether on every element of the list or selectively.

A more sophisticated implementation of Mediator can use events to allow participants to subscribe to (and unsubscribe from) things happening in the system. This way, messages sent from one component to another can be treated as events. In this setup, it is also easy for participants to unsubscribe from certain events if they are no longer interested in them or if they are about to leave the system altogether.

CHAPTER 20

Memento

When we looked at the Command design pattern, we noted that recording a list of every single change theoretically allows you to roll back the system to any point in time – after all, you've kept a record of all the modifications.

Sometimes, though, you don't really care about playing back through all the states of the system, but you *do* care about being able to roll back the system to a *particular* state, if need be.

This is precisely what the Memento pattern does: it typically stores the state of the system and returns it as a dedicated, read-only object with no behavior of its own. This "token," if you will, can be used only for feeding it back into the system to restore it to the state it represents.

Let's look at an example.

Bank Account

Let's use an example of a bank account that we've made before...

```
public class BankAccount
{
  private int balance;

  public BankAccount(int balance)
  {
    this.balance = balance;
  }

  // todo: everything else :)
}
```

© Dmitri Nesteruk 2022
D. Nesteruk, *Design Patterns in .NET 6*, https://doi.org/10.1007/978-1-4842-8245-8_20

...but now we decide to make a bank account with a Deposit(). Instead of it being void as in previous examples, Deposit() will now be made to return a Memento...

```
public Memento Deposit(int amount)
{
  balance += amount;
  return new Memento(balance);
}
```

...and the memento will then be usable for rolling back the account to the previous state:

```
public void Restore(Memento m)
{
  balance = m.Balance;
}
```

As for the memento itself, we can go for a trivial implementation:

```
public class Memento
{
  public int Balance { get; }
  public Memento(int balance)
  {
    Balance = balance;
  }
}
```

You'll notice that the Memento class is immutable. Imagine if you *could*, in fact, change the balance: you could roll back the account to a state it was never in!

And here is how one would go about using such a setup:

```
var ba = new BankAccount(100);
var m1 = ba.Deposit(50);
var m2 = ba.Deposit(25);
WriteLine(ba); // 175

// restore to m1
ba.Restore(m1);
```

```
WriteLine(ba); // 150

// restore back to m2
ba.Restore(m2);
WriteLine(ba); // 175
```

This implementation is good enough, through there are some things missing. For example, you never get a memento representing the opening balance because a constructor cannot return a value. You could add an out parameter, of course, but that's just too ugly.

Undo and Redo

What if you were to store *every* memento generated by BankAccount? In this case, you'd have a situation similar to our implementation of the Command pattern, where undo and redo operations are a byproduct of this recording. Let's see how we can get undo/redo functionality with a memento.

We'll introduce a new BankAccount class that's going to keep hold of every single memento it ever generates:

```
public class BankAccount
{
  private int balance;
  private List<Memento> changes = new();
  private int current;

  public BankAccount(int balance)
  {
    this.balance = balance;
    changes.Add(new Memento(balance));
  }
}
```

We have now solved the problem of returning to the initial balance: the memento for the initial change is stored as well. Of course, this memento isn't actually returned, so in order to roll back to it, well, I suppose you could implement some Reset() function or something – totally up to you.

The BankAccount class has a current member that stores the index of the latest memento. Hold on. Why do we need this? Isn't it the case that current will always be one less than the list of changes? Only if you want to support undo/rollback operations; if you want redo operations, too, you need this!

Now, here's the implementation of the Deposit() method:

```
public Memento Deposit(int amount)
{
  balance += amount;
  var m = new Memento(balance);
  changes.Add(m);
  ++current;
  return m;
}
```

There are several things that happen here:

- The balance is increased by the amount you want to deposit.

- A new memento is constructed with the new balance and added to the list of changes.

- We increase the current value (you can think of it as a pointer into the list of changes).

Now here comes the fun stuff. We add a method to restore the account state based on a memento:

```
public void Restore(Memento m)
{
  if (m != null)
  {
    balance = m.Balance;
    changes.Add(m);
    current = changes.Count - 1;
  }
}
```

The restoration process is significantly different from the one we've looked at earlier. First, we actually check that the memento is initialized – this is relevant because we now have a way of signaling no-ops: just return a default value. Also, when we restore a memento, we actually add that memento to the list of changes so an undo operation will work correctly on it.

Now, here is the (rather tricky) implementation of Undo():

```
public Memento Undo()
{
  if (current > 0)
  {
    var m = changes[--current];
    balance = m.Balance;
    return m;
  }
  return null;
}
```

We can only Undo() if current points to a change that is greater than zero. If that's the case, we move the pointer back, grab the change at that position, apply it, and then return that change. If we cannot roll back to a previous memento, we return null, which should explain why we check for null in Restore().

The implementation of Redo() is very similar:

```
public Memento Redo()
{
  if (current + 1 < changes.Count)
  {
    var m = changes[++current];
    balance = m.Balance;
    return m;
  }
  return null;
}
```

Again, we need to be able to redo something: if we can, we do it safely; if not, we do nothing and return null. Putting it all together, we can now start using the undo/redo functionality:

```
var ba = new BankAccount(100);
ba.Deposit(50);
ba.Deposit(25);
WriteLine(ba);

ba.Undo();
WriteLine($"Undo 1: {ba}"); // Undo 1: 150

ba.Undo();
WriteLine($"Undo 2: {ba}"); // Undo 2: 100

ba.Redo();
WriteLine($"Redo 2: {ba}"); // Redo 2: 150
```

Memento and Command

As I'm sure you've guessed, the creation of mementoes for every single change in the system is quite often unrealistic. But we've already seen the way undo/redo operations are defined in the Command design pattern. Just to recap, our approach to defining undo operations for Command basically meant that we would do the opposite of what the operation entailed. So, for a deposit operation, Undo() would take that money out of the account.

This is not always a realistic option either. Sometimes, the effects of an executed command are far-reaching and difficult to predict. Thus, it would make sense to use the Memento pattern to preserve the entire state of the system.

We can therefore put the Command and Memento approaches together as follows:

```
public class WithdrawCommand : ICommand
{
  public BankAccount Account;
  public decimal Amount;
  private Memento memento;
  private bool succeeded;
```

```csharp
public override void Call()
{
  succeeded = Account.Withdraw(Amount);
  memento = Account.Snapshot(); // memento-creating method
}

public override void Undo()
{
  if (succeeded && memento != null)
  {
    Account.RestoreTo(memento);
    memento = null; // prevent second undo
  }
}
}
```

One might argue that this approach simply added an extra level of indirection: instead of saving the state of the account directly, it is saved indirectly through the use of a memento. In this example, though, instead of having individual operations return memento objects, we create a memento explicitly. This process, in turn, could also leverage the Prototype pattern in situations where the state of the object you're trying to preserve is so complicated that writing explicit serialization code is tedious. But if that is the approach you take, you must distinguish between two types of data: the salient information about the system that must be persisted and any temporary information (e.g., private fields storing some temporary indicators) that need not be. The best advice I can give is to put all temporary information on the stack as return values – that way, you don't hold on to it longer than necessary.

Summary

The Memento pattern is all about handing out tokens that can be used to restore the system to a prior state. Typically, the token contains all the information necessary to move the system to a particular state, and if it's small enough, you can also use it to record *all* the states of the system so as to allow not just the arbitrary resetting of the system to a prior state, but controlled navigation backward (undo) and forward (redo) of all the states the system was in.

One design decision that I made in the preceding demos is to make the memento a `class`. This allows me to use the `null` value to encode the absence of a memento to operate upon. If we wanted to make it a `struct` instead, we would have to redesign the API so that, instead of `null`, the `Restore()` method would be able to take either a `Nullable<Memento>`, some `Option<Memento>` type (.NET doesn't have a built-in option type yet), or a memento possessing some easily identifiable trait (e.g., a balance of `int.MinValue`).

CHAPTER 21

Null Object

We don't always choose the interfaces we work with. For example, I'd rather have my car drive me to my destination by itself, without me having to give 100% of my attention to the road and the dangerous lunatics driving next to me. And it's the same with software: sometimes you don't really want a piece of functionality, but it's built into the interface. This means you have to provide some value even if you don't need this particular piece of functionality.

So what do you do? You make a null object.

Scenario

Suppose you inherited a library that uses the following interface:

```
public interface ILog
{
  void Info(string msg);
  void Warn(string msg);
}
```

The library uses this interface to operate on bank accounts such as

```
public class BankAccount
{
  private ILog log;
  private int balance;
```

© Dmitri Nesteruk 2022
D. Nesteruk, *Design Patterns in .NET 6*, https://doi.org/10.1007/978-1-4842-8245-8_21

```
  public BankAccount(ILog log)
  {
    this.log = log;
  }

  // more members here
}
```

In fact, BankAccount can have methods similar to

```
public void Deposit(int amount)
{
  balance += amount;
  log.Info($"Deposited ${amount}, balance is now {balance}");
}
```

So what's the problem here? Well, if you *do* need logging, there's no problem. You just implement your own logging class…

```
class ConsoleLog : ILog
{
  public void Info(string msg)
  {
    WriteLine(msg);
  }

  public void Warn(string msg)
  {
    WriteLine("WARNING: " + msg);
  }
}
```

…and you can use it straight away. But what if you *don't want logging at all*?

Intrusive Approaches

If you are prepared to break the Open-Closed Principle, there are a couple of intrusive approaches (with varying degrees of intrusiveness) that help you navigate around this situation.

The simplest approach, and also the ugliest, is to change the interface to an abstract class, that is, change ILog to

```
public abstract class ILog
{
  void Info(string msg) {}
  void Warn(string msg) {}
}
```

You might want to follow up this change with a rename refactoring from ILog to Log, but hopefully, the approach is obvious: by providing default no-op implementations in the base class, you can now simply make a dummy inheritor of this new ILog and supply it to whoever needs it. Or you can go further and make it non-abstract, and then ILog *is* your null object insofar as no-op behavior is concerned.

This approach can easily break things – after all, you might have clients who are explicitly assuming that ILog is an interface, so they could be implementing it *together with other interfaces* in their classes, which means this modification will break existing code.

Another alternative to this is to simply add null checks everywhere. You could then rewrite the BankAccount constructor to have a default null argument:

```
public BankAcccount(ILog log = null) { ... }
```

With this change, you now need to change every single call on the log to a safe call, for example, log?.Info(...). This will work, but it can result in a huge number of changes if the log is used all over the place. There's also a small issue with the fact that using null for absence is not idiomatically correct (not obvious) – perhaps a better approach would be to use some Option<T> type, but such use would result in even more drastic changes across the codebase.

Nullable Virtual Proxy

The final intrusive approach requires just one change inside the BankAccount class and is the least harmful: it involves the construction of a virtual proxy (see Chapter 13) over an ILog. Essentially, we make a proxy/decorator over a log where the underlying is allowed to be null:

```
class OptionalLog : ILog
{
  private ILog impl;
  public OptionalLog(ILog impl) { this.impl = impl; }

  public void Info(string msg) { impl?.Info(msg); }
  public void Warn(string msg) { impl?.Warn(msg); }
}
```

Then, we change the BankAccount constructor, adding both an optional null value and the use of the wrapper in the body. In fact, if you can bear just one more line in the BankAccount class, we can do a neat trick by introducing a nice, descriptive constant called NoLogging and using it instead:

```
private const ILog NoLogging = null;

public BankAccount([CanBeNull] ILog log = NoLogging)
{
  this.log = new OptionalLog(log);
}
```

This approach is probably the least intrusive and most hygienic, allowing a null where such a value was hitherto not allowed while, at the same time, using the name of the default value to hint at what's going on.[1]

---

[1] [CanBeNull] is an attribute that is part of the JetBrains.Annotations NuGet package. It is used to hint to the ReSharper/Rider static analyzers that the parameter can be assigned a null value.

Null Object

There are situations where none of the intrusive approaches will work, the most obvious being the case where you don't actually own the code that is using the relevant component. In this case, we need to construct a separate null object, which gives rise to the pattern we are discussing.

Look at BankAccount's constructor once again:

```
public BankAccount(ILog log)
{
  this.log = log;
}
```

Since the constructor takes a logger, it is *unsafe* to assume that you can get away with just passing it a null. BankAccount *could* be checking the reference internally before dispatching on it, but you don't know that it does, and without extra documentation it's impossible to tell.

As a consequence, the only thing that would be reasonable to pass into BankAccount is a *null object* – a class that conforms to the interface but contains no functionality:

```
public sealed class NullLog : ILog
{
  public void Info(string msg) { }
  public void Warn(string msg) { }
}
```

Notice that the class is sealed: this is a design choice that presupposes that there is no point in inheriting from an object that deliberately has no behavior. Essentially, NullLog is a worthless parent.

You would use such a class as follows:

```
var ba = new BankAccount(new NullLog());
ba.Deposit(100);
ba.Withdraw(200);
```

Null Object Singleton

It is completely reasonable to have a singleton null object, since making separate instances of null objects makes no sense. Furthermore, it would be beneficial if the Null class itself was not exposed directly as a type to the client.

We can easily implement this approach whether our null object inherits a class or implements an interface. Since in this chapter ILog is an interface, we can use default interface members to supply both the relevant member and an inner private class:

```csharp
interface ILog
{
  void Info(string msg);
  void Warn(string msg);

  public static ILog Null => NullLog.Instance;

  private sealed class NullLog : ILog
  {
    private NullLog() {}

    private static readonly Lazy<NullLog> instance = new ());

    public static ILog Instance => instance.Value;

    public void Info(string msg) { }
    public void Warn(string msg) { }
  }
}
```

I bet you never expected this! Our implementation augments the ILog interface to expose a Null member as a static member; furthermore, the interface contains within it a private class (not intended to be consumed directly) that, in turn, implements ILog with no-op operations.

The private class is constructed as a lazy singleton that is exposed as a static property in the class, which is further exposed as a static property by the containing interface.

The end result is you can write

```csharp
var ba = new BankAccount(ILog.Null);
// as before
```

Of course, it would be a bit more intuitive if we had a Log abstract class instead, because most C# developers, especially experienced ones, are unlikely to expect a static member incorporated within an interface!

Dynamic Null Object

In order to construct a correct null object, you have to implement every member of the required interface. Booo-ring! Can't we just write a single method that says "please just do nothing on *any* call"? Turns out we can, thanks to the DLR.

For this example, we are going to make a type called Null<T> that will inherit from DynamicObject and simply provide a no-op response to any method that's called on it:

```csharp
public class Null<T> : DynamicObject where T:class
{
  public override bool TryInvokeMember(InvokeMemberBinder binder,
    object[] args, out object result)
  {
    // cannot rely on binder.ReturnType
    var returnType = GetUnderlyingType(typeof(T).GetMember
    (binder.Name)[0]);
    if (returnType == typeof(void) || !returnType.IsValueType)
      result = null;
    else
      result = Activator.CreateInstance(returnType);
    return true;
  }
}
```

The result out parameter needs to be of the right type, and this presents a bit of a problem. Normally we'd look into binder.ReturnType for the type expected by the caller, but with ImpromptuInterface, this isn't an option. So what we do here is something different: we get the first member of the type with a matching name (because binder.Name is correct, luckily) and then attempt to get the underlying type by casting the MemberInfo into FieldInfo, PropertyInfo, and so on. Then, if it's a reference type we simply assign null, but if it's a value type we create a default instance of it: this way, an int will be 0 (zero), a bool will be false, and so on.

Now, I have neglected to mention what the T in Null<T> actually is. As you may have guessed, that's the interface that we need a no-op object for. We can create a utility property getter to actually construct instances of Null<T> that satisfy the interface T. For this, we are going to use the ImpromptuInterface library[2]:

```
public static T Instance
{
  get
  {
    if (!typeof(T).IsInterface)
      throw new ArgumentException("I must be an interface type");

    return new Null<T>().ActLike<T>();
  }
}
```

In the preceding code, the ActLike() method from ImpromptuInterface takes a dynamic object and conforms it at runtime to the required interface T.

Putting everything together, we can now write the following:

```
var log = Null<ILog>.Instance;
var ba = new BankAccount(log);
ba.Deposit(100);
ba.Withdraw(200);
```

Once again, this code has a computational cost related to the construction of a dynamic object that not only does no-ops but also conforms to the chosen interface.

Drawbacks

The dynamic null object has a large number of disadvantages.

First of all, it has a reasonably high computational cost because of the use of dynamic. This means that, while being suitable in settings where performance is not critical (e.g., tests), its use in production is not the best idea.

---

[2] ImpromptuInterface is an open source dynamic "duck casting" library built on top of the DLR and Reflection.Emit. Its source code is available at https://github.com/ekonbenefits/impromptu-interface, and you can install it directly from NuGet.

The second problem is that the dynamic null object is not a singleton. We ought to refactor it so that, for any given type T, only one adaptation (using ActLike()) is ever constructed. But even this optimization will not help much due to the dynamic nature of all the member calls.

Finally, it might be argued that a dynamic implementation is unnecessary. Assuming we are working with dependencies on interfaces rather than concrete classes, it is cleaner and much more efficient to use compile-time code generation (via T4 or source generators) to manufacture a "proper" null object without any use of the DLR.

Summary

The Null Object pattern raises an issue of API design: what kinds of assumptions can we make about the objects we depend upon? If we are taking a reference, do we then have an obligation to check this reference on every use? Or is it better to turn on C#'s nullability checks and assume that *nothing* can be null unless explicitly marked as such?

If you feel no such obligation, then the only way the client can implement a null object is to construct a no-op implementation of the required interface and pass that instance in. That said, this only works well with methods: if the object's fields are also being used, for example, then you are in real trouble. Same goes for non-void methods where the return values are actually used for something.

If you want to proactively support the idea of null objects being passed as arguments, you need to be explicit about it: either specify the parameter type as some Optional, give the parameter a default value that hints at a possible null, or just write documentation that explains what kind of value is expected at this location.

CHAPTER 22

Observer

The Observer pattern, quite simply, lets one component notify other components that something happened. The pattern is used all over the place: for example, when binding data to UI, we can program domain objects such that, when they change, they generate notifications that the UI can subscribe to and update the visuals. On the other hand, editing data in the UI should modify data behind the scenes, which requires the reverse set of operations to occur.

Events

The Observer pattern is a popular and necessary pattern, so it is not surprising that the designers of C# decided to incorporate it directly into the language wholesale with the `event` keyword. The use of events in C# typically employs a convention that mandates the following:

- Events can be members of a class and are decorated with the `event` keyword.

- Event handlers – methods that are called whenever an event is raised – are attached to the event with the `+=` operator and are detached with the `-=` operator.

- An event handler typically takes two arguments:

  - An `object` reference to who exactly fired the event

  - An object that (typically) derives from `EventArgs` that contains any necessary information about the event

The exact *type* of an event that is used is typically a delegate. Just like the `Action/Func` wrappers for lambdas, the delegate wrappers for events are called `EventHandler` and exist in both a nongeneric (that takes an `EventArgs`) and a generic (that takes a type

© Dmitri Nesteruk 2022
D. Nesteruk, *Design Patterns in .NET 6*, https://doi.org/10.1007/978-1-4842-8245-8_22

parameter that derives from EventArgs) second argument. The first argument is always an object:

```
public delegate void EventHandler(object sender, EventArgs e);
public delegate void EventHandler<TEventArgs>(object? sender,
TEventArgs e);
```

Here is a trivial example: suppose, whenever a person falls ill, we call a doctor. First of all we define event arguments; in our case we just need the address to send the doctor to:

```
public class FallsIllEventArgs : EventArgs
{
  public string Address;
}
```

Now, we can implement a Person type, which can look like this:

```
public class Person
{
  public void CatchACold()
  {
    FallsIll?.Invoke(this,
      new FallsIllEventArgs { Address = "123 London Road" });
  }

  public event EventHandler<FallsIllEventArgs> FallsIll;
}
```

We are using a strongly typed EventHandler delegate to expose a public event. The CatchACold() method is used to raise the event, with the safe access ?. operator being used to ensure that, if the event doesn't have any subscribers, we don't get a NullReferenceException.

All that remains is to set up a scenario and provide an event handler:

```
static void Main()
{
  var person = new Person();
  person.FallsIll += CallDoctor;
```

```
  person.CatchACold();
}

private static void CallDoctor(object sender, FallsIllEventArgs eventArgs)
{
  Console.WriteLine($"A doctor has been called to {eventArgs.Address}");
}
```

The event handler can be an ordinary (static or member) method, a local function, or a lambda – your choice. The signature is mandated by the original delegate; since we're using a strongly typed EventHandler variant, the second argument of the handler is FallsIllEventArgs. As soon as CatchACold() is called, the CallDoctor() method is triggered.

Any given event can have more than one handler (C# delegates are multicast, after all). Removal of event handlers is typically done with the -= operator. When all subscribers have unsubscribed from an event, the event instance is set to null.

Weak Event Pattern

Did you know that .NET programs can have memory leaks? Not in the C++ sense, of course, but it *is* possible to keep holding on to an object for longer than necessary. Specifically, you can make an object and set its reference to null, but it will still be alive, and events specifically are to blame for this. Why? Let me show you.

First, let's make a Button class:

```
public class Button
{
  public event EventHandler Clicked;

  public void Fire()
  {
    Clicked?.Invoke(this, EventArgs.Empty);
  }
}
```

In this class, `Fire()` simply fires the `Clicked` event. Now let's suppose we have this button shown inside a window. For the sake of simplicity, I'll just stick it into a `Window` constructor and subscribe to its `Clicked` event:

```
public class Window
{
  public Window(Button button)
  {
    button.Clicked += ButtonOnClicked;
  }

  private void ButtonOnClicked(object sender, EventArgs eventArgs)
  {
    WriteLine("Button clicked (Window handler)");
  }

  ~Window() { WriteLine("Window finalized"); }
}
```

Looks innocent enough, except it's not. If you make a button and a window and then set the window to `null`, the window will still be alive even though you no longer hold *explicit* references to it! Proof:

```
var btn = new Button();
var window = new Window(btn);
var windowRef = new WeakReference(window);
btn.Fire();

window = null;

FireGC(); // this forces GC
WriteLine($"Is window alive after GC? {windowRef.IsAlive}"); // True
```

The reason the window reference is still alive is that it has a subscription to the button. When a button is clicked, the expectation is that something sensible happens: since there is a subscription to this event, the object that happens to have made this subscription cannot be allowed to die, even if the only reference to that object has been set to `null`. This is a memory leak in the .NET sense.

How can we fix this? One approach would be to use the WeakEventManager class from System.Windows. This class is specifically designed to allow the listener's handlers to be garbage-collected even if the source object persists. This class is very simple to use:

```
public class Window2
{
  public Window2(Button button)
  {
    WeakEventManager<Button, EventArgs>
      .AddHandler(button, nameof(Button.Clicked), ButtonOnClicked);
  }
  // rest of class same as before
}
```

Repeating the scenario again, this Window2 implementation gives a windowRef. IsAlive result of False, as desired.

Event Streams

With all these discussions of Observer, you might be interested to learn that the .NET Framework comes with two interfaces: IObserver<T> and IObservable<T>. These interfaces, which were coincidental with the release of Reactive Extensions (Rx), are meant primarily to deal with reactive streams. While it is not my intention to discuss the entirety of Reactive Extensions, these two interfaces are worth mentioning.

Let's start with IObservable<T>. This is an interface that is generally similar to the interface of a typical .NET event. The only difference is that, instead of using the += operator for subscription, this interface requires that you implement a method called Subscribe(). This method takes an IObserver<T> as its only parameter. Remember, this is an interface, and unlike in the case of events/delegates, there is no prescribed storage mechanism. You are free to use anything you want.

There is some extra icing on the cake: the notion of *un*subscription is explicitly supported in the interface. The Subscribe() method returns an IDisposable with the understanding that the return token (the Memento pattern at work!) has a Dispose() method that unsubscribes the observer from the observable.

The second piece of the puzzle is the IObserver<T> interface. It is designed to provide push-based notifications through three specific methods:

- OnNext(T) gets invoked whenever a new event occurs.

- OnCompleted() gets invoked when the source has no more data to give.

- OnError() gets invoked whenever the observer has experienced an error condition.

Once again, this is just an interface, and how you handle this is up to you. For example, you can completely ignore both OnCompleted() and OnError().

So, given these two interfaces, the implementation of our trivial doctor-patient example is suddenly a lot less trivial. First of all, we need to encapsulate the idea of an *event subscription*. The reason this is required is because we need a memento[1] that implements IDisposable through which unsubscription can happen:

```
private class Subscription : IDisposable
{
  private Person person;
  public IObserver<Event> Observer;

  public Subscription(Person person, IObserver<Event> observer)
  {
    this.person = person;
    Observer = observer;
  }

  public void Dispose()
  {
    person.subscriptions.Remove(this);
  }
}
```

This class is an inner class of Person, which is a good hint at the growing complexity of any object that wants to support event streams. Now, coming back to Person, we want it to implement the IObservable<T> interface. But what is T? Unlike the conventional

---

[1] See Chapter 20 for more details.

events, there are no guidelines mandating that we inherit from EventArgs – sure, we could continue using that type,[2] or we could construct our own, completely arbitrary, hierarchy:

```csharp
public class Event
{
  // anything could be here
}

public class FallsIllEvent : Event
{
  public string Address;
}
```

Moving on, we now have a base class Event, so we can declare Person to be a generator of such events. As a consequence, our Person type would implement IObservable<Event> and would take an IObserver<Event> in its Subscribe() method. Here is the entire Person class with the body of the Subscription inner class omitted:

```csharp
public class Person : IObservable<Event>
{
  private readonly HashSet<Subscription> subscriptions = new ();

  public IDisposable Subscribe(IObserver<Event> observer)
  {
    var subscription = new Subscription(this, observer);
    subscriptions.Add(subscription);
    return subscription;
  }

  public void CatchACold()
  {
    foreach (var sub in subscriptions)
      sub.Observer.OnNext(new FallsIllEvent {Address = "123 London Road"});
  }
```

---

[2] By the way, System.EventArgs is an empty type. All it has is a default constructor (empty) and a static member EventArgs.Empty that is a singleton null object (double pattern headshot!) that indicates the event arguments have no data.

```
private class Subscription : IDisposable { ... }
}
```

I'm sure you'll agree that this is a lot more complicated than just publishing a single event for clients to subscribe to! But there are advantages to this: for example, you can choose your own policy with respect to repeat subscriptions, that is, situations where a subscriber is trying to subscribe to some event *again*. One thing worth noting is that HashSet<Subscription> is not a thread-safe container. This means that if you want Subscribe() and CatchACold() to be callable concurrently, you would need to either use a thread-safe collection, locking, or perhaps something even fancier, like an ImmutableList.

The problems don't end there. Remember, a subscriber has to implement an IObserver<Event> now. This means that, to support the scenario we've had previously shown, we would have to write the following:

```
public class Demo : IObserver<Event>
{
  static void Main(string[] args)
  {
    new Demo();
  }

  public Demo()
  {
    var person = new Person();
    var sub = person.Subscribe(this);
  }

  public void OnNext(Event value)
  {
    if (value is FallsIllEvent args)
      WriteLine($"A doctor has been called to {args.Address}");
  }

  public void OnError(Exception error){}
  public void OnCompleted(){}
}
```

This is, once again, quite a mouthful. We could have simplified the subscription by using a special `Observable.Subscribe()` static method, but `Observable` (without the `I`) is part of Reactive Extensions, a separate library that you may or may not want to use.

So this is how you can build an Observer pattern using .NET's own interfaces, without using the event keyword. The main advantage of this approach is that the stream of events that is generated by an `IObservable` can be directly fed into various Rx operators. For example, using `System.Reactive`, the entire demo program we've written can turn into a single statement:

```
person
  .OfType<FallsIllEvent>()
  .Subscribe(args =>
    WriteLine($"A doctor has been called to {args.Address}"));
```

Property Observers

One of the most common Observer implementations in .NET is getting notifications when a property changes. This is necessary, for example, to update UI when the underlying data changes. This mechanism uses ordinary events as well as some interfaces that have become standard within .NET.

Property observers can get really complicated, so we'll cover them in steps, starting from basic interfaces and operations and moving on to the more complicated scenarios.

Basic Change Notification

The central piece of change notification in .NET is an interface called `INotifyPropertyChanged`:

```
public interface INotifyPropertyChanged
{
  /// <summary>Occurs when a property value changes.</summary>
  event PropertyChangedEventHandler PropertyChanged;
}
```

All this interface does is expose an event that you're expected to use, defined as

```
public delegate void PropertyChangedEventHandler
  (object sender, PropertyChangedEventArgs e);
```

PropertyChangedEventArgs has a single member, PropertyName, that stores the name of the property that has been changed. Note that any additional information, such as information about the previous value, the new value, or *who* owns this property, simply isn't here. The owner of the property is typically the sender of the event (provided as the first argument to the handler). As for any extra information, well, if you do need it, you'd have to subclass PropertyChangedEventArgs and give it additional members yourself.

Given a class Person having a property called Age, the typical implementation of this interface looks as follows:

```
public class Person : INotifyPropertyChanged
{
  private int age;

  public int Age
  {
    get => age;
    set
    {
      if (value == age) return;
      age = value;
      OnPropertyChanged();
    }
  }

  public event PropertyChangedEventHandler PropertyChanged;

  [NotifyPropertyChangedInvocator]
  protected virtual void OnPropertyChanged(
    [CallerMemberName] string propertyName = null)
  {
    PropertyChanged?.Invoke(this,
      new PropertyChangedEventArgs(propertyName));
  }
}
```

There is a lot to discuss here. First of all, the property gets a backing field. This is required in order to look at the previous value of the property before it is assigned. Notice that the invocation of the `OnPropertyChanged()` method happens only if the property *did* change. If it didn't, there's no notification.

As far as the IDE-generated `OnPropertyChanged()` method is concerned, this method is designed to take in the name of the affected property via `[CallerMemberName]` metadata and then, provided the `PropertyChanged` event has subscribers, notify those subscribers that the property with that name did, in fact, change.

You can, of course, build your own change notification mechanisms, but both WinForms and WPF are intrinsically aware of `INotifyPropertyChanged`, as are many other frameworks. So, if you need change notifications, I'd stick to this interface.

A special note needs to be added about `INotifyPropertyChanging` – an interface that is intended to send events indicating that a property is in the process of changing. This interface is very rarely used, if ever. It would have been nice to be able to use this property to *cancel* a property change, but sadly the interface makes no provisions for this. In actual fact, cancelation of property changes can be one of the reasons you would want to implement *your own* interfaces instead of these.

Bidirectional Bindings

The `INotifyPropertyChanged` is very useful for notifying the user interface about the change of a property some label is bound to. But what if you have an edit box instead and that edit box also needs to update the code element behind the scenes?

This is actually doable and doesn't even result in infinite recursion! This problem generalizes to the following: how do you bind two properties such that changing the one changes the other, in other words, their values are always identical?

Let's try this. Suppose we have a `Product` that has a `Name` and we also have a `Window` that has a `ProductName`. We want `Name` and `ProductName` to be bound together:

```
var product = new Product{Name="Book"};
var window = new Window{ProductName = "Book"};

product.PropertyChanged += (sender, eventArgs) =>
{
  if (eventArgs.PropertyName == "Name")
  {
```

```
    Console.WriteLine("Name changed in Product");
    window.ProductName = product.Name;
  }
};

window.PropertyChanged += (sender, eventArgs) =>
{
  if (eventArgs.PropertyName == "ProductName")
  {
    Console.WriteLine("Name changed in Window");
    product.Name = window.ProductName;
  }
};
```

Common sense dictates that this code, when triggered, would cause a
StackOverflowException: window affects product, product affects window, and so on.
Except it doesn't happen. Why? Because the setter in both properties has a guard that
checks that the value did, in fact, change. If it didn't, it does a return, and no further
notifications take place. So we're safe here.

This solution works, but frameworks such as WinForms try to shrink-wrap situations
such as these into separate data binding objects. In a data binding, you specify the
objects and their properties and how they tie together. Windows Forms, for example,
uses property names (as strings), but nowadays we can be a little bit smarter and use
expression trees instead.

So let's construct a BidirectionalBinding class that will, in its constructor, bind
together two properties. For this, we need four pieces of information:

- The owner of the first property

- An expression tree accessing the first object's property

- The owner of the second property

- An expression tree accessing the second object's property

Sadly, it is impossible to reduce the number of parameters in this scenario, but at
least they will be more or less human-readable. We'll also avoid using generics here,
though they can, in theory, introduce additional type safety.

So here is the entire class:

```csharp
public sealed class BidirectionalBinding : IDisposable
{
  private bool disposed;

  public BidirectionalBinding(
    INotifyPropertyChanged first, Expression<Func<object>> firstProperty,
    INotifyPropertyChanged second, Expression<Func<object>> secondProperty)
  {
    if (firstProperty.Body is MemberExpression firstExpr
        && secondProperty.Body is MemberExpression secondExpr)
    {
      if (firstExpr.Member is PropertyInfo firstProp
          && secondExpr.Member is PropertyInfo secondProp)
      {
        first.PropertyChanged += (sender, args) =>
        {
          if (!disposed)
            secondProp.SetValue(second, firstProp.GetValue(first));
        };
        second.PropertyChanged += (sender, args) =>
        {
          if (!disposed)
            firstProp.SetValue(first, secondProp.GetValue(second));
        };
      }
    }
  }

  public void Dispose()
  {
    disposed = true;
  }
}
```

This code depends on a number of preconditions regarding the expression trees, specifically:

- Each expression tree is expected to be a `MemberExpression`.

- Each member expression is expected to access a property (thus, `PropertyInfo`).

If these conditions are met, we subscribe each property to each other's changes. There's an additional dispose guard added to this class to allow the user to stop processing the subscriptions if necessary.

This is a trivial example of the kinds of things that can happen behind the scenes in frameworks that intend to intrinsically support data binding.

Property Dependencies

In Microsoft Excel, spreadsheet cells can contain calculations using values from other cells. This is very convenient: whenever a particular cell value changes, Excel recalculates every single cell (including cells on other sheets) that this cell affects. And then *those* cells cause the recalculation of every cell dependent on *them*. And so it goes forever until the entire dependency graph is traversed, however long it takes. It's beautiful.

The problem with properties (and with the Observer pattern generally) is exactly the same: sometimes a part of a class not only generates notifications but affects other parts of the class, and then *those* members also generate their own event notifications. Unlike Excel, .NET doesn't have a built-in way of handling this, so such a situation can quickly turn into a real mess.

Let me illustrate. People aged 16 or older (could be different in your country) can vote, so suppose we want to be notified of changes to a person's voting rights:

```
public class Person : PropertyNotificationSupport
{
  private int age;

  public int Age
  {
    get => age;
```

```
    set
    {
      if (value == age) return;
      age = value;
      OnPropertyChanged();
    }
  }

  public bool CanVote => Age <= 16;
}
```

Clearly, changes to a person's age should affect their ability to vote. Thus, we would also need to generate appropriate change notifications for CanVote...but where? After all, CanVote has no setter!

You could try to put them into the Age setter, for example:

```
public int Age
{
  get => age;
  set
  {
    if (value == age) return;
    age = value;
    OnPropertyChanged();
    OnPropertyChanged(nameof(CanVote));
  }
}
```

This will work, but consider a scenario: what if age changes from 5 to 6? Sure, the age has changed, but CanVote has not, so why are we unconditionally doing a notification on it? This is incorrect. A functionally correct implementation would have to look something like the following:

```
set
{
  if (value == age) return;

  var oldCanVote = CanVote;
```

```
  age = value;
  OnPropertyChanged();

  if (oldCanVote != CanVote)
    OnPropertyChanged(nameof(CanVote));
}
```

As you can see, the only way to determine that CanVote has been affected is to cache its old value, perform the changes on age, then get its new value and check if it's been modified, and only then perform the notification.

Even without this particular pain point, the approach we've taken with property dependencies does not scale. In a complicated scenario where properties depend on other properties, how are we expected to track all the dependencies and make all the notifications? Clearly, some sort of centralized mechanism is needed to track all of this automatically.

Let us build such a mechanism. We'll construct a base class called PropertyNotificationSupport that will implement INotifyPropertyChanged and will also take care of dependencies. Here is its implementation:

```
public class PropertyNotificationSupport : INotifyPropertyChanged
{
  private readonly Dictionary<string, HashSet<string>> affectedBy = new();

  public event PropertyChangedEventHandler PropertyChanged;

  [NotifyPropertyChangedInvocator]
  protected virtual void OnPropertyChanged
    ([CallerMemberName] string propertyName = null)
  {
    PropertyChanged?.Invoke(this,
      new PropertyChangedEventArgs(propertyName));

    foreach (var affected in affectedBy.Keys)
      if (affectedBy[affected].Contains(propertyName))
        OnPropertyChanged(affected);
  }
```

```
  protected Func<T> property<T>(string name,
    Expression<Func<T>> expr) { ... }

  private class MemberAccessVisitor : ExpressionVisitor { ... }
}
```

This class is complicated, so let's go through this slowly and figure out what's going on here.

First, we have affectedBy, which is a dictionary that lists every property and a HashSet of properties affected by it. For example, if voting ability is affected by age and whether or not you're a citizen, this dictionary will contain a key of "CanVote" and values of {"Age", "Citizen"}.

We then modify the default OnPropertyChanged() implementation to ensure that the notifications happen both on the property itself and all properties it affects. The only question now is, How do properties get enlisted in this dictionary?

It would be too much to ask the developers to populate this dictionary by hand. Instead, we do it automatically with the use of expression trees. A getter for a read-only property is provided to the base class as an expression tree, which completely changes the way dependent properties are constructed:

```
public class Person : PropertyNotificationSupport
{
  private readonly Func<bool> canVote;
  public bool CanVote => canVote();

  public Person()
  {
    canVote = property(nameof(CanVote),
      () => Citizen && Age >= 16);
  }

  // other members here
}
```

Clearly, everything has changed. The property is now initialized inside the constructor using the base class' property() method. This method takes an *expression tree*, parses it to find the dependent properties, and then compiles the expression into an ordinary Func<T>:

```csharp
protected Func<T> property<T>(string name, Expression<Func<T>> expr)
{
  Console.WriteLine($"Creating computed property for expression {expr}");

  var visitor = new MemberAccessVisitor(GetType());
  visitor.Visit(expr);

  if (visitor.PropertyNames.Any())
  {
    if (!affectedBy.ContainsKey(name))
      affectedBy.Add(name, new HashSet<string>());

    foreach (var propName in visitor.PropertyNames)
      if (propName != name)
        affectedBy[name].Add(propName);
  }

  return expr.Compile();
}
```

The parsing of the expression tree is done using a MemberAccessVisitor, a private, nested class that we've created. This class goes through the expression tree looking for member access and collects all the property names into a simple list:

```csharp
private class MemberAccessVisitor : ExpressionVisitor
{
  private readonly Type declaringType;
  public readonly IList<string> PropertyNames = new List<string>();

  public MemberAccessVisitor(Type declaringType)
  {
    this.declaringType = declaringType;
  }

  public override Expression Visit(Expression expr)
  {
    if (expr != null && expr.NodeType == ExpressionType.MemberAccess)
    {
      var memberExpr = (MemberExpression)expr;
```

```
    if (memberExpr.Member.DeclaringType == declaringType)
    {
      PropertyNames.Add(memberExpr.Member.Name);
    }
  }

  return base.Visit(expr);
  }
}
```

Notice that we restrict ourselves to the declaring type of the owning class – handling a situation with property dependencies between classes is doable, but a lot more complicated.

Putting all of this together, we can now write something like the following:

```
var p = new Person();
p.PropertyChanged += (sender, eventArgs) =>
{
  Console.WriteLine($"{eventArgs.PropertyName} has changed");
};
p.Age = 16;
// Age has changed
// CanVote has changed
p.Citizen = true;
// Citizen has changed
// CanVote has changed
```

So it works. But our implementation is still far from ideal. If we were to change the age to 10, CanVote would still receive a notification, even though it shouldn't! That's because, at the moment, we're firing these notifications unconditionally. If we wanted to fire these only when the dependent properties have changed, we would have to resort to INotifyPropertyChanging (or a similar interface) where we would have to cache the old value of every affected property until the INotifyPropertyChanged call and then check that those have, in fact, changed. I leave this as an exercise for you.

Finally, a small note: You can see some overcrowding happening inside property setters. Three lines is already a lot, but if you factor in additional calls, such as the use of INotifyPropertyChanging, then it makes sense to externalize the entire property setter. Turning each property into a Property<T> (see the "Property Proxy" section of Chapter 13) is a bit overkill, but we can imbue the base class with something like…

```
protected void setValue<T>(T value, ref T field,
  [CallerMemberName] string propertyName = null)
{
  if (value.Equals(field)) return;
  OnPropertyChanging(propertyName);
  field = value;
  OnPropertyChanged(propertyName);
}
```

…with properties now simplifying to

```
public int Age
{
  get => age;
  set => setValue(value, ref age);
}
```

Notice that, in this code, we must perform propertyName propagation in calls to OnPropertyXxx() because the [CallerMemberName] attribute inside the method will no longer work for us out of the box.

Views

There's a big, huge, glaring problem with property observers: the approach is intrusive and clearly goes against the idea of Separation of Concerns. Change notification is a separate concern, so adding it right into your domain objects might not be the best idea – especially considering that it is only one of a number of concerns (others including validation, automatic data type conversions, etc.) that may become evident at a later stage once the domain is already well-defined.

Suppose you decide to change your mind and move from the use of INPC to the use of the IObservable interface. If you were to scatter INPC use throughout your domain objects, you'd have to meticulously go through each one, modifying each property to use the new paradigm, not to mention the fact that you'd have to modify the owning classes as well to stop using the old interfaces and start using the new ones. This is tedious and error-prone and precisely the kind of thing we want to avoid.

So, if you want change notifications handled outside of the objects that change, where would you add them? It shouldn't be hard – after all, we've seen patterns such as Decorator that are designed for this exact purpose.

One approach is to put another object in front of your domain object that would handle change notifications and other things besides. This is what we would typically call a *view* – it is this thing that would be bound to UI, for example.

To use views, you would keep your objects simple, using ordinary properties (or even public fields!) without embellishing them with any extra behaviors:

```
public class Person
{
  public string Name;
}
```

The view is then simply a wrapper, of sorts, around the underlying object that can incorporate other concerns, including property observers:

```
public class PersonView : View
{
  protected Person person;
  public PersonView(Person person)
  {
    this.person = person;
  }

  public string Name
  {
    get => person.Name;
    set => setValue(value, () => person.Name);
  }
}
```

373

This view is, of course, a decorator. It wraps the underlying object with mirroring getters/setters that perform the necessary notifications. If you need even more complexity, this is the place to add it. For example, if you want property dependencies tracked in an expression tree, you'd do it in the view constructor rather than in the constructor of the underlying object.

You'll notice that, in the preceding listing, we're trying to be sly by hiding implementation details. We simply inherit from some class `View,` and we don't really care how it handles notifications: maybe it uses `INotifyPropertyChanged`, maybe it uses `IObservable`, or maybe something else. This accentuates adherence to the DIP: we separate the low-level modules that implement basic mechanics from the higher-level View construct.

The only real issue is how to call this class' setter considering that we want it to have information about both the name of the property we're assigning (just in case it's needed) and the value being assigned. There's no uniform solution to this problem; and, obviously, the more information you pack into this improvised `setValue()` method, the better. If `person.Name` had been a field, things would be greatly simplified because we could simply pass a reference to that field to be assigned, but we'd still have to pass a `nameof()` for the base class to notify via INPC if necessary.

Case Study: Quadratic Equation Solver

Consider a piece of code designed to solve quadratic equations, that is, equations in the form $ax^2 + bx + c = 0$. This equation can have one or two solutions depending on the values of a, b and c; furthermore, the solutions may be real numbers or complex numbers.

Ignoring data loss issues,[3] we shall adopt the closed-form solution most of us know from our school years

$$x_{1,2} = \frac{-b \pm \sqrt{\Delta}}{2a}$$

---

[3] Real-world implementations of a quadratic equation solver use a different formula than the one you learned in school so as to preserve numerical stability, particularly in cases where the value of a is really small.

where the so-called *discriminant* Δ is defined as $\Delta = b^2 - 4ac$. A quadratic equation yields two complex roots if $\Delta < 0$, a single real solution if $\Delta = 0$, and two real solutions if $\Delta > 0$. For the sake of simplicity, we'll use the Complex type for all calculations.

We begin our implementation by defining a simple class that exposes both the equation's inputs (a, b, and c) and its outputs (x_1 and x_2) as public fields:

```csharp
public class QuadraticEquationSolver
{
  public Complex A, B, C;

  public Complex Discriminant => B * B - 4 * A * C;

  public Tuple<Complex, Complex> Solve()
  {
    var rootDisc = Complex.Sqrt(Discriminant);
    return Tuple.Create(
      (-B + rootDisc) / (2 * A),
      (-B - rootDisc) / (2 * A));
  }
}
```

If we decide to build a user interface around a class such as this, the approach we would take is a lot more flexible than simply making a static method. Imagine a simple user interface such as

```
a:  |  1
----+-----
b:  | 10
----+-----
c:  | 16
----+-----
x1: | -2
----+-----
x2: | -8
```

Now let's introduce some requirements to our application:

1. When any of the a, b, or c values is changed, the values of x_1 and x_2 are recalculated.

2. If $x_{1,2}$ are not complex (i.e., are real), they are *shown* as real and not as complex numbers with a zero and an imaginary component.

These requirements are *presentation* requirements, not related directly to the domain model as such. It makes no sense to incorporate them into the QuadraticEquationSolver. What we do instead is build a view that takes care of some of these requirements. Notice that, since the equation data does not need to be transformed in any way, we won't need to build a separate model (as part of MVVM) for this example.

Circular Recalculation Limitations

Our example presents an interesting challenge. We know that the solutions $x_{1,2}$ depend on a,b,c and vice versa. However, the underlying data type of Complex is double, which has finite precision. This means that, were we to base our recalculations on PropertyChanged subscriptions, we would cause an infinite loop! Here, let me illustrate:

-   We try to solve the (rather trivial) equation $x^2 - 2 = 0$.

-   We plug in the coefficients $a = 1$, $b = 0$, and $c = -2$.

-   A PropertyChanged notification fires, causing the recalculation of $x_{1,2}$.

-   The values of $x_{1,2}$ are set to $\pm\sqrt{2}$.

-   Another PropertyChanged notification fires to recalculate the values $a,b,$c.

-   We calculate a and b correctly, but when calculating $c = x_1 x_2$, we hit a problem because

```
> Math.Sqrt(2)*Math.Sqrt(2)
2.0000000000000004
```

Oops! So instead of getting $c = -2$, we get $c = -2.0000000000000004$, which causes another round of recalculation, then another and another, and so on.

Observable Collections

If you bind a `List<T>` to a list box in either WinForms or WPF, changing the list won't update the UI. Why not? Because `List<T>` does not support the Observer pattern, of course – its individual members might, but the list as a whole has no explicit way of notifying that its contents have changed. Admittedly, you could just make a wrapper where methods such as `Add()` and `Remove()` generate notifications. However, both WinForms and WPF come with *observable collections* – the `BindingList<T>` and `ObservableCollection<T>` classes, respectively.

Both of these types behave as a `Collection<T>`, but the operations generate additional notifications that can be used, for example, by UI components to update the presentation layer when the collections change. For example, `ObservableCollection<T>` implements the `INotifyCollectionChanged` interface, which, in turn, has a `CollectionChanged` event. This event will tell you what action has been applied to the collection and will give you a list of both old and new items, as well as information about old and new starting indices: in other words, you get everything that you need in order to, say, redraw a list box correctly depending on the operation.

This functionality must be used with care! If you modify a collection many times over in, say, some iterative setting, it's best to temporarily disable notifications so that the bound UI gets redrawn only ones instead of hundreds of times! This functionality is available in the frameworks themselves (e.g., WinForms' `SuspendLayout()` temporarily suspends the processing of change notifications), but a more robust strategy is to simply subclass the observable collection and introduce a flag that you can toggle to prevent notifications. For example, you could inherit from `ObservableCollection<T>` and override its `OnCollectionChanged()` method, calling the `base` method conditionally.

One important thing to note is that neither `BindingList<T>` nor `ObservableCollection<T>` is thread-safe. So if you plan to read/write these collections from multiple threads, you'd need to build a threading proxy (hey, Proxy pattern!). There are, in fact, two options here:

- Inherit from an observable collection and just put common collection operations such as `Add()` behind a lock.

- Inherit from a concurrent collection (e.g., a `ConcurrentBag<T>`) and add `INotifyCollectionChanged` functionality.

You can find implementations of both of these approaches on Stack Overflow and elsewhere. I prefer the first option as it's a lot simpler.

Observable LINQ

When we discussed property observers, we also managed to discuss the idea of properties that affect other properties. But that's not all they affect. For example, a property might be involved in a LINQ query, which yields some result. So how can we know that we need to re-query the data in a particular query when a property it depends on changes?

Over time, there had been frameworks such as CLINQ (Continuous LINQ) and Bindable LINQ that attempted to solve the problem of a LINQ query generating the necessary events (i.e., CollectionChanged) when one of its constituent parts failed. Other frameworks exist, and I can offer no recommendations here about which one you use. Keep in mind that these frameworks are attempting to solve a really difficult problem.

Declarative Subscriptions in Autofac

So far, most of our discussions have centered around the idea of *explicit*, imperative subscription to events, whether via the usual .NET mechanisms, Reactive Extensions, or something else. However, that's not the only way event subscriptions can happen.

You can also define event subscriptions *declaratively*. This is often made possible by the fact that applications make use of a central IoC container where the declarations can be found and event wireups can be made behind the scenes.

There are two popular approaches for declarative event wireups. The first uses attribute: you simply mark some method as [Publishes("foo")] and some other method, in some other class, as [Subscribes("foo")]; and the IoC container makes a connection behind the scenes.

The second is to use interfaces, and that is what we are going to demonstrate, together with the use of the Autofac library. First, we define the notion of an event and flesh out interfaces for the sending of the event and its handling:

```
public interface IEvent {}

public interface ISend<TEvent> where TEvent : IEvent
{
  event EventHandler<TEvent> Sender;
}
```

```csharp
public interface IHandle<TEvent> where TEvent : IEvent
{
  void Handle(object sender, TEvent args);
}
```

We can now manufacture concrete implementations of events. For example, suppose we are handling click events, where a user can click a button a certain number of times (e.g., double-click it):

```csharp
public class ButtonPressedEvent : IEvent
{
  public int NumberOfClicks;
}
```

We can now make a Button class that generates such events. For simplicity, we'll simply add a Fire() method that fires off the event. Adopting a declarative approach, we decorate the Button with the ISend<ButtonPressedEvent> interface:

```csharp
public class Button : ISend<ButtonPressedEvent>
{
  public event EventHandler<ButtonPressedEvent> Sender;

  public void Fire(int clicks)
  {
    Sender?.Invoke(this, new ButtonPressedEvent
    {
      NumberOfClicks = clicks
    });
  }
}
```

And now, for the receiving side. Suppose we want to log button clicks. This means we want to handle ButtonPressedEvents. Luckily, we already have an interface for this too:

```csharp
public class Logging : IHandle<ButtonPressedEvent>
{
  public void Handle(object sender, ButtonPressedEvent args)
  {
    Console.WriteLine(
```

```
        $"Button clicked {args.NumberOfClicks} times");
  }
}
```

Now, what we want, behind the scenes, is for our IoC container to automatically subscribe Logging to the Button.Sender event behind the scenes, without us having to do this manually. Let me first of all show you the monstrous piece of code that you would require to do this:

```
var cb = new ContainerBuilder();
var ass = Assembly.GetExecutingAssembly();

// register publish interfaces
cb.RegisterAssemblyTypes(ass)
  .AsClosedTypesOf(typeof(ISend<>))
  .SingleInstance();

// register subscribers
cb.RegisterAssemblyTypes(ass)
  .Where(t =>
    t.GetInterfaces()
      .Any(i =>
        i.IsGenericType &&
        i.GetGenericTypeDefinition() == typeof(IHandle<>)))
  .OnActivated(act =>
  {
    var instanceType = act.Instance.GetType();
    var interfaces = instanceType.GetInterfaces();
    foreach (var i in interfaces)
    {
      if (i.IsGenericType
          && i.GetGenericTypeDefinition() == typeof(IHandle<>))
      {
        var arg0 = i.GetGenericArguments()[0];
        var senderType = typeof(ISend<>).MakeGenericType(arg0);
        var allSenderTypes =
          typeof(IEnumerable<>).MakeGenericType(senderType);
        var allServices = act.Context.Resolve(allSenderTypes);
```

```
    foreach (var service in (IEnumerable) allServices)
    {
      var eventInfo = service.GetType().GetEvent("Sender");
      var handleMethod = instanceType.GetMethod("Handle");
      var handler = Delegate.CreateDelegate(
        eventInfo.EventHandlerType, null, handleMethod);
      eventInfo.AddEventHandler(service, handler);
    }
  }
}
})
.SingleInstance()
.AsSelf();
```

Let's go through what's happening in the preceding code step-by-step:

- First, we register all assembly types that implement ISend<>. There are no special steps that need to be taken there because they just need to exist somewhere. For the sake of simplicity, we register them as singletons – if that were not the case, the situation with the wireups would become even more complicated because the system would have to track each constructed instance.[4]

- We then register the types that implement IHandle<>. This is where things get crazy because we specify an additional OnActivated() step that must be performed before an object is returned.

- In this step, given this IHandle<Foo> type, we locate all types that implement the ISend<Foo> interface using reflection. This is a rather tedious process.

- For each of the located types, we wire up the subscription. Again, this is done using reflection, and you can also see some magic strings here and there.

---

[4] From personal experience, there are many situations where you *do* need your IoC container to track all instances that have been constructed. One example is the Dynamic Prototyping approach (see the "Dynamic Prototyping Bridge" section of Chapter 8), where an in-process change of an object mandates an immediate replacement of all such objects that have been constructed during the application's lifetime.

With this setup in place, we can build the container and resolve both a `Button` and a `Logging` component, and the subscriptions will be done behind the scenes:

```
var container = cb.Build();

var button = container.Resolve<Button>();
var logging = container.Resolve<Logging>();

button.Fire(1); // Button clicked 1 times
button.Fire(2); // Button clicked 2 times
```

In a similar fashion, you could implement declarative subscriptions using attributes instead. And if you don't use Autofac, don't worry: most popular IoC containers are capable of implementing these sorts of declarative event wireups.

Summary

Generally speaking, we could have avoided discussing the Observer pattern in C# because the pattern itself is baked right into the language. That said, I have demonstrated some of the practical uses of Observer (property change notifications) as well as some of the issues related to that (dependent properties). Furthermore, we looked at the way in which the Observer pattern is supported for reactive streams.

Thread safety is one concern when it comes to Observer, whether we are talking about individual events or entire collections. The reason it shows up is because several observers on one component form a list (or similar structure), and then the question immediately arises as to whether that list is thread-safe and what exactly happens when it's being modified and iterated upon (for purposes of notification) at the same time.

CHAPTER 23

State

I must confess: my behavior is governed by my state. If I didn't get enough sleep, I'm going to be a bit tired. If I had a drink, I wouldn't get behind the wheel. All of these are *states*, and they govern my behavior: how I feel and what I can and cannot do.

I can, of course, transition from one state to another. I can go get a coffee, and this will take me from sleepy to alert (I hope!). So we can think of coffee as a *trigger* that causes a transition of yours truly from sleepy to alert. Here, let me clumsily illustrate it for you:

```
        coffee
sleepy --------> alert
```

The State design pattern is a very simple idea: state controls behavior, state can be changed, and the only thing that the jury is out on is *who* triggers the change from one state to another.

There are two ways in which we can model states:

- States are actual classes with behaviors, and these behaviors cause the transition from this state to another. In other words, a state's members are the options in terms of where we can go from that state.

- States and transitions are just enumerations. We have a special component called a *state machine* that performs the actual transitions.

Both of these approaches are viable, but it's really the second approach that is the most common. We'll take a look at both of them, but I must warn that I'll glance over the first one, since this isn't how people typically do things.

D. Nesteruk, *Design Patterns in .NET 6*, https://doi.org/10.1007/978-1-4842-8245-8_23

State-Driven State Transitions

We'll begin with the most trivial example out there: a light switch that can only be in the *on* and *off* states. The reason we are choosing such a simple domain is that I want to highlight the madness (there's no other word for it) that a classic implementation of State brings, and this example is simple enough to do so without generating pages of code listings.

We are going to build a model where any state is capable of switching to some other state: this reflects the "classic" implementation of the State design pattern (as per the GoF book). First, let's model the light switch. All it has is a state and some means of switching from one state to another:

```
public class Switch
{
  public State State = new OffState();
}
```

This all looks perfectly reasonable. We have a switch that's in some state (either *on* or *off*). We can now define the State, which, in this particular case, is going to be an actual class:

```
public abstract class State
{
  public virtual void On(Switch sw)
  {
    Console.WriteLine("Light is already on.");
  }

  public virtual void Off(Switch sw)
  {
    Console.WriteLine("Light is already off.");
  }
}
```

This implementation is far from intuitive, so much so that we need to discuss it slowly and carefully, because from the outset, nothing about the State class makes sense.

While the State is abstract (meaning you cannot instantiate it), it has non-abstract members that allow the switching from one state to another. This, to a reasonable person, makes no sense. Imagine the light switch: it's the switch that changes states. The state itself isn't expected to change *itself*, and yet it appears this is exactly what it does.

Perhaps most bewildering, though, the default behavior of State.On()/Off() claims that we are *already* in this state! Note that these methods are virtual. This will come together, somewhat, as we implement the rest of the example.

We now implement the on and off states:

```
public class OnState : State
{
  public OnState()
  {
    Console.WriteLine("Light turned on.");
  }
  public override void Off(Switch sw)
  {
    Console.WriteLine("Turning light off...");
    sw.State = new OffState();
  }
}
// similarly for OffState
```

The constructor of each state simply informs us that we have *completed* the transition. But the transition itself happens in OnState.Off() and OffState.On(). That is where the switching happens.

We can now complete the Switch class by giving it methods to actually switch the light on and off:

```
public class Switch
{
  public State State = new OffState();
  public void On()  { State.On(this);  }
  public void Off() { State.Off(this); }
}
```

So, putting it all together, we can run the following scenario:

```
LightSwitch ls = new LightSwitch(); // Light turned off
ls.On();  // Switching light on...
          // Light turned on
ls.Off(); // Switching light off...
          // Light turned off
ls.Off(); // Light is already off
```

Here is an illustrated transition from OffState to OnState:

```
          LightSwitch.On() -> OffState.On()
OffState -------------------------------> OnState
```

On the other hand, the transition from OnState to OnState uses the base State class, the one that tells you that you are already in that state:

```
          LightSwitch.On() -> State.On()
OnState ----------------------------> OnState
```

Let me be the first to say that the implementation presented here is *terrible*. While being a nice demonstration of OOP equilibristics, it is an unreadable, unintuitive mess that goes against everything we learn about both OOP generally and design patterns in particular, specifically:

- A state typically does not switch itself.

- A list of possible transitions should not appear all over the place; it's best to keep it in one place (SRP).

- There is no need to have actual classes modeling states unless they have class-specific behaviors; this example could be reduced to something much simpler.

Maybe we should have been using enums to begin with?

Enum-Based State Machine

Let's try to define a state machine for a typical phone conversation.

First of all, we'll describe the states of a phone:

```
public enum State
{
  OffHook,
  Connecting,
  Connected,
  OnHold
}
```

We can now also define transitions between states, also as an enum:

```
public enum Trigger
{
  CallDialed,
  HungUp,
  CallConnected,
  PlacedOnHold,
  TakenOffHold,
  LeftMessage
}
```

Now, the exact *rules* of this state machine, that is, what transitions are possible, need to be stored somewhere. Here is a UML state machine diagram showing what kind of transitions we want.

Let's use a dictionary of state-to-trigger/state pairs to model the state diagram presented in Figure 23-1:

```
private static Dictionary<State, List<(Trigger, State)>> rules
  = new() { /* todo */ }
```

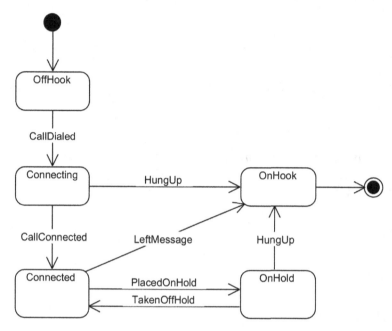

Figure 23-1. *Phone call state diagram*

This is a little clumsy, but essentially the key of the dictionary is the State we're moving *from*, and the value is a list of Trigger-State pairs representing possible triggers while in this state and the state you move into when you use a trigger.

Let's initialize this data structure:

```
private static Dictionary<State, List<(Trigger, State)>> rules
  = new ()
  {
    [State.OffHook] = new()
    {
      (Trigger.CallDialed, State.Connecting)
    },
    [State.Connecting] = new()
    {
```

```
      (Trigger.HungUp, State.OffHook),
      (Trigger.CallConnected, State.Connected)
    },
    // more rules here
  };
```

We also need a starting (current) state, and we can also add an exit (terminal) state if we want the state machine to stop executing once that state is reached:

```
State state = State.OffHook, exitState = State.OnHook;
```

So in the preceding line, we start out with the OffHook state (when you're ready to make the call), and the exit state is when the phone is placed OnHook and the call is finished.

Having made this, we don't necessarily have to build a separate component for actually running (we use the term *orchestrating*) a state machine. For example, if we wanted to build an interactive model of the telephone, we could do it like this:

```csharp
do
{
  Console.WriteLine($"The phone is currently {state}");
  Console.WriteLine("Select a trigger:");

  for (var i = 0; i < rules[state].Count; i++)
  {
    var (t, _) = rules[state][i];
    Console.WriteLine($"{i}. {t}");
  }

  int input = int.Parse(Console.ReadLine());

  var (_, s) = rules[state][input];
  state = s;
} while (state != exitState);
Console.WriteLine("We are done using the phone.");
```

Here's how it works: we let the user select one of the available triggers on the current state, and provided the trigger is valid, we transition to the right state by using that rules dictionary that we created earlier.

If the state we've reached is the exit state, we just jump out of the loop. Here's a sample interaction with the program:

```
The phone is currently OffHook
Select a trigger:
0. CallDialed
0
The phone is currently Connecting
Select a trigger:
0. HungUp
1. CallConnected
1
The phone is currently Connected
Select a trigger:
0. LeftMessage
1. HungUp
2. PlacedOnHold
2
The phone is currently OnHold
Select a trigger:
0. TakenOffHold
1. HungUp
1
We are done using the phone.
```

This hand-rolled state machine's main benefit is that it is very easy to understand: states and transitions are ordinary enumerations, the set of transitions is defined in a `Dictionary`, and the start and end states are simple variables. I'm sure you'll agree this is much easier to understand than the example we started the chapter with.

Switch-Based State Machine

In our exploration of state machines, we have progressed from the needlessly complicated classic example where states are represented by classes to a handcrafted example where states are represented as enumeration members, and now we shall experience one final step of degradation as we stop using dedicated data types for transitions.

But our simplifications won't end there: instead of jumping from one method call to another, we'll confine ourselves to an infinitely repeating `switch` statement where state will be examined and transitions will happen by virtue of the state changing.

The scenario I want you to consider is a combination lock. The lock has a four-digit code (e.g., 1234) that you enter one digit at a time. As you enter the code, if you make a mistake, you get the "FAILED" output, but if you enter all digits correctly, you get "UNLOCKED" instead and you exit the state machine.

We shall still encode the states using an enumeration:

```
enum State
{
  Locked,
  Failed,
  Unlocked
}
```

The entire scenario that we want to run can fit into a single listing:

```
string code = "1234";
var state = State.Locked;
var entry = new StringBuilder();

while (true)
{
  switch (state)
  {
    case State.Locked:
      entry.Append(Console.ReadKey().KeyChar);

      if (entry.ToString() == code)
      {
        state = State.Unlocked;
        break;
      }

      if (!code.StartsWith(entry.ToString()))
      {
        // the code is blatantly wrong
```

```
      state = State.Failed;
    }
    break;
  case State.Failed:
    Console.CursorLeft = 0;
    Console.WriteLine("FAILED");
    entry.Clear();
    state = State.Locked;
    break;
  case State.Unlocked:
    Console.CursorLeft = 0;
    Console.WriteLine("UNLOCKED");
    return;
  }
}
```

As you can see, this is very much a state machine, albeit one that lacks any structure. You couldn't examine it from the top level and be able to tell what all the possible states and transitions are. It is not clear, unless you really examine the code, how the transitions happen – and we're lucky there are no goto statements here to make jumps between the cases!

This Switch-Based State Machine approach is viable for scenarios with very small numbers of states and transitions. It loses out on structure, readability, and maintainability, but can work as a quick patch if you do need a state machine quickly and are too lazy to make enum cases.

Overall, this approach does not scale and is difficult to manage, so I would not recommend it in production code. The only exception would be if such a machine was made using code generation on the basis of some external model.

Encoding Transitions with Switch Expressions

The switch-based state machine may be unwieldy, but that's partly due to the way information about states and transitions is structured (because it's not). But there is a different kind of switch – a switch *expression* (as opposed to *statement*) that, thanks to pattern matching, allows us to neatly define state transitions.

Okay, time for a simple example. You're on a hunt for treasure and find a treasure chest that you can open or close...unless it's locked, in which case the situation is a bit more complicated (you need to have a key to lock or unlock a chest). Thus, we can encode the states and possible transitions as follows:

```
enum Chest { Open, Closed, Locked }
enum Action { Open, Close }
```

With this definition, we can write a method called `Manipulate` that takes us from one state to another. The general rules of chest operation are as follows:

- If the chest is locked, you can only open it if you have the key.

- If the chest is open and you close it while having the key, you lock it.

- If the chest is open and you don't have the key, you just close it.

- A closed (but not locked) chest can be opened whether you have the key or not.

The set of possible transitions can be encoded right in the structure of the pattern matching expression. Without further ado, here it is:

```
static Chest Manipulate(Chest chest,
  Action action, bool haveKey) =>
  (chest, action, haveKey) switch
  {
    (Chest.Closed, Action.Open, _) => Chest.Open,
    (Chest.Locked, Action.Open, true) => Chest.Open,
    (Chest.Open, Action.Close, true) => Chest.Locked,
    (Chest.Open, Action.Close, false) => Chest.Closed,

    _ => chest
  };
```

This approach has a number of advantages and disadvantages. The advantages are that

- This state machine is easy to read.

- Guard conditions such as `haveKey` are easy to incorporate and fit nice into pattern matching.

There are disadvantages too:

- The formal set of rules for this state machine is defined in a way that cannot be extracted. There's no data store where the rules are kept, so you cannot generate a report or a diagram or run any verification checks beyond those that are done by the compiler (it only checks for exhaustiveness).

- If you need any behaviors, such as state entry or exit behaviors, this cannot be done easily in a switch expression – you would need to define a good old-fashioned method with a switch statement in it.

To sum up, this approach is great for simple state machines because it results in very readable code. But it's not exactly an "enterprise" solution.

State Machines with Stateless

While hand-rolling a state machine works for the simplest of cases, you probably want to leverage an industrial-strength state machine framework. That way, you get a tested library with a lot more functionality. It's also fitting because we need to discuss additional state machine–related concepts, and implementing them by hand is rather tedious.

Before we move on to the concepts I want to discuss, let us first of all reconstruct our previous phone call example using Stateless.[1] Assuming the existence of the same enumerations State and Trigger as before, the definition of a state machine is very simple:

```
var call = new StateMachine<State, Trigger>(State.OffHook);

phoneCall.Configure(State.OffHook)
  .Permit(Trigger.CallDialed, State.CallConnected);

// and so on, then, to cause a transition, we do

call.Fire(Trigger.CallDialed); // call.State is now State.CallConnected
```

---

[1] Stateless can be found at https://github.com/dotnet-state-machine/stateless. It's worth noting that the phone call example actually comes from the authors of SimpleStateMachine, a project on which Stateless is based.

As you can see, Stateless' `StateMachine` class is a builder with a fluent interface. The motivation behind this API design will become apparent as we discuss the different intricacies of Stateless.

Types, Actions, and Ignoring Transitions

Let's talk about the many features of Stateless and state machines generally.

First and foremost, Stateless supports states and triggers of *any* .NET type – it's not constrained to enums. You can use strings, numbers, anything you want. For example, a light switch could use a `bool` for states (`false` = off, `true` = on); we'll keep using enums for triggers. Here is how one would implement the `LightSwitch` example:

```
enum Trigger { On, Off }
var light = new StateMachine<bool, Trigger>(false);

light.Configure(false)          // if the light is off...
  .Permit(Trigger.On, true)     // we can turn it on
  .Ignore(Trigger.Off);         // but if it's already off we do nothing

// same for when the light is on
light.Configure(true)
  .Permit(Trigger.Off, false)
  .Ignore(Trigger.On)
  .OnEntry(() => timer.Start())
  .OnExit(() => timer.Stop());  // calculate time spent in this state

light.Fire(Trigger.On);  // Turning light on
light.Fire(Trigger.Off); // Turning light off
light.Fire(Trigger.Off); // Light is already off!
```

There are a few interesting things worth discussing here. First of all, this state machine has *actions* – things that happen as we enter a particular state. These are defined in `OnEntry()`, where you can provide a lambda that does something; similarly, you could invoke something at the moment the state is exited using `OnExit()`. One use of such transition actions would be to start a timer when entering a transition and stop it when exiting one, which could be used for tracking the amount of time spent in each state. For example, you might want to measure the time the light stays on for purposes of verifying electricity costs.

Another thing worth noting is the use of `Ignore()` builder methods. This basically tells the state machine to ignore the transition completely: if the light is already off and we try to switch it off (as in the last line of the preceding listing), we instruct the state machine to simply ignore it, so no output is produced in that case.

Why is this important? Because, if you forget to `Ignore()` this transition or fail to specify it explicitly, Stateless will throw an `InvalidOperationException`:

> "No valid leaving transitions are permitted from state 'False' for trigger 'False.' Consider ignoring the trigger."

Reentrancy Again

Another alternative to the "redundant switching" conundrum is Stateless' support for reentrant states. To replicate the light switch example from the start of this chapter, we can configure the state machine so that, in the case of reentry into a state (meaning that we transition, say, from false to false), an action is invoked. Here is how one would configure it:

```
var light = new StateMachine<bool, Trigger>(false);

light.Configure(false) // if the light is off...
  .Permit(Trigger.On, true)  // we can turn it on
  .OnEntry(transition =>
  {
    if (transition.IsReentry)
      WriteLine("Light is already off!");
    else
      WriteLine("Turning light off");
  })
  .PermitReentry(Trigger.Off);

// same for when the light is on

light.Fire(Trigger.On);  // Turning light on
light.Fire(Trigger.Off); // Turning light off
light.Fire(Trigger.Off); // Light is already off!
```

In the last line of the configuration code, `PermitReentry()` allows us to return to the `false` (off) state on a `Trigger.Off` trigger. Notice that, in order to output a corresponding message to the console, we use a different lambda: one that has a parameter of type `Transition`. The parameter has public members that describe the transition fully. This includes `Source` (the state we're transitioning from), `Destination` (the state we're going to), `Trigger` (what caused the transition), and `IsReentry`, a Boolean flag that we use to determine if this is a reentrant transition.

Hierarchical States

In the context of a phone call, it can be argued that the `OnHold` state is a substate of the `Connected` state, implying that when we're on hold, we're also connected. Stateless lets us configure the state machine like this:

```
phoneCall.Configure(State.OnHold)
  .SubstateOf(State.Connected)
  // etc.
```

Now, if we are in the `OnHold` state, `phoneCall.State` will give us `OnHold`, but there's also a `phoneCall.IsInState(State)` method that will return `true` when called with either `State.Connected` or `State.OnHold`.

More Features

Let's talk about a few more features related to state machines that are implemented in Stateless.

Guard clauses allow you to enable and disable transitions at will by calling `PermitIf()` and providing `bool`-returning lambda functions, for example:

```
phoneCall.Configure(State.OffHook)
  .PermitIf(Trigger.CallDialled, State.Connecting, () => IsValidNumber)
  .PermitIf(Trigger.CallDialled, State.Beeping, () => !IsValidNumber);
```

Parameterized triggers are an interesting concept. Essentially, you can attach parameters to triggers such that, in addition to the trigger itself, there's also additional information that can be passed along. For example, if a state machine needs to notify a particular employee, you can specify an email to be used for notification:

```
var notifyTrigger = workflow.SetTriggerParameters<string>(Trigger.Notify);
workflow.Configure(State.Notified)
  .OnEntryFrom(assignTrigger, email => SendEmail(email));
workflow.Fire(notifyTrigger, "foo@bar.com");
```

External storage is a feature of Stateless that lets you store the internal state of a state machine externally (e.g., in a database) instead of using the StateMachine class itself. To use it, you simply define the getter and setter methods in the StateMachine constructor:

```
var stateMachine = new StateMachine<State, Trigger>(
  () => database.ReadState(),
  s => database.WriteState(s));
```

Introspection allows us to actually look at the table of triggers that can be fired from the current state through the PermittedTriggers property.

This is far from an exhaustive list of features that Stateless offers, but it covers all the important parts.

Concurrent State Machines

Due to the conciseness of our examples, we may have given the impression that any given system has just one, rather manageable, state machine that governs the overall behavior of the system. This is not always correct: sometimes the operation of the system is governed by several independent states. As soon as such a situation is reached, the level of complexity jumps since the interaction between two or more state machines may introduce additional logic that must be incorporated.

For example, consider an automated trading system that trades cryptocurrency. We can have one state machine for the status of our connection to the system (connected, disconnected, faulted, etc.) and another state machine indicating our trading strategies (not in market, high-frequency trading, holding on to long-term positions).

Now imagine our reaction to a surprise disconnect. If we don't have a position open, a disconnection may not be such a big deal. A disconnection with long-term positions is also manageable, though we definitely need to inform the system owner just in case. But a disconnection in the middle of a trading session with many positions open (especially when not governed by server-side stop-loss rules) can be a disaster, so we need to try and salvage the situation – reconnect as quickly as possible to recover a situation; notify the owner ASAP; if the reconnection fails after X attempts, let the owner know so they may attempt other means of closing positions (either by using a different terminal/client or by physically calling the broker or exchange).

Implicit State Machines

The C# programming language has two language constructs that turn into state machines behind the scenes.

The first construct is `yield`, which allows resumable iteration by constructing a state machine behind the scenes. Check out the decompiled version of `MoveNext()` to see the internal implementation details.

The second construct is, of course, `async/await`. Prior to its introduction in C#, asynchronous processing of this sort was effectively emulated using `yield`, as demonstrated by `AsyncEnumerator` in Jeffrey Richter's PowerThreading library.[2]

Summary

The operation of state machines extends way beyond simple transitions: it allows a lot of complexity to handle the most demanding business cases. Let us recap some of the state machine features we've discussed:

- State machines involve two collections: states and triggers. States model the possible states of the system, and triggers transition us from one state to another. You are not limited to enumerations: you can use ordinary data types.

- Attempting a transition that's not configured will result in an exception.

- It is possible to explicitly configure entry and exit actions for each state.

- Reentrancy can be explicitly allowed in the API, and furthermore, you can determine whether or not a reentry is occurring in the entry/exit action.

---

[2] `https://github.com/Wintellect/PowerThreading`

- Transitions can be turned on an off through guard conditions. They can also be parameterized.

- States can be hierarchical, that is, they can be substates of other states. An additional method is then required to determine whether you're in a particular (parent) state.

While most of the preceding features might seem like overengineering, these features provide great flexibility in defining real-world state machines.

CHAPTER 24

Strategy

Suppose you decide to take an array or vector of several strings and output them as a list:

- just

- like

- this

If you think about the different output formats, you probably know that you need to take each element and output it with some additional markup. But in the case of languages such as HTML or LaTeX, the list will also need the start and end tags or markers.

We can formulate a strategy for rendering a list:

- Render the opening tag/element.

- For each of the list items, render that item.

- Render the closing tag/element.

Different strategies can be formulated for different output formats, and these strategies can be then fed into a general, non-changing algorithm to generate the text.

This is yet another pattern that exists in dynamic (runtime-replaceable) and static (generics-based, fixed) incarnations. Let's take a look at both of them.

Dynamic Strategy

So our goal is to print a simple list of text items in the following formats:

```
public enum OutputFormat
{
  Markdown,
  Html
}
```

401

The skeleton of our strategy will be defined in the following base class:

```
public interface IListStrategy
{
  void Start(StringBuilder sb);
  void AddListItem(StringBuilder sb, string item);
  void End(StringBuilder sb);
}
```

Now let us jump to our text processing component. This component would have a list-specific method called, say, AppendList():

```
public class TextProcessor
{
  private StringBuilder sb = new StringBuilder();
  private IListStrategy listStrategy;

  public void AppendList(IEnumerable<string> items)
  {
    listStrategy.Start(sb);
    foreach (var item in items)
      listStrategy.AddListItem(sb, item);
    listStrategy.End(sb);
  }

  public override string ToString() => sb.ToString();
}
```

So we've got a buffer called sb where all the output goes, the listStrategy that we're using for rendering lists, and of course AppendList(), which specifies the set of steps that need to be taken to actually render a list with a given strategy.

Now, pay attention here. Composition, as used previously, is one of two possible options that can be taken to allow concrete implementations of a skeleton algorithm. Instead, we could add functions such as AddListItem() as abstract or virtual members to be overridden by derived classes: that's what the Template Method pattern does.

Anyways, back to our discussion. We can now go ahead and implement different strategies for lists, such as a HtmlListStrategy:

```csharp
public class HtmlListStrategy : IListStrategy
{
  public void Start(StringBuilder sb) => sb.AppendLine("<ul>");
  public void End(StringBuilder sb) => sb.AppendLine("</ul>");

  public void AddListItem(StringBuilder sb, string item)
  {
    sb.AppendLine($"  <li>{item}</li>");
  }
}
```

By implementing the overrides, we fill in the gaps that specify how to process lists. We implement a MarkdownListStrategy in a similar fashion, but because Markdown does not need opening/closing tags, we only do work in the AddListItem() method:

```csharp
public class MarkdownListStrategy : IListStrategy
{
  // markdown doesn't require list start/end tags
  public void Start(StringBuilder sb) {}
  public void End(StringBuilder sb) {}

  public void AddListItem(StringBuilder sb, string item)
  {
    sb.AppendLine($" * {item}");
  }
}
```

We can now start using the TextProcessor, feeding it different strategies and getting different results, for example:

```csharp
var tp = new TextProcessor();
tp.SetOutputFormat(OutputFormat.Markdown);
tp.AppendList(new []{"foo", "bar", "baz"});
WriteLine(tp);

// Output:
// * foo
// * bar
// * baz
```

We can make provisions for strategies to be switchable at runtime – this is precisely why we call this implementation a *dynamic* strategy. This is done in the SetOutputFormat() method, whose implementation is trivial:

```
public void SetOutputFormat(OutputFormat format)
{
  switch (format) {
    case OutputFormat.Markdown:
      listStrategy = new MarkdownListStrategy();
      break;
    case OutputFormat.Html:
      listStrategy = new HtmlListStrategy();
      break;
    default:
      throw new ArgumentOutOfRangeException(nameof(format), format, null);
  }
}
```

Now, switching from one strategy to another is trivial, and you get to see the results straight away:

```
tp.Clear(); // erases underlying buffer
tp.SetOutputFormat(OutputFormat.Html);
tp.AppendList(new[] { "foo", "bar", "baz" });
WriteLine(tp);

// Output:
// <ul>
//   <li>foo</li>
//   <li>bar</li>
//   <li>baz</li>
// </ul>
```

Static Strategy

Thanks to the magic of generics, you can bake any strategy right into the type. Only minimal changes are necessary to the TextStrategy class:

```
public class TextProcessor<LS>
  where LS : IListStrategy, new()
{
  private StringBuilder sb = new StringBuilder();
  private IListStrategy listStrategy = new LS();

  public void AppendList(IEnumerable<string> items)
  {
    listStrategy.Start(sb);
    foreach (var item in items)
      listStrategy.AddListItem(sb, item);
    listStrategy.End(sb);
  }

  public override string ToString() => return sb.ToString();
}
```

What changed in the dynamic implementation is as follows: we added the LS generic argument, made a listStrategy member with this type, and started using it instead of the reference we had previously. The results of calling the adjusted AppendList() are identical to what we had before:

```
var tp = new TextProcessor<MarkdownListStrategy>();
tp.AppendList(new []{"foo", "bar", "baz"});
WriteLine(tp);

var tp2 = new TextProcessor<HtmlListStrategy>();
tp2.AppendList(new[] { "foo", "bar", "baz" });
WriteLine(tp2);
```

The textual output of this example is exactly the same as for the dynamic strategy. Note that we've had to make two instances of TextProcessor, each with a distinct list-handling strategy, since it is impossible to switch a type's strategy midstream: it is baked right into the type.

Equality and Comparison Strategies

The most well-known use of the Strategy pattern inside .NET is, of course, the use of equality and comparison strategies.

Consider a simple class such as the following:

```
class Person
{
  public int Id;
  public string Name;
  public int Age;
}
```

As it stands, you can put several `Person` instances inside a `List`, but calling `Sort()` on such a list would be meaningless:

```
var people = new List<Person>();
people.Sort(); // does not do what you want
```

The same goes for comparisons using the `==` and `!=` operators: at the moment, all these involve reference-based comparison.

We need to clearly distinguish two types of operations:

- *Equality* checks whether or not two instances of an object are equal, according to the rules you define. This is covered by the `IEquatable<T>` interface (the `Equals()` method) as well as operators `==` and `!=,` which typically use the `Equals()` method internally.

- *Comparison* allows you to compare two objects and find which one is less than, equal to, or greater than another. This is covered by the `IComparable<T>` interface and is required for things like sorting.

By implementing `IEquatable<T>` and `IComparable<T>`, every object can expose its own comparison and equality strategies. For example, if we assume that people have unique `Id`s, we can use this value for comparison:

```
public int CompareTo(Person other)
{
  if (ReferenceEquals(this, other)) return 0;
  if (ReferenceEquals(null, other)) return 1;
  return Id.CompareTo(other.Id);
}
```

So now, calling people.Sort() makes sense – it will use the built-in CompareTo() method that we've written. But there is a problem: a typical class can only have one default CompareTo() implementation for comparing the class with itself. The same goes for equality. So what if your comparison strategy changes at runtime?

Luckily, BCL designers have thought of that too. We can specify the comparison strategy right at the call site, simply by passing in a lambda:

```
people.Sort((x, y) => x.Name.CompareTo(y.Name));
```

This way, even though Person's default comparison behavior is to compare by id, we can compare by name if we need to.

But that's not all! There is a third way in which a comparison strategy can be defined. This way is useful if some strategies are common and you want to preserve them inside the class itself.

The idea is this: you define a nested class that implements the IComparer<T> interface. You then expose this class as a static variable:

```
public class Person
{
  // ... other members here
  private sealed class NameRelationalComparer : IComparer<Person>
  {
    public int Compare(Person x, Person y)
    {
      if (ReferenceEquals(x, y)) return 0;
      if (ReferenceEquals(null, y)) return 1;
      if (ReferenceEquals(null, x)) return -1;
      return string.Compare(x.Name, y.Name,
        StringComparison.Ordinal);
    }
  }
```

```
public static IComparer<Person> NameComparer { get; }
  = new NameRelationalComparer();
}
```

As you can see, this class (which could easily be a struct instead) defines a standalone strategy for comparing two Person instances using their names. We can now simply take a static instance of this class and feed it into the Sort() method:

```
people.Sort(Person.NameComparer);
```

As you may have guessed, the situation with equality comparison is fairly similar: you can use an IEquatable<T>, pass in a lambda, or generate a class that implements an IEqualityComparer<T>. Your choice!

Functional Strategy

The functional variation of the Strategy pattern is simple: all OOP constructs are simply replaced by functions. First of all, TextProcessor devolves from being a class to being a function. This is actually idiomatic (i.e., the right thing to do) because TextProcessor has a single operation:

```
let processList items startToken itemAction endToken =
  let mid = items |> (Seq.map itemAction) |> (String.concat "\n")
  [startToken; mid; endToken] |> String.concat "\n"
```

In functional programming parlance, any function that takes one or more functions as parameters is called a *higher-order function*. processList() is precisely this type of function, as it takes four arguments: a sequence of items, the starting token (note: it's a token, not a function), a function for processing each element, and the ending token. Since this is a function, this approach assumes that processList is stateless, that is, it does not keep any state beyond the duration of the call.

The algorithm presented here is the same as before, but since it's in functional form, let's discuss how it is implemented:

- The set of items is first "mapped" using Seq.map (this is equivalent to LINQ's Select()) using the itemAction provided.

- All items are concatenated together with the line break separator.

- The start token, middle part (from the previous step), and end token are all concatenated together using the line break separator.

Our strategy is not just a single, neatly self-contained element, but rather a combination of three different items: the start and end tokens as well as a function that operates upon each of the elements in the sequence. We can now specialize `processList` in order to implement HTML and Markdown processing as before:

```
let processListHtml items =
  processList items "<ul>" (fun i -> "  <li>" + i + "</li>") "</ul>"

let processListMarkdown items =
  processList items "" (fun i -> " * " + i) ""
```

Here is how you would use these specializations, with predictable results:

```
let items = ["hello"; "world"]
printfn "%s" (processListHtml items)
printfn "%s" (processListMarkdown items)
```

This approach, admittedly, lacks in usability because the interface of `processList` gives absolutely no hints whatsoever as to what the client is supposed to provide as the `itemAction`. All they know is it's an `'a -> string`, so we rely on them to guess correctly what it's actually for.

Declarative Strategies

We've looked at two ways of specifying strategies: either as references provided directly into a class constructor or as a type parameter in a generic class. Another very common way of specifying a strategy is declarative, for example, by using attributes.

There is no *one true way* of specifying strategies in a declarative way because different frameworks do it differently. Here are a few examples of using attributes as strategies:

- Compile-time decorations using packages such as `JetBrains.Annotations` are used to specify analysis strategies that need to be adopted by static analysis tools such as JetBrains ReSharper or Rider.

- Attributes applied to types can be parsed by an IoC container and incorporated during the construction of the object. This is mentioned in Chapter 22, where we auto-wire event subscriptions.

- Attributes applied to properties, specifying validation rules, are located and used by frameworks such as ASP.NET.

- Additional strategies, often affecting large areas of code, can be specified using attributes and then applied using IL weavers such as Fody or PostSharp.

Just like the Static Strategy approach, the declarative approach is more or less set in stone at compile time. Of course, if you are using reflection to detect the attributes at runtime, then you can affect the resulting behavior.

Summary

The Strategy design pattern allows you to define a skeleton of an algorithm and then use composition to supply the missing implementation details related to a particular strategy. This approach exists in two incarnations:

- *Dynamic strategy* simply keeps a reference to the strategy currently being used. Want to change to a different strategy? Just change the reference. Easy!

- *Static strategy* requires that you choose the strategy at compile time and stick with it – there is no scope for changing your mind later on.

- *Functional strategy* receives a function or function wrapper and invokes it whenever required. This reference is typically not kept beyond the duration of the higher-order function.

Should one use dynamic or static strategies? Well, dynamic ones allow you reconfiguration of the objects after they have been constructed. Imagine a UI setting that controls the form of the textual output: what would you rather have, a switchable `TextProcessor` or two variables of type `TextProcessor<MarkdownStrategy>` and `TextProcessor<HtmlStrategy>`? It's really up to you.

CHAPTER 25

Template Method

The Strategy and Template Method design patterns are very similar, so much so that, just like with factories, I would be very tempted to merge those patterns into some sort of "Skeleton Method" design pattern. I will resist the urge.

The difference between Strategy and Template Method is that Strategy uses composition (whether static or dynamic), whereas Template Method uses inheritance. But the core principle of defining the skeleton of an algorithm in one place and its implementation details in other places remains, once again observing the OCP (we simply *extend* systems).

Game Simulation

Most board games are very similar: the game starts (some sort of setup takes place), players take turns until a winner is decided, and then the winner can be announced. It doesn't matter what the game is – chess, checkers, something else. We can define the algorithm as follows:

```
public abstract class Game
{
  public void Run()
  {
    Start();
    while (!HaveWinner)
      TakeTurn();
    WriteLine($"Player {WinningPlayer} wins.");
  }
}
```

411

© Dmitri Nesteruk 2022
D. Nesteruk, *Design Patterns in .NET 6*, https://doi.org/10.1007/978-1-4842-8245-8_25

As you can see, the run() method, which runs the game, simply uses a set of other methods and properties. Those methods are abstract and also have protected visibility, so they don't get called from the outside:

```
protected abstract void Start();
protected abstract bool HaveWinner { get; }
protected abstract void TakeTurn();
protected abstract int WinningPlayer { get; }
```

To be fair, some of the preceding members, especially void-returning ones, do not necessarily have to be abstract. For example, if some games have no explicit start() procedure, having start() as abstract violates the ISP since members that do not need it would still have to implement it. In Chapter 24 we deliberately made an interface, but with Template Method, the case is not so clear-cut.

Now, in addition to the preceding members, we can have certain protected fields that are relevant to all games – the number of players and the index of the current player:

```
public abstract class Game
{
  public Game(int numberOfPlayers)
  {
    this.numberOfPlayers = numberOfPlayers;
  }

  protected int currentPlayer;
  protected readonly int numberOfPlayers;
  // other members omitted
}
```

From here on out, the Game class can be extended to implement a game of chess:

```
public class Chess : Game
{
  public Chess() : base(2) { /* 2 players */ }

  protected override void Start()
  {
    WriteLine($"Starting a game of chess with {numberOfPlayers} players.");
  }
```

```
protected override bool HaveWinner => turn == maxTurns;

protected override void TakeTurn()
{
  WriteLine($"Turn {turn++} taken by player {currentPlayer}.");
  currentPlayer = (currentPlayer + 1) % numberOfPlayers;
}

protected override int WinningPlayer => currentPlayer;

private int maxTurns = 10;
private int turn = 1;
}
```

A game of chess involves two players, so that's the value fed into the base class' constructor. We then proceed to override all the necessary methods, implementing some very simple simulation logic for ending the game after ten turns. We can now use the class with new Chess().Run() – here is the output:

```
Starting a game of chess with 2 players
Turn 0 taken by player 0
Turn 1 taken by player 1
...
Turn 8 taken by player 0
Turn 9 taken by player 1
Player 0 wins.
```

And that's pretty much all there is to it!

Template Method Mixin

The scenario we have looked at so far had a class with a *single* template method, the presumed implementation of which would be done through subclassing. But, thanks to default interface methods, there is an alternative implementation that we'll call *Template Method Mixin*. The idea is to construct a functional equivalent of a base class, but in an interface! For example, instead of baking an abstract Game, you'd make an IGame:

```
interface IGame
{
  public void Run()
  {
    Start();
    while (!HaveWinner)
      TakeTurn();
    WriteLine($"Player {WinningPlayer} wins.");
  }

  void Start();
  bool HaveWinner { get; }
  void TakeTurn();
  int WinningPlayer { get; }
}
```

Of course, interfaces don't have constructors, but apart from that, this is something that can now be mixed (hence the *mixin* part) into any class, including classes that have inheritors already. Thus, a class can implement a template method without using its inheritance characteristics directly, but using an interface instead.

The implementation of the IGame interface in the Chess and similar classes is almost identical to Game inheritance from before, but with subtle differences. The interface members are likely to be public; this is somewhat annoying since you probably want to hide details and not let anyone use them.

The implementation of empty methods is the same as with abstract classes: you either leave a method signature with no body, or you give it an empty body. If you do not implement it in the related class (note there is no override keyword), you will get a no-op, and things will function just fine, and there will be no warning.

The invocation is also different; you need to make sure the variable is of the interface type before you use it, that is:

```
IGame chess = new Chess();
chess.Run();
```

This approach is great in terms of flexibility. You can now add a template method to a class without modifying its parent or if a parent already exists. Also, a class can now be given two or more template methods without any contention over inheritance. Overall, it's a very flexible mechanism provided you are happy with the way default interface methods function in C#.

Functional Template Method

As you may have guessed, the functional approach to Template Method is to simply define a standalone function runGame() that takes the templated parts as parameters. The only problem is that a game is an *inherently mutable* scenario, which means we have to have some sort of container representing the state of the game. We can try using a record type:

```
type GameState = {
  CurrentPlayer: int;
  NumberOfPlayers: int;
  WinningPlayer: int;
}
```

With this setup, we end up having to pass an instance of GameState into every function that is part of the template method. The method itself, mind you, is rather simple:

```
let runGame initialState startAction takeTurnAction haveWinnerAction =
  let state = initialState
  startAction state
  while not (haveWinnerAction state) do
    takeTurnAction state
  printfn "Player %i wins." state.WinningPlayer
```

The implementation of a chess game isn't a particularly difficult affair either, the only real problem being the initialization and modification of internal state:

```
let chess() =
  let mutable turn = 0
  let mutable maxTurns = 10
  let state = {
    NumberOfPlayers = 2;
    CurrentPlayer = 0;
    WinningPlayer = -1;
```

```
  }
  let start state =
    printfn "Starting a game of chess with %i players" state.
    NumberOfPlayers

  let takeTurn state =
    printfn "Turn %i taken by player %i." turn state.CurrentPlayer
    state.CurrentPlayer <- (state.CurrentPlayer+1) % state.NumberOfPlayers
    turn <- turn + 1
    state.WinningPlayer <- state.CurrentPlayer

  let haveWinner state =
    turn = maxTurns

runGame state start takeTurn haveWinner
```

So, just to recap, what we're doing here is initializing all the functions required by the method/function right inside the outer function (this is completely legitimate in both C# and F#) and then passing each of those functions into runGame. Notice also that we have some mutable state that is used throughout the sub-function calls.

Overall, implementation of Template Method using functions instead of objects is quite possible if you're prepared to introduce record types and mutability into your code. And sure, theoretically, you could rewrite this example and get rid of mutable state by essentially storing a snapshot of each game state and passing that in a recursive setting – this would effectively turn a template method into a kind of templated state pattern. Try it!

Summary

Unlike Strategy, which uses composition and thus branches into static and dynamic variations, Template Method uses inheritance, and as a consequence, it can only be static, since there is no way to manipulate the inheritance characteristics of an object once it's been constructed.

The only design decision in a template method is whether you want the methods used by the template method to be abstract or actually have a body, even if that body is empty. If you foresee some methods unnecessary for *all* inheritors, go ahead and make them empty/non-abstract so as to comply with the ISP.

CHAPTER 26

Visitor

To explain this pattern, I'm going to jump into an example first and then discuss the pattern itself. Hope you don't mind! Suppose you have parsed a mathematical expression (with the use of the Interpreter pattern, of course!) composed of double values and addition operators, for example:

```
(1.0 + (2.0 + 3.0))
```

This expression can be represented using an object hierarchy similar to the following:

```csharp
public abstract class Expression { /* nothing here (yet) */ }

public class DoubleExpression : Expression
{
  private double value;

  public DoubleExpression(double value) { this.value = value; }
}

public class AdditionExpression : Expression
{
  private Expression left, right;

  public AdditionExpression(Expression left, Expression right)
  {
    this.left = left;
    this.right = right;
  }
}
```

© Dmitri Nesteruk 2022
D. Nesteruk, *Design Patterns in .NET 6*, https://doi.org/10.1007/978-1-4842-8245-8_26

Given this setup, you are interested in two things:

- Printing the OOP expression as text

- Evaluating the expression's value

You also want to do those two things (and many other possible operations on these trees) as uniformly and succinctly as possible. How would you do it? Well, there are many ways, and we'll take a look at them all, starting with the implementation of the printing operation.

Intrusive Visitor

The simplest solution is to take the base `Expression` class and add an abstract member to it:

```
public abstract class Expression
{
  // adding a new operation
  public abstract void Print(StringBuilder sb);
}
```

In addition to breaking the OCP, this modification hinges on the assumption that you actually have access to the hierarchy's source code – something that's not always guaranteed. But we've got to start somewhere, right? So with this change, we need to implement `Print()` in `DoubleExpression` (that's easy, so I'll omit it here) as well as in `AdditionExpression`:

```
public class AdditionExpression : Expression
{
  ...
  public override void Print(StringBuilder sb)
  {
    sb.Append(value: "(");
    left.Print(sb);
    sb.Append(value: "+");
```

```
    right.Print(sb);
    sb.Append(value: ")");
  }
}
```

Ooh, this is fun! We are polymorphically and recursively calling `Print()` on subexpressions. Wonderful, let's test this out:

```
var e = new AdditionExpression(
  new DoubleExpression(1),
  new AdditionExpression(
    new DoubleExpression(2),
    new DoubleExpression(3)));
var sb = new StringBuilder();
e.Print(sb);
WriteLine(sb); // (1.0 + (2.0 + 3.0))
```

Well, this was easy. But now imagine you've got ten inheritors in the hierarchy (not uncommon, by the way, in real-world scenarios) and you need to add some new `Eval()` operation. That's ten modifications that need to be done in ten different classes. But the OCP isn't the real problem.

The real problem is the SRP. You see, a problem such as printing is a special concern. Rather than stating that every expression should print itself, why not introduce an `ExpessionPrinter` that knows how to print expressions? And, later on, you can introduce an `ExpressionEvaluator` that knows how to perform the actual calculations. All without affecting the `Expression` hierarchy in any way.

Reflective Visitor

Now that we've decided to make a *separate* printer component, let's get rid of `Print()` member functions (but keep the base class, of course):

```
abstract class Expression
{
  // nothing here!
};
```

Now let's try to implement an ExpressionPrinter. My first instinct would be to write something like this[1]:

```
public static class ExpressionPrinter
{
  public static void Print(DoubleExpression e, StringBuilder sb)
  {
    sb.Append(de.Value);
  }

  public static void Print(AdditionExpression ae, StringBuilder sb)
  {
    sb.Append("(");
    Print(ae.Left, sb);   // will not compile!!!
    sb.Append("+");
    Print(ae.Right, sb); // will not compile!!!
    sb.Append(")");
  }
}
```

This code will not compile. C# knows that, say, ae.Left is an Expression, but since it doesn't check the type at runtime (unlike various dynamically typed languages), it doesn't know which overload to call. Too bad!

What can be done here? Well, only one thing – remove the overloads and check the type at runtime:

```
public static class ExpressionPrinter
{
  public static void Print(Expression e, StringBuilder sb)
  {
    switch (e)
    {
      case DoubleExpression de:
        sb.Append(de.Value);
        break;
```

---

[1] Notice that in this example, and in all further examples in this book, we have broken encapsulation by exposing the members of visitable classes as public and mutable.

```
    case AdditionExpression ae:
      sb.Append("(");
      Print(ae.Left, sb);
      sb.Append("+");
      Print(ae.Right, sb);
      sb.Append(")");
      break;
    default:
      // your choice what to do here
      throw new Exception("Unsupported expression type");
  }
 }
}
```

Using a fancy switch statement, we try to typecast to every known expression type and process things accordingly. The choice of what to do in the default case is yours, with the two most obvious choices being the following:

- Do nothing. Kust skip over a type if you don't know it.

- Throw an exception.

With all that said, we've actually arrived at a viable solution that we can use:

```
var e = new AdditionExpression(
  left: new DoubleExpression(1),
  right: new AdditionExpression(
    left: new DoubleExpression(2),
    right: new DoubleExpression(3)));
var sb = new StringBuilder();
ExpressionPrinter.Print(e, sb);
WriteLine(sb);
```

This approach is simple, but has several disadvantages.

First, there are no compiler checks that you *have*, in fact, implemented printing for every single element in the hierarchy. When a new element gets added, you can keep using ExpressionPrinter without modification, and it will just revert to whatever behavior the default case defines, and you end up with either a no-op or a runtime exception – neither of those is desirable.

Second, the `case` statements are order-sensitive and dependent on the hierarchy of types. If you have types `Parent` and `Child`, the check against `Child` has to come first before `Parent`. If it comes after, `Child` nodes will never be processed. This may be easy to handle in simple hierarchies, but in complicated ones, having to manage this list correctly can be a challenge.

Nonetheless, this is a viable solution. Seriously, it's quite possible to stop here and never go any further in the Visitor pattern: the `is` operator isn't *that* expensive, and I think many developers will remember to cover every single type of object in that `if` statement.

Extension Methods?

You could be forgiven for thinking that the problem of separating out an `ExpressionPrinter` can be somehow solved without the use of type checks. Sadly, this setup also devolves to the use of the reflective visitor.

Sure, you can take both `DoubleExpression` and `AdditionExpression` and give them `Print()` extension methods that would be callable directly on the object, while residing elsewhere. However, your implementation of `AdditionExpression.Print()` will still have several problems:

```
public static void Print(this AdditionExpression ae, StringBuilder sb)
{
  sb.Append("(");
  ae.Left.Print(sb); // oops
  sb.Append("+");
  ae.Right.Print(sb);
  sb.Append(")");
}
```

The first problem is that, since this is an extension method, we need to make the `Left` and `Right` members public so that the extension method can access them.

But that's not the real problem. The main issue here is that `ae.Left.Print()` cannot be called because `ae.Left` is a general `Expression`. How would you support it? Well, this is where you would devolve to a reflective printer by implementing an extension method on the root element of the hierarchy and perform type checks:

```
public static void Print(this Expression e, StringBuilder sb)
{
  switch (e)
  {
    case DoubleExpression de:
      de.Print(sb);
      break;
    case AdditionExpression ae:
      ae.Print(sb);
      break;
    // and so on
  }
}
```

This solution runs into the same problem as the original, namely, the issue that there's no verification to ensure that *every* inheritor of Expression is covered by the switch statement. Now, admittedly, this is something that we can actually force, thus lending the reflective printer its true name by using...reflection!

Extension method classes are static and can have both static fields and constructors, so we can map out all the inheritors and attempt to find the methods that handle them:

```
public static class ExpressionPrinter
{
  private static Dictionary<Type, MethodInfo> methods
    = new Dictionary<Type, MethodInfo>();

  static ExpressionPrinter()
  {
    var a = typeof(Expression).Assembly;
    var classes = a.GetTypes()
      .Where(t => t.IsSubclassOf(typeof(Expression)));
    var printMethods = typeof(ExpressionPrinter).GetMethods();
    foreach (var c in classes)
    {
      // find extension method that takes this class
      var pm = printMethods.FirstOrDefault(m =>
```

```
        m.Name.Equals(nameof(Print)) &&
        m.GetParameters()?[0]?.ParameterType == c);

    methods.Add(c, pm);
  }
 }
}
```

With this setup, the extension method `Print()` implemented for the base type `Expression` now devolves to

```
public static void Print(this Expression e, StringBuilder sb)
{
  methods[e.GetType()].Invoke(null, new object[] {e, sb});
}
```

Naturally, this approach has significant performance costs. There are ways to offset these costs, such as using `Delegate.CreateDelegate()` to avoid storing those `MethodInfo` objects and instead having ready-to-call delegates when the need arises.

Finally, there's always the "nuclear option": generating code that creates those calls at runtime. Of course, this comes with its own set of problems: you'll be generating code either on the basis of reflection (which means that you're almost always one step behind, because you need a binary in order to extract type information), or alternatively, you'll be inspecting actual written code using a parser framework provided by Roslyn, ReSharper, Rider, or some similar mechanism.

Functional Reflective Visitor (C#)

In our discussion of the reflective visitor variation, we saw that with a lot of type casts, we can keep all visitor logic constrained to the visitor itself, at the expense of the visitor having to be aware of the structure of the hierarchy it's working with. The weakness of that approach is that any other visitor has to, in effect, replicate this, since knowledge of how to handle a particular hierarchy is not kept in a central place.

Since this knowledge is necessary, we can delegate it to the root of our hierarchy. This is no greater an OCP violation than that implied in the reflective visitor and, in fact, directly supports the SRP since there is only one place that needs to be modified to incorporate a new type. Yes, the root being aware of its descendants is not the prettiest of things, but assuming the hierarchy is stable, you only have to define it once.

What I propose is embellishing the root of the hierarchy with a method such as the following:

```csharp
public void Match(
  Action<DoubleExpression> visitDoubleExpression,
  Action<AdditionExpression> visitAdditionExpression,
  Action<Expression> visitUnknownExpression = null)
{
  switch (this)
  {
    case DoubleExpression e:
      visitDoubleExpression(e);
      break;
    case AdditionExpression e:
      visitAdditionExpression(e);
      break;
    default:
      visitUnknownExpression?.Invoke(this);
      break;
  }
}
```

This method takes a set of `Actions` corresponding to the different types of the hierarchy. It then performs a type cast equivalent to the reflective visitor to determine which type we received and calls the appropriate function. The functions are provided externally. I have also included an optional handler for unknown hierarchy types, so the caller can provide an action to process that type if needed.

As always, this method is order-sensitive: any `Child` class *must* appear before its `Parent` in order to maintain correct functioning.

With this approach, our visitor is able to provide a single entry point and invoke a single method to get its work done:

```csharp
public class ExpressionPrinter
{
  private readonly StringBuilder sb = new();
```

```
public string Print(Expression e)
{
  e.Match(VisitDoubleExpression,  VisitAdditionExpression);
  return sb.ToString();
}

private void VisitAdditionExpression(AdditionExpression ae) { ... }
private void VisitDoubleExpression(DoubleExpression de) { ... }
}
```

Now, an ExpressionPrinter can just call Print() on any Expression and have some meaningful output. While this approach does not check for exhaustiveness, it is robust in the sense that, if some type is not handled, this will not cause a crash.

An interesting point here is that the naming of VisitXxx methods is redundant. We could have overloaded a single Visit() method and invoke e.Match(Visit, Visit) with no loss of generality, since C# is smart enough to figure out which overload to take for each argument. It will work just fine even if some classes in the hierarchy inherit from others, and if you want one parent handler to handle several children, that's not a problem either – you'll just have to provide the same argument in all locations where the specific types are expected.

A possible variation of this approach is to modify the Match() method to turn it into a generic Match<T>(...), accepting a set of Func<T, Expression> delegates. Such a method could propagate return values without temporaries (allowing visitors to become static/singleton-like) and handle map-reduce behaviors as described in the "Reductions and Transforms" section of this chapter.

Functional Reflective Visitor (F#)

It's worth noting that the approach adopted in the reflective visitor implementation is *precisely* the approach you would adopt in a language such as F#, the only difference being that, instead of inheritance hierarchies, you would mainly be dealing with functions.

If, instead of a hierarchy, you defined your expression types in a discriminated union such as...

```
type Expression =
  | Add of Expression * Expression
  | Mul of Expression * Expression
..
```

...then any visitor you would implement would, most likely, have a structure similar to the following:

```
let rec process expr =
  match expr with
  | And(lhs, rhs) -> ...
  | Mul(lhs, rhs) -> ...
  ...
```

This approach is precisely equivalent to the approach taken in our C# implementation. Each of the cases in a match expression would effectively be turned into an is check. There are major differences, however. First of all, concrete case filters and guard conditions in F# are easier to read than nested if statements in C#. The possible recursiveness of the entire process is a lot more expressive, particularly with the use of partial patterns, should you need them. Also note that a discriminated union cannot leverage proper inheritance/polymorphism, so it is not possible to group several cases by functionality unless you introduce additional discriminated unions.

Improvements

While it's not possible to statically enforce the presence of every single necessary type check in the preceding example, it *is* possible to generate exceptions if the appropriate implementation is missing. To do this, simply make a dictionary that maps the supported types to lambda functions that process those types, that is:

```
private static DictType actions = new DictType
{
  [typeof(DoubleExpression)] = (e, sb) =>
  {
    var de = (DoubleExpression) e;
    sb.Append(de.Value);
  },
```

```
[typeof(AdditionExpression)] = (e, sb) =>
{
  var ae = (AdditionExpression) e;
  sb.Append("(");
  Print(ae.Left, sb);
  sb.Append("+");
  Print(ae.Right, sb);
  sb.Append(")");
}
};
```

Now you can implement a top-level `Print()` method in a much simpler fashion. In fact, for bonus points, you can use the C# extension method mechanic to add `Print()` as a method of any `Expression`:

```
public static void Print(this Expression e, StringBuilder sb)
{
  actions[e.GetType()](e, sb);
}
// sample use:
myExpression.Print(sb);
```

Whether or not you use extension methods or just ordinary static or instance methods on a `Printer` is completely irrelevant for the purposes of the SRP. Both an ordinary class and an extension method class serve to isolate printing functionality from the data structures themselves, the only difference being whether or not you consider printing part of `Expression`'s API, which I personally think is reasonable: I like the idea of `expression.Print()`, `expression.Eval()`, and so on. However, if you are an OOP purist, you might hate this approach.

What Is Dispatch?

Whenever people speak of visitors, the word *dispatch* is brought up. What is it? Well, put simply, "dispatch" is a problem of figuring out which methods to call – specifically, how many pieces of information are required in order to make the call.

Here's a simple example:

```
interface IStuff { }
class Foo : IStuff { }
class Bar : IStuff { }

public class Something
{
  static void func(Foo foo) { }
  static void func(Bar bar) { }
}
```

Now, if I make an ordinary Foo object, I'll have no problem calling func() with it:

```
Foo foo = new Foo();
func(foo); // this is fine
```

But if I decide to cast it to a base type (interface or class), the compiler will not know which overload to call:

```
Stuff stuff = new Foo;
func(stuff); // oops!
```

Now, let's think about this polymorphically: is there *any* way we can coerce the system to invoke the correct overload without any runtime (is, as, and similar) checks? Turns out there is.

See, when you call something on an IStuff, that call *can* be polymorphic, and it can be dispatched right to the necessary component. This in turn can call the necessary overload. This is called *double dispatch* because

1. First, you do a polymorphic call on the actual object.

2. Inside the polymorphic call, you call the overload. Since, inside the object, this has a precise type (e.g., a Foo or Bar), the right overload is triggered.

Here's what I mean:

```
interface Stuff {
  void call();
}
```

```
class Foo : Stuff {
  void call() { func(this); }
}
class Bar : Stuff {
  void call() { func(this); }
}

void func(Foo foo) {}
void func(Bar bar) {}
```

Can you see what's happening here? We cannot just stick one generic call() implementation into Stuff: the distinct implementations *must* be in their respective classes so that the this pointer is suitably typed.

This implementation lets you write the following:

```
Stuff foo = new Foo;
foo.call();
```

And here is a schematic showing what's going on:

```
           this = Foo
foo.call() ------------> func(foo)
```

Dynamic Visitor

Let's come back to the ExpressionPrinter example that I claimed has no zero chance of working:

```
public class ExpressionPrinter
{
  public void Print(AdditionExpression ae, StringBuilder sb)
  {
    sb.Append("(");
    Print(ae.Left, sb);
    sb.Append("+");
    Print(ae.Right, sb);
    sb.Append(")");
  }
```

```
  public void Print(DoubleExpression de, StringBuilder sb)
  {
    sb.Append(de.Value);
  }
}
```

What if I told you I could make it work as is just by adding two keywords and raising the computational cost of the `Print(ae,sb)` method? I'm sure you can guess what I'm talking about already. Yeah, I'm talking about dynamic dispatch:

```
public void Print(AdditionExpression ae, StringBuilder sb)
{
  sb.Append("(");
  Print((dynamic)ae.Left, sb);    // <-- look closely here
  sb.Append("+");
  Print((dynamic)ae.Right, sb); // <-- and here
  sb.Append(")");
}
```

The whole business of `dynamic` was added to C# in order to support dynamically typed languages. One aspect of some of those languages is the ability to dynamically dispatch, that is, to make call decisions at runtime as opposed to compile- time. And that's exactly what we're doing here!

Here's how you would call it:

```
var e = ...; // as before
var ep = new ExpressionPrinter();
var sb = new StringBuilder();
ep.Print((dynamic)e, sb); // <-- note the cast here
WriteLine(sb);
```

By casting a variable to `dynamic`, we defer dispatch decisions until runtime. Thus, we get the correct calls happening; there are only a few problems, namely:

- There is a fairly significant performance penalty related to this type of dispatching.

- If a needed method is missing, you will get a runtime error.

A dynamic visitor is a good solution if you expect the object graph you visit to be small and the calls to be infrequent. Otherwise, the performance penalty might make the entire endeavor untenable.

Classic Visitor

The "classic" implementation of the Visitor design pattern uses *double dispatch*. There are conventions as to what the visitor member functions are called:

- Methods of the visitor are typically called Visit().

- Methods implemented throughout the hierarchy are typically called Accept().

So now, once again, we have something to put into the base Expression class – the Accept() method:

```
public abstract class Expression
{
  public abstract void Accept(IExpressionVisitor visitor);
}
```

As you can see, the preceding code refers to an interface type named IExpressionVisitor that can serve as a base type for various visitors such as ExpressionPrinter, ExpressionEvaluator, and similar. Now, every single implementor of Expression is now *required* to implement Accept() in an identical way, specifically:

```
public override void Accept(IExpressionVisitor visitor)
{
  visitor.Visit(this);
}
```

On the surface of it, this looks like a violation of DRY (Don't Repeat Yourself), another self-descriptive principle. However, if you think about it, every implementor will have a differently typed this reference, so this is not another case of cut-and-paste programming that static analysis tools like to complain about so much.

Now, on the other side, we can define the IExpressionVisitor interface as follows:

```
public interface IExpressionVisitor
{
  void Visit(DoubleExpression de);
  void Visit(AdditionExpression ae);
}
```

Notice that we *absolutely must* define overloads for all expression objects; otherwise, we would get a compilation error when implementing the corresponding Accept(). We can now implement this interface to define our ExpressionPrinter:

```
public class ExpressionPrinter : IExpressionVisitor
{
  StringBuilder sb = new();

  public void Visit(DoubleExpression de)
  {
    sb.Append(de.Value);
  }

  public void Visit(AdditionExpression ae)
  {
    // wait for it!
  }

  public override string ToString() => sb.ToString();
}
```

The implementation for a DoubleExpression is fairly obvious, but here's the implementation for an AdditionExpression:

```
public void Visit(AdditionExpression ae)
{
  sb.Append("(");
  ae.Left.Accept(this);
  sb.Append("+");
  ae.Right.Accept(this);
  sb.Append(")");
}
```

Notice how the calls now happen *on* the subexpressions themselves, leveraging double dispatch once again. As for the usage of the new double-dispatch visitor, here it is:

```
var e = new AdditionExpression(
  new DoubleExpression(1),
  new AdditionExpression(
    new DoubleExpression(2),
    new DoubleExpression(3)));
var ep = new ExpressionPrinter();
ep.Visit(e);
WriteLine(ep.ToString()); // (1 + (2 + 3))
```

Sadly, it's impossible to construct an extension method analogue to the preceding implementation because extension methods are static and cannot implement interfaces. If you want to hide the expression printer behind a slightly nicer API, you can go with the following:

```
public static class ExtensionMethods
{
  public static string Print(this DoubleExpression e)
  {
    var ep = new ExpressionPrinter();
    ep.Visit(e);
    return ep.ToString();
  }
}
```

This allows you to write `e.Print()` to get a string representation of the expression; sadly, using `ToString()` is not possible because extension methods cannot override it.

Of course, it's up to you to implement all the correct overloads, so this approach doesn't really help much and provides no safety checks to ensure you've overloaded for every single `Expression` inheritor.

Abstract Classes and Virtual Methods

One very important discussion to be had is whether the Visitor pattern is better using interfaces or with abstract classes. After all, if you don't need the root of the hierarchy to contain anything, why not make it an interface?

This mainly depends on what kind of hierarchy of visitable objects we want to create.

If we have a hierarchy with a single root and several inheritors, where the root serves as a kind of marker interface glue to join together objects with similar functionality, everything is fine: we can continue using an interface or, if need be, an abstract class with an abstract `Accept()` member.

If we do plan for inheritance, however, I would argue that there is a clear advantage of having the base of the hierarchy be an abstract class. This advantage has to do with the way `Accept()` is defined in our hierarchy of classes.

You see, in order to adhere to the LSP, any inheritor of our hierarchy of nodes has to function correctly when substituted for the original node. So if I define something like...

```
public class AbsoluteDoubleExpression : DoubleExpression
{
  public AbsoluteDoubleExpression(double value) : base(value) {}
}
```

...then, unfortunately, any `Accept()` call on this will invoke `Visitor.VisitDoubleExpression` because the implementation will be taken from the base class. As it stands, it is *impossible* to override `Accept()` if it's defined in an interface.

Now consider when the root of the hierarchy is an abstract class that provides a default no-op `Accept()` implementation.[2] Now, `IExpressionVisitor.Visit(AbsoluteDoubleExpression)` makes sense because we can invoke it:

```
public class AbsoluteDoubleExpression : DoubleExpression
{
  public AbsoluteDoubleExpression(double value) : base(value) {}
  public override void Accept(IExpressionVisitor visitor)
```

---

[2] Sure, we could continue using interfaces and just selectively make some `Accept()` methods virtual in the implemented classes. But this is a very wishy-washy approach. How do we know which methods to make virtual? We typically do not. And if we make them *all* virtual? That's right, and it's a lot easier to do it in an abstract base class!

435

```
  {
    visitor.Visit(this);
  }
}
```

This allows us to get the intended results provided we adjust the visitor hierarchy to accommodate the new type:

```
var e = new AbsoluteDoubleExpression(-3);
var ev = new ExpressionCalculator();
var ep = new ExpressionPrinter();
e.Accept(ep, ev); // extension method!
WriteLine($"{ep} = {ev.Result}"); // |-3| = 3
```

This listing uses a variadic extension method for `Accept()`, which is completely superfluous except for this particular demo or similar situations where one object needs to be fed to more than one visitor at the same time.

There are two more options that are available to you if you decide to use virtual members.

First, you can deliberately opt in to have the visitor process your class as a base class. To do this, simply avoid overriding `Accept()`, and you're good to go. This may be relevant in situations where you are forced to create two nodes that mean the same thing: to save effort, you can inherit `PlusExpression` from `SumExpression` – there is no need for a separate visitor method, so you can allow the system to treat those two in the same way.

The other option is the visitable null object where you don't want the node to be processed. In this particular case, you can override `Accept()`, but leave the body empty. This approach is similar to the all-cancelling element we discussed in Chain of Responsibility, the one that fails to propagate processing on the entire chain. Well, it's a similar idea here: if `Accept()` doesn't call `Visit()`, the visitor just ignores it.

Finally, when it comes to the base type of visitors, is it worth having an interface or a class? Once again, I would argue that it's better to have a base class with virtual members. First, you get some convenient no-op implementations, should you wish to skip on a node. And of course your visitors can now be efficiently inherited and customized in the inheriting methods. Just make sure to avoid private visitor members in favor of protected ones, and you're good to go!

Reducing Boilerplate

Every single class of our visitable hierarchy implements the same exact `Accept()` method that simply calls `visitor.Visit(this)`. It is very tempting to somehow reduce the number of places where this line of code is repeated, perhaps by defining something like

```
interface IVisitable<T>
{
  public void Accept(IExpressionVisitor v)
  {
    v.Visit((T)this);
  }
}
```

Unfortunately, unlike in C++, C# will not be able to determine at compile time that an overload for type T actually exists. We *could*, of course, cast v to a `dynamic`, but this just turns it into a reflective visitor with unnecessary extra steps.

Another way of fixing this is with source generators. We would need to declare every visitable class as `partial` and find a place in our code where we want to indicate that the source generator should do its work – there are many options here, for example, we could decorate every class with `[Visitable]`. We would then use a source generator to generate an `Accept()` for every class behind the scenes.

Implementing an Additional Visitor

So what is the advantage of the double-dispatch approach? The advantage is you have to implement the `Accept()` member through the hierarchy *just once*. You'll never have to touch a member of the hierarchy again. For example, suppose you now want to have a way of evaluating the result of the expression. This is easy...

```
public class ExpressionCalculator : IExpressionVisitor
{
  public double Result;

  public void Visit(DoubleExpression de)
  {
    Result = de.Value;
  }
```

```
public void Visit(AdditionExpression ae)
{
  // in a moment!
}
}
```

...but one needs to keep in mind that Visit() is currently declared as a void method, so the implementation for an AdditionExpression might look a little bit weird:

```
public void Visit(AdditionExpression ae)
{
  ae.Left.Accept(this);
  var a = Result;
  ae.Right.Accept(this);
  var b = Result;
  Result = a + b;
}
```

The preceding code is a byproduct of an inability to return from Accept(), so we cache the results in variables a and b and then return their sum. It works just fine:

```
var calc = new ExpressionCalculator();
calc.Visit(e);
WriteLine($"{ep} = {calc.Result}");
// prints "(1+(2+3)) = 6"
```

The interesting thing about this approach is that you can now write new visitors, in separate classes, even if you don't have access to the source code of the hierarchy itself. This lets you stay true to both the SRP and OCP, in addition to making your code a lot easier to understand. Figure 26-1 shows all the classes involved in our Visitor construction.

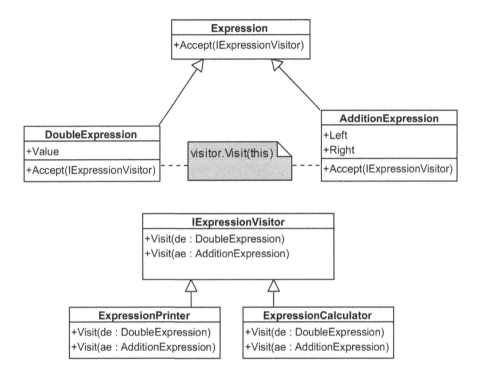

Figure 26-1. *Classic visitor implementation*

Type Checks Are Unavoidable

In practice, regardless of which implementation of visitor you go for, type checks are often unavoidable. For example, in our demo, we print the expression 1+2+3 as ((1+2)+3), while the parentheses, in this case, are completely unnecessary. They are only really necessary if, for example, we have a MultiplicationExpression also as part of a hierarchy. Then, (1+2)*3 and 1+2*3 would have different results, so braces would be required.

So, assuming we've created a MultiplicationExpression class (not exactly difficult), how can we make a printer that only adds parentheses when they actually matter?

This requires, first of all, a modification of the base Expression class to

```
public abstract class Expression
{
  public Expression Parent;
  public abstract void Accept(IExpressionVisitor visitor);
}
```

The construction of AdditionExpression then needs to be modified to

```
public AdditionExpression(Expression left, Expression right)
{
  Left = left;
  Right = right;
  Left.Parent = Right.Parent = this;
}
```

Same goes for MultiplicationExpression, naturally. Now, we assume that we only need braces when

- The expression we're in is an AdditionExpression.

- The parent expression is of type MultiplicationExpression.

This means that a print visitor for AdditionExpression would be performing type checks, that is:

```
public void Visit(AdditionExpression ae)
{
  bool needBraces = ae.Parent is MultiplicationExpression;
  if (needBraces) sb.Append("(");
  ae.Left.Accept(this);
  sb.Append("+");
  ae.Right.Accept(this);
  if (needBraces) sb.Append(")");
}
```

This now gives us the correct set of braces:

```
var e2 = new MultiplicationExpression(
  new DoubleExpression(1),
  new AdditionExpression(
    new DoubleExpression(2),
    new DoubleExpression(3)));
ep = new ExpressionPrinter();
ep.Visit(e2);
WriteLine(ep.ToString()); // 1*(2+3)
```

See? Type checks are often unavoidable. And in this particular case, we're only considering a very simplistic case of looking at a parent node. Now imagine if we have to start traversing the tree in an arbitrary manner, say, with pattern matching.

Acyclic Visitor

Now is a good time to mention that there are actually two strains, if you will, of the Visitor design pattern. They are

- *Cyclic visitor*, which is based on function overloading. Due to the cyclic dependency between the hierarchy (which must be aware of the visitor's type) and the visitor (which must be aware of *every* class in the hierarchy), the use of the approach is limited to stable hierarchies that are infrequently updated.

- *Acyclic visitor*, which is also based on type casting. The advantage here is the absence of limitations on visited hierarchies, but, as you may have guessed, there are performance implications.

The first step in the implementation of the acyclic visitor is the actual visitor interface. Instead of defining a `Visit()` overload for every single type in the hierarchy, we make things as generic as possible:

```
public interface IVisitor<in TVisitable>
{
  void Visit(TVisitable obj);
}
```

We need each element in our domain model to be able to accept such a visitor, but since every specialization is unique, what we do is introduce a *marker interface* – an empty interface with absolutely nothing in it:

```
public interface IVisitor {} // marker interface
```

This interface has no members, but we *will* use it as an argument to an `Accept()` method in whichever object we want to actually visit. Now, what we can do is redefine our `Expression` class from before as follows:

```
public abstract class Expression
{
  public virtual void Accept(IVisitor visitor)
  {
    if (visitor is IVisitor<Expression> typed)
      typed.Visit(this);
  }
}
```

So here's how the new Accept() method works: we take an IVisitor but then try to cast it to an IVisitor<T> where T is the type we're currently in. If the cast succeeds, the visitor in question knows how to visit our type, and so we call its Visit() method. If it fails, it's a no-op. It is *critical* to understand why typed itself does not have a Visit() that we could call on it. If it did, it would require an overload for every single type that would be interested in calling it, which is precisely what introduces a cyclic dependency.

After implementing Accept() in other parts of our model (once again, the implementation in each Expression class is identical), we can put everything together by once again defining an ExpressionPrinter, but this time round, it would look as follows:

```
public class ExpressionPrinter : IVisitor,
  IVisitor<Expression>,
  IVisitor<DoubleExpression>,
  IVisitor<AdditionExpression>
{
  StringBuilder sb = new StringBuilder();

  public void Visit(DoubleExpression de) { ... }

  public void Visit(AdditionExpression ae) { ... }

  public void Visit(Expression obj)
  {
    // default handler?
  }

  public override string ToString() => sb.ToString();
}
```

As you can see, we implement the IVisitor marker interface as well as a Visitor<T> for every T that we like to visit. If we omit a particular type T (e.g., suppose I comment out Visitor<DoubleExpression>), the program will still compile, and the corresponding Accept() call, if it comes, will simply execute as a no-op.

In the preceding code, the implementations of the Visit() methods are identical to what we had in the classic visitor implementation, and so are the results.

There is, however, a fundamental difference between this example and the classic visitor. The classic visitor used an interface, whereas our acyclic visitor has an abstract class as the root of the hierarchy. What does this mean? Well, an abstract class can have an implementation that can be used as a "fallback," which is why in the definition of ExpressionPrinter, I can implement IVisitor<Expression> and provide a Visit(Expression obj) method that can be used to handle a missing Visit() overload. For example, you could add logging there or throw an exception.

Figure 26-2 provides a visual illustration of the classes used to construct the acyclic visitor.

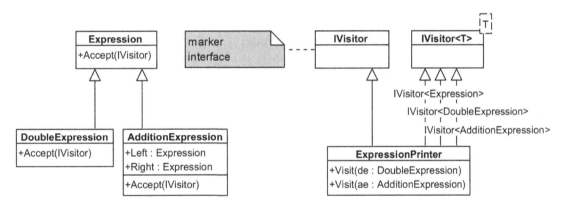

Figure 26-2. *Acyclic visitor class diagram*

Visitable Null Object

The Null Object pattern can sometimes interact with the Visitor design pattern. Let us construct a very simple example where a null object is necessary in order for things to function properly.

Consider mathematical expressions such as 1+2-3 and similar. Let's assume that every mathematical expression is represented by either a Literal, representing a value, or a BinaryExpression, representing an addition or a subtraction:

```
public interface INode {}
public record Literal(double Value) : INode;
public record BinaryExpression(INode Left, INode Right, char Op) : INode;
```

Thus, an expression 1+2-3 would be defined, in code, as

```
var exp = new BinaryExpression(
  new BinaryExpression(new Literal(1), new Literal(2), '+'),
  new Literal(3), '-'
);
```

A printer visitor defined, say, as a dynamic visitor would traverse this expression and print ((1+2)-3), assuming that we want to bracket each binary expression for safety. We can expand our model to support named variables such as

```
public record Variable(string Name) : INode;
```

But now consider a more complicated example. Let's say we decide to support unary expressions. A unary expression such as -5 is easy because it is simply a Literal(-5), since a numeric value carries the sign with it. But what about the expression -X? We *could* try to express this as BinaryExpression(Literal(0), Variable("X"), '-'). And, if we use an evaluation visitor, we'll get the correct value, since in fact 0 - X == -X. But if we feed this to a printer visitor, our output will be 0-X, which is not what we want!

So how to fix this? There are several ways of handling this:

1. Introduce a new type called UnaryExpression that knows how to print itself correctly. Note that any new type automatically requires that any visitor that processes a hierarchy of types be modified to handle this new type.

2. Reuse the BinaryExpression type, but instead of Literal(0) use a null on the left side of the printer. This is a very expensive approach because it requires every visitor in the application to be modified to perform null checks on every node being accessed.

3. Reuse the `BinaryExpression` type, but instead of `Literal(0)`
    use a null object on the left side that the printer and other
    visitors simply ignore. This implies that all the visitors need to be
    modified.

While in many cases the first option is quite sensible, we shall instead consider the
third option – creating a reusable null object that does nothing at all as far as expression
processing goes:

```csharp
public sealed class Null : INode {}
```

Our expression can now be defined thus:

```csharp
var exp = new BinaryExpression(new Null(), new Variable("X"), '-');
```

Now, the final question is how to get any visitor to successfully ignore any `Null` it
encounters. This largely depends on the kind of visitor implementation you choose to
use, since there are many. If you decide to go for the dynamic variation, your expression
printer can appear as follows:

```csharp
public class ExpressionPrinter
{
  private readonly StringBuilder sb = new();

  public void Visit(INode node) {}

  public void Visit(BinaryExpression exp)
  {
    sb.Append("(");
    Visit((dynamic)exp.Left);
    sb.Append(exp.Op);
    Visit((dynamic)exp.Right);
    sb.Append(")");
  }

  // other Visit() members omitted

  public override string ToString() => sb.ToString();
}
```

What's interesting about the preceding implementation is a Visit() method taking an INode. This method happens to be the catch-all method for all arguments for which overloads cannot be found after they're cast to a dynamic. Consequently, providing a Null here results in a no-op. Putting everything together, we can finally get the desired output:

```
var exp = new BinaryExpression(new Null(), new Variable("X"), '-');
var printer = new ExpressionPrinter();
printer.Visit(exp);
Console.WriteLine(printer); // (-X)
```

One disappointing thing about the dynamic visitor variation is that we would have to be putting this catch-all Visit() method manually into every single visitor class that we need. It is impossible to put it into a base class and then reuse it because we are doing a dynamic call, which will simply fail, and as mentioned earlier, dynamic calls do not happen on inherited members.

Now, consider a scenario where you are using double dispatch. Would it be possible to simply define such a Null class that would work unintrusively with existing structures? Sadly, the answer is *no*. What we would ideally want is something like

```
public sealed record NullLiteral() : Literal(0)
{
  public override void Accept(IVisitor visitor)
  {
    if (visitor is not ExpressionPrinter)
    base.Accept(visitor);
  }
}
```

This may seem as a null visitable of last resort, because it tightly couples itself to the type of visitor it accepts. But the reason it cannot exist is because of the override keyword. Sure, inheriting from Literal is a great idea to sneak this class into the hierarchy, but it is extremely unlikely that the author of Literal deliberately made the Accept() method virtual (unless they followed my advice, of course). If they did, well, great. We can override it in our class, and everything works. If they didn't, there's no way we can affect visitation behavior.

Interestingly, we have a symmetrical problem if we decide to preserve the OCP on the visitor side. Suppose we decide to introduce an `ExpressionAwarePrinter` through inheritance. But, by default, our original printer doesn't have any virtual members, so we cannot override things as we see fit – all we can do is reimplement every single `Visit()` method, and in this case, why do we need inheritance at all?

Visitor Adapter

All our visitor examples have been based on strong typing: each element of the hierarchy has a concrete type, and when you need to process something new, you introduce a new type. This maximizes flexibility (e.g., in terms of adding new visitors), but raises additional concerns. For example, should our visitables or visitors have virtual methods? Does inheritance make sense? Should we, perhaps, replace interfaces by abstract classes just in case?

If all we want from a hierarchy is traversal with a visitor and our situation is sufficiently simple, instead of building a hierarchy we can have just a single, suitably general, type. Say we're using a web service that returns a logical expression as JSON:

```
{ "Name": "Operator",
  "Value": "And",
  "Children": [
    {
      "Name": "Operator",
      "Value": "Greater",
      "Children": [
        {
          "Name": "Age",
          "Value": "16",
          "Children": []
        }
      ]
    },
    {
      "Name": "Operator",
      "Value": "Equal",
```

```
  "Children": [
    {
      "Name": "Citizen",
      "Value": "True",
      "Children": []
    }]}]} // compacted braces to save space
```

Now, we could create types such as AndOperator, EqualOperator, etc. in order to process this. But bear in mind that the construction of these types would have to involve reflection (finding the type by name), and if all you're interested in is just transforming this JSON into some other textual expression, there's little point in constructing an OOP-heavy solution. Perhaps something as simple as the following will suffice:

```
public sealed record Node(string Name, string Value, List<Node> Children);
```

Our node is a simple record that we don't want to imbue with additional behaviors. It works just fine – we can easily serialize the aforementioned piece of JSON into it. Now what we need is to be able to convert it to some other format using a visitor.

As always, there are many possibilities here, but let us assume that we still want our visitor to be organized and to process each of the operators in a distinct method. To accommodate this, we can introduce the following types:

```
public interface IVisitable
{
  void Accept(IVisitor visitor);
}
```

```
public interface IVisitor
{
  void VisitAnd(IVisitable visitable);
  void VisitEquals(IVisitable visitable);
  void VisitGreater(IVisitable visitable);
}
```

Only one problem remains: Node does not implement IVisitable, and the process of calling Accept() on it is not particularly straightforward. After all, we need to first check its internals and then dispatch onto the appropriate VisitXxx() method. Where to do this?

448

The answer is that we'll have to construct an additional object: a visitor adapter. This adapter will implement IVisitable and handle the dispatch for us:

```
public class VisitableNode : IVisitable
{
  private readonly Node node;
  public VisitableNode(Node node) => this.node = node;

  public void Accept(IVisitor visitor)
  {
    if (node.Name == "Operator")
    {
      switch (node.Value)
      {
        case "And": visitor.VisitAnd(node); break;
        case "Greater": visitor.VisitGreater(node); break;
        case "Equal": visitor.VisitEquals(node); break;
      }
    }
  }
}
```

Such an adapter can be constructed *in situ* or with the help of an extension method:

```
public static class NodeExtensions
{
  public static IVisitable ToVisitable(this Node node)
  {
    return new VisitableNode(node);
  }
}
```

The rest of the implementation would be pretty much the same as it is in an ordinary visitor implementation. The only difference is that whenever we visit the nodes recursively, we need to use the adapter, that is:

```
public class NodePrinter : IVisitor
{
  ...
```

```csharp
public void VisitBinaryOp(Node node, string op)
{
  sb.Append("(");
  node.Children[0].ToVisitable().Accept(this); // here
  sb.Append($" {op} ");
  node.Children[1].ToVisitable().Accept(this); // here
  sb.Append(")");
}
}
```

And that's it. We can now deserialize into our record class, create a visitor, cast the top node to a visitable, and use it:

```csharp
var node = JsonConvert.DeserializeObject<Node>(
  File.ReadAllText("input.json"));
NodePrinter p = new();
node.ToVisitable().Accept(p);
Console.WriteLine(p);
// ((Age > 16) && (Citizen == True))
```

This example, like a few others, essentially investigates the cat-and-mouse game of introducing some part of the Visitor pattern post hoc. Of course, it's nice when you plan for it from the outset, but sometimes that's just not possible, so you end up having to go around various C# limitations.

Reductions and Transforms

When we calculated the final numeric value in our ExpressionEvaluator, we relied on this value being stored inside the visitor as a temporary. This led to some rather strange-looking code where, at times, we had to cache the result because it was about to be overwritten by the next step of the calculation. That was because the only way we could collate the results of a traversal was by taking its side effect.

An alternative to this approach is to implement a transformer. This interface is similar to an ordinary visitor, except that it attempts to perform what's essentially a reduce operation. Reduction operations can be defined in a generic manner such as

```
public abstract class Expression
{
  public abstract T Reduce<T>(ITransformer<T> transformer);
}
```

This means that we can choose different data types depending on what we need to reduce our hierarchy to:

- For evaluation, the entire expression will reduce to a `double`.

- For printing, the expression will reduce to a `string`.

- For calculating the depth of our expression tree or the number of elements in it, the expression will reduce to a `uint`.

As in the previous implementations, we shall adopt a double-dispatch dual interface such that

- Visitable members will implement `Reduce<T>(ITransformer<T>)`.

- Visitors shall implement overloaded versions of `Transform` for different node types.

We shall define our visitor interface as

```
public interface ITransformer<T>
{
  T Transform(DoubleExpression de);
  T Transform(AdditionExpression ae, T left, T right);
}
```

Notice that, since `AdditionExpression` is a composite that deterministically produces values of type `T` in its `Left` and `Right` reductions, we can incorporate them directly into the interface.

With this setup, `AdditionExpression` can be implemented as follows:

```
public class AdditionExpression : Expression
{
  public Expression Left, Right;

  public AdditionExpression(Expression left, Expression right)
  {
```

```
    Left = left;
    Right = right;
  }

  public override T Reduce<T>(ITransformer<T> transformer)
  {
    var left = Left.Reduce(transformer);
    var right = Right.Reduce(transformer);
    return transformer.Transform(this, left, right);
  }
}
```

The key difference here is that the method returns something, and that something is a generic that will be defined later.[3]

Our evaluation visitor now has slightly more sensible code:

```
public class EvaluationTransformer : ITransformer<double>
{
  public double Transform(DoubleExpression de) => de.Value;

  public double Transform(AdditionExpression ae, double left, double right)
  {
    return left + right;
  }
}
```

The evaluator is a specialization for double. Here's a printer, which specializes for a string:

```
public class PrintTransformer : ITransformer<string>
{
  public string Transform(DoubleExpression de)
  {
    return de.Value.ToString();
  }
```

---

[3] We must take pause and thank C# designers for virtual generic methods. We take these methods for granted in languages such as C# or Java, but in languages such as C++ where they are unavailable, their lack leads to the creation of additional IVisitable<T>-related interfaces – something that we luckily don't have to worry about.

```
public string Transform(AdditionExpression ae, string left, string right)
{
    return $"({left} + {right})";
}
}
```

We can use both of these transformers exactly as before, that is:

```
var expr = new AdditionExpression(
    new DoubleExpression(1), new DoubleExpression(2));
var et = new EvaluationTransformer();
var result = expr.Reduce(et);
var pt = new PrintTransformer();
var text = expr.Reduce(pt);
Console.WriteLine($"{text} = {result}"); // (1 + 2) = 3
```

But there's a burning question: why did we call the visitors transformers? It looks like they just evaluate things, not really transform them into anything. Well, the answer is that, in this paradigm, we've made it really easy to replace one tree with another, modified tree, should we need to. All we have to do in this case is set `T = Expression`, and we're good to go.

Here's a simple example: we'll take each double value in the tree and square it – not by changing the `Value` of the original node but by replacing the node entirely. Here is how this can be done:

```
public class SquareTransformer : ITransformer<Expression>
{
    public Expression Transform(DoubleExpression de)
    {
        // square the value and return a new object
        return new DoubleExpression(de.Value * de.Value);
    }

    public Expression Transform(AdditionExpression ae)
    {
        return new AdditionExpression(
```

```
        ae.Left.Reduce(this),
        ae.Right.Reduce(this));
  }
}
```

This is a rather different implementation from what we've seen before because this time round we're leveraging polymorphism! Consequently, running this transformer on an expression tree gives you a brand-new tree:

```
var expr = new AdditionExpression(
  new DoubleExpression(2), new DoubleExpression(3));
var st = new SquareTransformer();
var newExpr = expr.Reduce(st);
var text = newExpr.Reduce(pt);
Console.WriteLine(text); // (4 + 9)
```

Wholesale tree transformations are quite common in the real world. For example, if you wished to calculate $ax^2 + bx$, a compiler might transform an expression a*x*x + b*x into the expression (a*x + b)*x so as to reduce the number of multiplications.

You'll notice that we changed the nomenclature from Visitor/Visit/Accept to Transformer/Transform/Reduce. This is a stylistic choice: you can continue using prior nomenclature if all your visitor use cases involve a reduce-style operation. If, however, you envisage having visitors that do not perform any transforms, you can adapt a dual interface that would support both modalities.

Functional Visitor in F#

We have already looked at implementing a visitor in F# when we discussed the Interpreter design pattern, so I won't repeat it here. The general approach boils down to a traversal of a recursive discriminated union using pattern matching on types together with other useful features such as list comprehensions (assuming you're using lists, of course).

The visitor in a functional paradigm is fundamentally different from that in OOP. In object-oriented programming, a visitor is a mechanism for giving a set of related classes additional functionality "on the side" while ideally being able to

- Group the functionality together.

- Avoid type checks, instead relying on interfaces.

Pattern matching on a discriminated union is the equivalent of using the `is` C# keyword (`isinst` IL instruction) to check each type. Unlike C#, however, F# will tell you about the missing cases, so it offers greater compile-time safety.

Thus, compared with the OOP implementation, the canonical F# visitor would implement a *reflective visitor* approach.

The implementation of Visitor in F# is problematic for many reasons. First, as we've mentioned before, discriminated unions themselves break the OCP since there's no way to extend them other than to change their definitions. But the Visitor implementation compounds the problem further: since our functional visitor is essentially a huge `switch` statement, the only way to add support for a particular type is to violate the OCP in the visitor too!

Summary

The Visitor design pattern allows us to add some distinct behavior to every element in a hierarchy of objects. The approaches we have seen include

- *Intrusive*: Adding a method to every single object in the hierarchy. Possible (assuming you have access to source code) but breaks the OCP.

- *Reflective*: Adding a separate visitor that requires no changes to the objects; uses `is`/`as` whenever runtime dispatch is needed.

- *Dynamic*: Forces runtime dispatch via the DLR by casting hierarchy objects to `dynamic`. This gives the nicest interface at very large computational cost.

- *Classic* (double dispatch): The entire hierarchy *does* get modified, but just once and in a very generic way. Each element of the hierarchy learns to `Accept()` a visitor. We then subclass the visitor to enhance the hierarchy's functionality in all sorts of directions. This approach also has a transforming variation where visitor methods return values.

- *Acyclic*: Just like the reflective variety, it performs casting in order to dispatch correctly. However, it breaks the circular dependency between visitor and visitee and allows for more flexible composition of visitors.

Visitor appears quite often in tandem with the Interpreter pattern: having interpreted some textual input and transformed it into object-oriented structures, we need to, for example, render the abstract syntax tree in a particular way. Visitor helps propagate a `StringBuilder` (or similar accumulator object) throughout the entire hierarchy and collate the data together.

Index

A

AbsorbCyclePolicy, 194, 196, 199

Abstract factory, 73, 79–82, 91, 216

Accept() method, 432, 433, 436, 437, 442, 446

ActLike() method, 244, 350

Acyclic visitor, 441–443

Adapter
    decorator, 185
    definition, 135
    dependency injection, 152–155
    hashing problem, 140–142
    iterator, 315, 316
    .NET Framework, 156, 157
    scenario, 133, 134
    temporaries, 136–140

Add() method, 5, 25, 28, 263

AddChild() method, 40, 41

AddListItem(), 402, 403

AddRoom() method, 318

Aggregation, 53, 131, 180

Ambient Context pattern, 122–126

Anonymous functions, 27, 28

Array-backed properties, 235–237, 306–309

AsString() method, 191–193, 199, 200

Asynchronous factory method, 76, 77

Azure Service Bus, 333

B

Behavioral subtyping, 13

BetterFormattedText class, 224, 225

Bidirectional adapter, 155, 156

Bidirectional bindings, 363–366

Bidirectional iterator, 305, 314

Binary serialization, 107, 108

Bitmap class, 134, 237–239

Bridge class diagram, 163

Bridge pattern, 159

Broker chain, 265–269

Build() method, 44, 49, 63

Builder
    communicating intent, 42, 44
    component, renders web pages, 37–39
    decorator, 65–67
    DSL construction in F#, 69, 70
    extension with recursive generics, 58–62
    marker interfaces, 49
    parameter, 56, 58
    piecewise construction, 40, 41
    static initialization, 41

Builder interfaces, 50, 51

Builder marker interfaces, 49–51

Builder pattern
    marker interfaces, 51

Bulk modifications, 87, 88, 90

C

Capitalize() method, 223, 224

CatchACold() method, 354, 355, 360

Chain of Responsibility (CoR)
    broker chain, 265–269
    functional, 270–271
    method chain, 262–265
    scenario, 261

© Dmitri Nesteruk 2022
D. Nesteruk, *Design Patterns in .NET 6*, https://doi.org/10.1007/978-1-4842-8245-8

Printed in the United States
by Baker & Taylor Publisher Services